The Sleeping Sovereign

Richard Tuck traces the history of the distinction between
sovereignty and government and its relevance to the development
of democratic thought. Tuck shows that this was a central issue in
the political debates of the seventeenth and eighteenth centuries, and
provides a new interpretation of the political thought of Bodin,
Hobbes and Rousseau. Integrating legal theory and the history of
political thought, he also provides one of the first modern
histories of the constitutional referendum, and shows the
importance of the United States in the history of the referendum.
The book derives from the John Robert Seeley Lectures delivered
by Richard Tuck at the University of Cambridge in 2012, and will
appeal to students and scholars of the history of ideas, political
theory and political philosophy.

RICHARD TUCK is Frank G. Thomson Professor of Government at
Harvard University. He is the author of *Natural Rights Theories*
(Cambridge University Press, 1979), *Hobbes* (1989), *Philosophy
and Government 1572–1651* (Cambridge University Press, 1993),
*The Rights of War and Peace: Political Thought and the International
Order from Grotius to Kant* (1999) and *Free Riding* (2008). He is also
the editor of standard editions of Hobbes and Grotius.

THE SEELEY LECTURES

The John Robert Seeley Lectures have been established by the
University of Cambridge as a biennial lecture series in social and
political studies, sponsored jointly by the faculty of History and
Cambridge University Press. The Seeley Lectures provide a unique
forum for distinguished scholars of international reputation to address,
in an accessible manner, topics of broad interest in social and political
studies. Subsequent to their public delivery in Cambridge, the
University Press publishes suitably modified versions of each set of
lectures. Professor James Tully delivered the inaugural series of
Seeley Lectures in 1994 on the theme of 'Constitutionalism in an
Age of Diversity'.

The Seeley Lectures include

Strange Multiplicity: Constitutionalism in an Age of Diversity
JAMES TULLY
ISBN 978 0 521 47694 2 (paperback)
Published 1995

The Dignity of Legislation
JEREMY WALDRON
ISBN 978 0 521 65092 2 (hardback), 978 0 521 65883 6 (paperback)
Published 1999

Women and Human Development: The Capabilities Approach
MARTHA C. NUSSBAUM
ISBN 978 0 521 66086 0 (hardback), 978 0 521 00385 8 (paperback)
Published 2000

Value, Respect, and Attachment
JOSEPH RAZ
ISBN 978 0 521 80180 5 (hardback), 978 0 521 00022 2 (paperback)
Published 2001

The Rights of Others: Aliens, Residents, and Citizens
SEYLA BENHABIB
ISBN 978 0 521 83134 5 (hardback), 978 0 521 53860 2 (paperback)
Published 2004

Laws of Fear: Beyond the Precautionary Principle
CASS R. SUNSTEIN
ISBN 978 0 521 84823 7 (hardback), 978 0 521 61512 9 (paperback)
Published 2005

Counter-Democracy: Politics in an Age of Distrust
PIERRE ROSANVALLON
ISBN 978 0 521 86622 2 (hardback), 978 0 521 71383 2 (paperback)
Published 2008

On the People's Terms: A Republican Theory and Model of Democracy
PHILIP PETTIT
ISBN 978 1 107 00511 2 (hardback), 978 0 521 18212 6 (paperback)
Published 2012

The Politics of the Human
ANNE PHILLIPS
ISBN 978 1 107 093973 (hardback), 978 1 107 475830 (paperback)
Published 2015

THE SLEEPING SOVEREIGN

The Invention of Modern Democracy

RICHARD TUCK
Harvard University

 CAMBRIDGE
UNIVERSITY PRESS

CAMBRIDGE
UNIVERSITY PRESS

University Printing House, Cambridge CB2 8BS, United Kingdom

Cambridge University Press is part of the University of Cambridge.

It furthers the University's mission by disseminating knowledge in the pursuit of education, learning and research at the highest international levels of excellence.

www.cambridge.org
Information on this title: www.cambridge.org/9781107130142

© Richard Tuck 2015

First published 2016

Printed in the United Kingdom by Clays, St Ives plc

A catalogue record for this publication is available from the British Library

Library of Congress Cataloguing in Publication data
Tuck, Richard, 1949–
The sleeping sovereign : the invention of modern democracy / Richard Tuck.
    pages cm. – (The Seeley lectures)
Includes bibliographical references and index.
ISBN 978-1-107-13014-2 (Hardback)
1. Democracy–Philosophy. 2. Sovereignty–Philosophy. 3. Bodin, Jean,
1530–1596. 4. Hobbes, Thomas, 1588–1679. 5. Rousseau, Jean-Jacques, 1712–1778.
6. Referendum–United States–History. I. Title.
JC423.T76 2015
321.8–dc23   2015020179

ISBN 978-1-107-13014-2 Hardback
ISBN 978-1-107-57058-0 Paperback

CONTENTS

vii

This book is an expanded version of the Seeley Lectures, which I delivered to the University of Cambridge in May 2012. I would like to thank John Robertson and the History faculty of the university, as well as Richard Fisher and Cambridge University Press, for the invitation to give the lectures, and for their continued help and advice over their publication. Though I have added a significant amount of material, I have chosen to retain the structure that I used originally, namely four chapters on, respectively, 'Jean Bodin', 'Grotius, Hobbes and Pufendorf', 'The eighteenth century' and 'America'; but I have added a conclusion in which I have briefly developed some of the general implications of what I am saying.

The title of the book refers to a long passage in Thomas Hobbes's *De Cive* of 1642, in which Hobbes worked systematically through an extensive analogy between a democratic sovereign and a sleeping monarch, a passage I discuss in detail in the second chapter. Remarkably, it is one of the first full accounts of how we might think about democracies to be found in the literature of political theory after the disappearance of the ancient republics, despite the fact that Hobbes was primarily interested in defending the sovereignty of the kings of England. In it, Hobbes argued that a sovereign democracy need not be involved at all in the ordinary business of government; it could simply determine who should rule on its behalf and how in general they should behave, and then retire into the shadows, just as a monarch might appoint a vizier to govern in his place before going to sleep. Government – the prime activity of the ancient democracies, with their constant meetings of citizens to decide all kinds of matters including court cases – need not in fact be the activity of a democracy at all.

This is a graphic image, typical of Hobbes's writings, but he himself did little with it other than offer it as a theoretical possibility to his readers. The person for whom an idea of this kind really mattered was Jean-Jacques Rousseau; indeed, I would argue that as a result of neglecting his use of the distinction we have seriously misunderstood the degree to which Rousseau accepted the practical exigencies of modern politics. Contrary to what many of his recent readers have thought, Rousseau believed that ancient democracy was not an appropriate model for modern societies, in which constant political participation by all the citizens is not feasible. However, he did think that modern societies can be democracies if they are what we might call the Hobbesian kind. We will have to accept that *governing* is not the same as *authorising* the actions of a government, but at the same time we must find some means of allowing the mass electorate of a modern state to pass fundamental legislation. Merely electing representatives was not (Rousseau thought) enough to count as the action of a democratic sovereign, and his successors' search for the appropriate means of institutionalising this fundamental legislative power is a large part of my theme.

So it is Rousseau's various discussions of the difference between 'sovereignty' and 'government' that form the centrepiece of this book and from which I look both backwards and forwards. In the first chapter I move from Rousseau back to the first appearance of a clear distinction between sovereignty and government, in the work of the sixteenth-century French theorist Jean Bodin, and in the second chapter I discuss Hobbes's use of the distinction and the opposition it aroused among contemporaries. The third chapter deals expressly with Rousseau, and the men who (I argue) applied Rousseau's ideas in this area to practical constitution-making in the French Revolution via the idea of a constitutional plebiscite, in which the sovereign people can indeed act as a genuine legislator and then withdraw from the activity of government. As with Hobbes, there was strenuous opposition to this idea; unlike most modern writers on the subject, I treat the great constitutional theorist the Abbé Sieyès as an opponent of the way the distinction between sovereign and government was implemented in the Revolutionary constitutions, and the politicians associated with the Girondin party as the true heirs (in this respect) of Rousseau. The fourth chapter continues the theme of constitution-making, this time in the newly independent American republic, where (I argue) there came to be a similar reliance upon a plebiscitary model of popular sovereignty, at least at the state level; even at the federal level, I think, there was an attempt to structure the new constitution in a way that reflected the fundamental division between acts of sovereignty and acts of government. And, as I said, I have added a conclusion in which the implications of this story for modern constitutional thought are outlined.

In addition to giving the Seeley Lectures, I presented some of the material at Jena University, the Yale Law School

Legal Theory Workshop, the Popular Sovereignty Workshop at Queen Mary University of London, and as a Safra Center Lecture at Harvard; for these invitations, and for their extremely helpful comments, I would like to thank Alexander Schmidt at Jena, Scott Shapiro at Yale, Richard Bourke and Quentin Skinner at Queen Mary and Larry Lessig at Harvard. Many other colleagues and students have read drafts or have attended these lectures and given me their thoughts; among them Bruce Ackerman, Duncan Bell, Seyla Benhabib, Ann Blair, Annabel Brett, Daniela Cammack, Graham Clure, Greg Conti, Alan Cromartie, Noah Dauber, John Dunn, Katrina Forrester, Ben Friedman, Bryan Garsten, Mark Goldie, Alex Gourevitch, Mark Hanin, Kinch Hoekstra, Duncan Kelly, Sungho Kimlee, Madhav Khosla, James Kloppenberg, Tsin Yen Koh, Melissa Lane, Adam Lebovitz, Daniel Lee, Michael Lesley, Karuna Mantena, Michael Mencher, Isaac Nakhimovsky, David Runciman, Magnus Ryan, Paul Sagar, Sophie Smith, Mark Somos, Michael Sonenscher, Sophy Tuck, James Tully, Namita Wahi and Daniel Wikler. I am particularly indebted to Michael Lesley and Daniela Cammack for helping me with the proofs.

I would like to thank three people in particular for their extensive help and detailed advice. One is my colleague at Harvard, Eric Nelson, whose own work on eighteenth-century America turned out to run parallel in interesting ways to mine, and who read and commented on the final draft. Another is my former student, now an Associate Professor at the Yale Law School, David Grewal, who provided me with the fullest possible comments on the draft, and who has been a constant source of support and inspiration. But the third, alas, I can no longer thank in person. That is Istvan Hont, for many years a friend and a colleague at Cambridge, who always understood what I was thinking better than I did myself, and to whom I was talking about this material even in the last months of his life. He died on 29 March 2013, and this book is dedicated to his memory.

1

Jean Bodin

In his eighth *Letter from the Mountain*, written in 1764 in defence of his *Social Contract* and *Emile*, against attacks made on them in Geneva, Rousseau declared that 'Up to the present the democratic Constitution has been poorly examined. All those who have spoken about it either did not know it, or took too little interest in it, or had an interest in presenting it in a false light. None of them have sufficiently distinguished the Sovereign from the Government'.[1] What he meant by this, he made clear both in the *Social Contract* and elsewhere in the *Letters from the Mountain*, was that the ancient democracies, in which the citizens gathered in an assembly on a regular basis to administer their societies and make judgements of policy about all matters of concern to them, were not an appropriate model for the kind of democracy he advocated. They had not distinguished between 'government' and 'sovereignty', and had treated both day-to-day policy questions and fundamental decisions about the organisation of their societies as falling within the scope of the democratic assembly.

[1] Michel Launay (ed.), *Oeuvres complètes* (Paris: Éditions du Seuil, 1971), vol. III, p. 465; for translation, see translation by Christopher Kelly and Judith Bush, in Christopher Kelly and Eve Grace (eds.), *Letter to Beaumont, Letters Written from the Mountain, and Related Writings* (Hanover, NH: University Press of New England, 2001), p. 257.

Against this view, Rousseau insisted that his democracy would be restricted to acts of sovereignty, affecting the fundamental legal structure, and that government – including even such things as decisions on going to war – would not ideally be democratic in character (his own preference was for aristocracy). In the *Social Contract* he described this kind of democracy as a 'republic', partly in order precisely to avoid the implication in the familiar notion of a democracy that it must have a democratic *government*. But in the *Letters from the Mountain* he was happy to apply the term *democracy* to his kind of republic, and in the ninth *Letter* he made clear (much clearer, in fact, than he had done in the *Social Contract* itself) that a distinction of this kind permitted the reappearance of democracy in the modern world, a world in which citizens simply could not give the time and attention to government that had been possible for their ancient predecessors. Even in a city the size of Geneva, he wrote, ancient politics could not be revived:

> Ancient Peoples are no longer a model for modern ones;
> they are too alien to them in every respect. You above all,
> Genevans, keep your place, and do not go for the lofty
> objects that are presented to you in order to hide the
> abyss that is being dug in front of you. You are neither
> Romans, nor Spartans; you are not even Athenians.
> Leave aside these great names that do not suit you. You
> are Merchants, Artisans, Bourgeois, always occupied with
> their private interests, with their work, with their
> trafficking, with their gain; people for whom even liberty is
> only a means for acquiring without obstacle and for
> possessing in safety.

This situation demands maxims particular to you. Not being idle as ancient Peoples were, you cannot ceaselessly occupy yourselves with the Government as they did: but by that very fact that you can less constantly keep watch over it, it should be instituted in such a way that it might be easier for you to see its intrigues and provide for abuses. Every public effort that your interest demands ought to be made all the easier for you to fulfil since it is an effort that costs you and that you do not make willingly. For to wish to unburden yourselves of them completely is to wish to cease being free. 'It is necessary to choose,' says the beneficent Philosopher, 'and those who cannot bear work have only to seek rest in servitude'.[2]

In the *Letters* he was chiefly concerned with the inapplicability of ancient democratic government even to a small city such as Geneva, because modern commercial conditions meant that citizens, even if they could meet in an assembly, could not do so in the near-continuous session that ancient politics demanded. But in his *Considerations on the Government of Poland* (1772) he used the same distinction between *sovereign* and *government* to recommend a constitutional restructuring for a large modern state in which it was physically impossible for the citizens to meet

---

[2] Launay (ed.), *Oeuvres complètes*, vol. III, p. 483; *Letter to Beaumont, Letters Written from the Mountain, and Related Writings*, pp. 292–3. The 'beneficent Philosopher' is Stanislas Leszczynski, and the quotation is from his *La voix libre du citoyen, ou Observations sur le gouvernement de Pologne* (n.p., 1749) Part I, p. 195.

together.[3] It is clear that in his eyes the distinction was absolutely essential if democratic politics were to be reintroduced to a world of large commercial states, and his early readers immediately saw its significance. When Turgot wrote to Hume in 1767 about Rousseau, he said of the *Social Contract* that 'this book is in essence a precise distinction between the sovereign and the government; but that distinction reveals to us an extremely illuminating truth, and seems to me to have established for all time the idea of the inalienability of the people's sovereignty under whatever government they find themselves'.[4] Similarly, Pierre-Samuel du Pont de Nemours wrote in his copy of the first edition of the *Social Contract*, 'It is in this excellent terminology [*nomenclature*], in the precise and accurate notion which Rousseau gives of the *Sovereign*, and in the distinction between it and *Government* that the principal merit of the book consists. This merit is very great and is a part of

---

[3.] For example, 'One of the vices of the Polish constitution is that it fails to distinguish sufficiently clearly between legislation and administration, and that in the course of exercising legislative power, the Diet mixes in bits of administration, performing indifferently acts of sovereignty and acts of government, often even mixed acts in which its members are simultaneously magistrates and legislators' (chapter 9). Launay (ed.), *Oeuvres complètes*, vol. III, p. 546; translation from Victor Gourevitch (ed.), *The Social Contract and Other Later Political Writings* (Cambridge University Press, 1997), p. 217.

[4.] 'ce livre se réduit à la distinction précise du souverain et du gouvernment; mais cette distinction présente une vérité bien lumineuse, et qui me paraît fixer à jamais les idées sur l'inaliénabilité de la souveraineté du peuple dans quelque gouvernement que se soit'. *Oeuvres de Turgot et documents le concernant*, ed. Gustave Schelle (Paris: F.Alcan, 1913–23), vol. II, p. 660.

4

the science of political economy which belongs to Jean-Jacques and only to him'.[5]

Two innovations were needed before a theory of this kind could be put forward, a theory that (as we shall see) corresponds to what has become the default constitutional structure of most modern states, in which a procedure such as a plebiscite is used to ratify fundamental constitutional legislation, whereas an elected assembly or set of assemblies legislate on less fundamental matters. Both are to be found in Rousseau. One was the idea that sovereignty and government can be distinguished, and that different kinds of legislation are appropriate to the different levels – this idea is going to be the principal subject of this book. The other is less obvious but still contributed importantly to the creation of a new way of thinking about democracy: it was that it is possible or even desirable to restrict democratic action to a final judgement about what should be binding on the society, and to exclude from democracy to a great extent the process of *collective deliberation*. That exclusion seems surprising to many modern theorists of democracy, for whom (following an idealised and in many ways unhistorical picture of an ancient assembly) the activity of citizens conferring and arguing about their collective decisions is central to the nature of democratic politics. But part of Rousseau's claim that modern states can be democratic was that the principal act of the democratic citizen is the *vote* and not the discussion; indeed, he strikingly

---

[5.] Jean A. Perkins, 'Rousseau jugé par Du Pont de Nemours', *Annales de la Société J.-J. Rousseau* 39 (1972), p. 186. I am indebted to Graham Clure for directing me to this work.

remarked in the *Social Contract* that the ideal democratic moment would be 'if, when the people, being furnished with adequate information, held its deliberations, the citizens had no communication one with another', and went on to say that it was the activity of communicating with one another that gave rise eventually to what he called 'partial associations' and the eventual corruption of the state.[6] Like much in Rousseau, as we shall see, this looked back to Hobbes, who had famously denounced deliberative assemblies but was willing to concede that non-deliberative democracy could be a reasonable means of organising a state.[7]

The objection to ancient democracy in a modern state had always been presented as primarily logistical (so to speak), in that the citizens of a modern state could not physically gather together or could not find the time to do so. But implicit in this as an objection was the conviction that the gathering would be to discuss legislation. This was why the election of representatives (which had after all been part of

---

[6.] Book II, chapter 3. Launay (ed.), *Oeuvres complètes*, vol. II, p. 527; G. D. H. Cole (ed. and trans.), *The Social Contract and Discourses*, rev. by J. H. Brumfitt and John C. Hall (London: J. M. Dent, 1973), p. 185.

[7.] He said this clearly in *De Cive*, x.15: 'if in a *Democracy* the *people* should choose to concentrate deliberations about war and peace and legislation in the hands of just one man or of a very small number of men, and were happy to appoint magistrates and public ministers, i.e. to have authority without executive power [*authoritate sine ministerio*], then it must be admitted that *Democracy* and *Monarchy* would be equal in this matter'. Richard Tuck and Michael Silverthorne (eds.), *On the Citizen* (Cambridge University Press, 1998), p. 125. For the Latin text see Howard Warrender (ed.), *De Cive: The Latin Version* (Oxford University Press, 1983), p. 179.

the basic structure of government in most Western states for 500 years or more) was not seen as the act of a democracy, for the deliberative and legislative activity of the society was restricted to those representatives.[8] Once it was recognised

8. See for a full discussion of this, see Nadia Urbinati, *Representative Democracy: Principles and Genealogy* (Chicago University Press, 2006). As Gerald Stourzh first observed (I believe), the term *representative democracy* appeared for the first time in a letter of Alexander Hamilton commending the new constitution of New York State in 1777 (Gerald Stourzh, *Alexander Hamilton and the Idea of Representative Government* (Stanford: Stanford University Press, 1970), p. 49 and p. 223, n. 36; see also Pierre Rosanvallon, *Le peuple introuvable* (Paris: Gallimard, 1998), p. 11, n. 2). Hamilton's letter was not published until 1904 (in Henry Cabot Lodge's edition of *Hamilton's Works* (New York: G.P. Putnam's Sons, 1904), vol. IX, p. 72), so the first appearance in print seems to have been in the lexicographer Noah Webster's *Sketches of American Policy* (Hartford, CT, 1785), in the context (curiously) of a series of unacknowledged extracts from the *Social Contract* in the form of the standard eighteenth-century English translation of the work *A Treatise on the Social Compact; or The Principles of Politic Law* (London, 1764). After faithfully rehearsing Rousseau's views, Webster suddenly concluded that 'In large communities, the individuals are too numerous to assemble for the purpose of legislation; for which reason, the people appear by substitutes or agents; persons of their own choice. A representative democracy seems therefore to be the most perfect system of government that is practicable on earth' (p. 11). In French, the term first appears (as *démocratie représentative*) in Condorcet's *Lettres d'un bourgeois de New-Heaven* [sic] *à un citoyen de Virginie*, in Philip Mazzei's *Recherches Historiques et Politiques sur les États-Unis de l'Amérique Septentrionale* (Paris, 1788), vol. I, p. 361; presumably Condorcet picked it up from Webster rather than from Hamilton. A puzzle remains about the use of the term in an essay by Mazzei himself. His *Memorie della vita e delle peregrinazioni del fiorentino Filippo Mazzei* (published posthumously at Lugano in 1846, but written c.1813) includes *Frammenti di scritti pubblicati nelle gazzette al*

that the element of discussion in their activity could be slight or even non-existent, and once it was recognised that the important acts of democratic sovereignty were by their very nature infrequent, the way was open to recreate democracy in a modern setting and get the citizens as a whole to legislate as well as to elect. And as we shall see, the opportunity to do so was taken in the generation immediately after Rousseau, on both sides of the Atlantic.

Although in the *Letters* Rousseau claimed that no one had used the distinction between *sovereign* and *government* to interpret democratic constitutions, and while in the *Social Contract* he warned that his long discussion of the distinction in Book III 'requires careful reading' (with the implication that it was unfamiliar and difficult to follow), he must in fact have been well aware that he was not the first person to use it, and furthermore that

principio della rivoluzione americana da un citadino di Virginia ['citizen of Virginia', a nom de plume Mazzei used in his American writings; see below p. 149]'. In these *frammenti* he praises *democrazia (voglio dire una democrazia rappresentativa)* as the only government under which one can enjoy liberty (vol. II, p. 287). The *frammenti* are principally an attack on the British constitution, something which in the *Memorie* Mazzei said he had been attacking in print and in conversation in 1776 (vol. I, p. 367), and which is criticised in various manuscripts among Mazzei's surviving papers which seem to date from that year, though their status and indeed authorship is not at all clear (Philip Mazzei, *Selected Writings and Correspondence*, ed. Margherita Marchione [Prato: Edizioni del Palazzo, 1983], vol. I, pp. 98, 102, 106, 112). But no article in any journal of the period has turned up to correspond to what Mazzei recalled, nor do his papers include the *frammenti* that he reproduced in his *Memorie*.

he was not even the first person to apply it to the question of democracy. His remark in Book III, chapter 1 that 'government' is 'often wrongly confused with the Sovereign, whose minister it is' indeed suggests that he recognised that sometimes it had *not* been wrongly confused. But (as we shall see later in this book) for more or less a century the distinction had been either disregarded or expressly repudiated by the principal European political theorists, so that it was not unreasonable for Rousseau to present his own extensive use of it as an innovation. And, I think, it was no accident that Rousseau revived it in the context of a defence of democracy, because as we shall also see it had been its association with democracy that had led to its repudiation in the first place.

The first person to insist on the importance of a distinction of this kind, as his contemporaries and successors well understood, had in fact been Jean Bodin, writing in the 1560s and 1570s. It is a central feature of his theory of sovereignty, something that should have puzzled Bodin's modern readers more than it generally has done: for, as Rousseau's use of the distinction illustrates, it seems to fit more naturally into a defence of modern democratic politics than into the kind of 'absolutist' theory commonly ascribed to Bodin. But as we shall see, though Bodin's principal objective in formulating the distinction was not to defend democratic politics of a Rousseauian kind, he was more sympathetic to them than one might have expected, and furthermore his actual objective was much less 'absolutist' than we have been led to think. I shall argue that he was fundamentally more interested in defending the independence and standing of the French parlements than in constructing a theory of absolute monarchical power.[9]

The distinction made its first appearance in chapter 6 of his *Methodus ad facilem historiarum cognitionem* of 1566, a long chapter devoted to the *status Rerumpublicarum*.[10] Though this has, I think, not been observed before, the chapter is structured as a fairly methodical and radical critique of Aristotle's *Politics* Books III to VIII in which Bodin moved through the various arguments of Aristotle about the nature of states, systematically refuting them.[11] Towards the beginning

[9.] Bodin's use of the distinction is beginning to attract the attention of scholars after many years of neglect; see in particular Daniel Lee, 'Office is a thing borrowed: Jean Bodin on offices and seigneurial government', *Political Theory* 41 (2013), pp. 409–40 and Kinch Hoekstra, 'Early modern absolutism and constitutionalism', *Cardozo Law Review* 34 (2012–13), pp. 1079–98.

[10.] There are important differences between the first and second editions of Bodin's *Methodus*, which have recently been clarified in Sara Miglietti's critical edition of the work: see Bodin, *Methodus ad facilem historiarum cognitionem*, trans. into Italian by Sara Miglietti (ed.), (Pisa: Edizioni della Normale, 2013). For convenience, I will give references to Miglietti's edition, to the first edition (Paris, 1566), to the second edition (Paris, 1572), and to the English translation by Beatrice Reynolds, *Method for the Easy Comprehension of History* (New York: Columbia University Press, 1945).

[11.] One can see this particularly clearly if one compares the sequence of discussions in chapter 6 with Jacques Lefèvre d'Etaples's *In Politica Aristotelis Introductio* (1508, but regularly reprinted in the early sixteenth century), with which Bodin was no doubt extremely familiar. This was a précis of the *Politics*, which highlighted exactly the topics Bodin dealt with in chapter 6, in the order in which he dealt with them. Only the first part of the *Introductio*, on the household, and the last part, on education, were not used in Bodin's critique (though there is a brief discussion

of the chapter, Bodin said that Aristotle had failed to define sovereignty, *summum imperium*, and instead had simply described 'the government of a state', *Reipublicae*

of the household in the *Methodus*). Even Bodin's well-known polemic against mixed constitutions was, I think, linked to his critique of Lefèvre's Aristotelianism. Bodin acknowledged that Aristotle himself had not said very much about mixed constitutions, but he said that Aristotle had 'offered an opportunity for error' in his remarks about Sparta (p. 414 of Miglietti, p. 216 of the 1566 edition, p. 282 of the second edition and p. 185 of Reynolds). The obvious reference here is to Lefèvre, who was one of the first people to use Polybius's account of the Roman constitution (which had only recently been rediscovered), in his other work on the *Politics*, the commentary that he annexed to his 1506 revision of Bruni's translation. Lefèvre observed in one of his annotations that

> the types [of constitution] which [Aristotle] lists here are the pure kind [*simplices*]. They ought also to be mixed [*volunt . . . componi*] in *civitates*, as in the Spartan and Roman republics according to Polybius . . . Surely if either two or three of these types are linked together [*iungantur*] in some *civitas*, nothing stops us from saying that the *respublica* is mixed. If however one of the types is superior to [*praeficiatur*] the others, the *summa reipublicae* is said to be there, and the republic is named on the basis of the dominant type. (III.5 [what we would now call III.7], p. 42)

This is more or less contemporary with the first known use of Book VI of Polybius (by Bernardo Rucellai in his *Liber de urbe Roma*), but is much more significant because Rucellai's book was not printed until the eighteenth century. On Rucellai, see Arnaldo Momigliano, 'Polybius' reappearance in Western Europe' in his *Essays in Ancient and Modern Historiography* (Oxford: Basil Blackwell, 1977), pp. 87–8; Momigliano uncharacteristically overlooked Lefèvre's citation of Polybius. See also J. H. Hexter, 'Seyssel, Machiavelli and Polybius, VI: the mystery of the missing translation', *Studies in the Renaissance* 3 (1956), pp. 75–96.

administratio;[12] this contrast between the terms *summum imperium* and *administratio* would henceforward remain the standard way of describing the distinction between the 'sovereign' and the 'government' in the Latin texts of Renaissance and post-Renaissance Europe.

To understand what Bodin meant, we have first to remember that he was well aware that Aristotle's *Politics* does employ the language of 'sovereignty', in a way: in many places Aristotle talks about one part of a *polis* being κύριον, which we might translate as 'dominant', and he often uses the term πολίτευμα to describe this dominant part, as in a passage in Book III, chapter 7: 'the πολίτευμα, which is the dominant part of a city [κύριον τῶν πόλεων], must be in the hands of one, or of a few, or of the many' (1279a25). In a couple of places Aristotle also says that the πολίτευμα is, or means the same as, the πολιτεία (which since the Jowett version in 1885 has often been translated as 'constitution').[13] Bodin's objection to Aristotle was not that Aristotle had no concept

---

[12.] Page 358 of Miglietti, p. 181 of the 1566 edition, p. 235 of the second edition and p. 156 of Reynolds. It is interesting that Jean-François Champagne in his translation of Aristotle's *Politics*, which appeared in 'l'An 5' of the Revolution (1796–7) made the same point, expressly as a follower not of Bodin but of Rousseau: he annotated III.6 with the observation that Aristotle *confond ici le souverain et le prince*, i.e. *puissance législative* with *puissance exécutive* (*La Politique d'Aristote, ou La Science des Gouvernemens* (Paris: An V), vol. I, p. 188). The whole translation is expressly Rousseauian, see p. lxii.

[13.] '[T]he πολιτεία is in fact the πολίτευμα' (πολίτευμα δ᾽ἐστὶν ἡ πολιτεία) (1278b10, III.6); 'the words πολιτεία and πολίτευμα have the same meaning' (1279a25, III.7).

of sovereignty, but that he was not clear about what it meant to be 'dominant' in a city. As he said in chapter 6,

> [Aristotle] nowhere defines *summum imperium*,
> which he himself calls κύριον πολίτευμα and κυρίαν
> ἀρχὴ, and in which the *Reipublicae status* consists.
> Unless we are to suppose that he meant to do so when
> he stated that there are altogether three parts to a
> *Respublica*; one being deliberation, another choosing
> magistrates, and the last jurisdiction.[14]

This last remark was a reference to Book IV, chapter 14 of the *Politics*, 1297b38, in which Aristotle indeed said that there are three 'elements' (μόρια) in any constitution, the 'deliberative element' (τὸ βουλευόμενον), the element 'concerned with the magistracies' (περὶ τὰς ἀρχάς), and 'that which has judicial power' (τὸ δικάζον). Aristotle went on to say that τὸ βουλευόμενον 'has authority [is κύριον] in matters or war and peace, in making and unmaking alliances; it passes laws, inflicts death, exile, confiscation, elects magistrates and audits their accounts', but he also thought that it was possible for these powers to be distributed between two 'elements'. Only if enough of these powers were in the hands of the people as a whole, for example, would the constitution be democratic; so that 'where particular persons have authority in particular matters – for example, when the whole people decide about peace and war and hold scrutinies, but the magistrates regulate everything else, and they are elected by vote or lot – there is an aristocracy or a polity

---

[14.] Page 356 of Miglietti, p. 181 of the 1566 edition, p. 234 of the 1572 edition and p. 156 of Reynolds.

[πολιτεία]' (1298b5).[15] So it was not unreasonable for Bodin (from his own perspective) to complain that Aristotle did not give a precise account of what the defining characteristic of being τὸ κύριον might be, and which powers were necessarily in the hands of a sovereign.

The difficulty involved in working out what Aristotle meant in these passages had been reflected in the different translations for the key term πολίτευμα in the Latin versions of the *Politics*, which were current in Bodin's lifetime. William of Moerbeke, in the standard medieval translation, characteristically left both πολιτεία and πολίτευμα untranslated (as *politia* and *politeuma*), thereby evading the interpretative questions. But Aquinas in his (partial) commentary on Book III rather accurately said that *politeuma* 'means the ruling class [*ordo dominantium*] in the *civitas*'.[16] This concrete sense of what Aristotle

[15.] This is from the Stephen Everson edition of the *Politics* (Cambridge University Press, 1988), p. 103, which uses Jonathan Barnes's revision of the Jowett text; I have slightly emended it, changing 'there the government is an aristocracy or a constitutional government' to 'there is an aristocracy or a polity', as the original reads simply 'ἀριστοκρατία ἡ πολιτεία', i.e. with no word corresponding to 'government'. Πολιτεία here of course has the technical Aristotelian meaning of a mixed or moderated regime.

[16.] *Opera omnia iussu Leonis XIII P. M. edita* 48 (Rome: Ad Sanctae Sabinae, 1971) XXXI.6, n. 2. Nicolas Oresme in his fourteenth-century French translation of the *Politics* followed Moerbeke in leaving the key terms untranslated: *policie* for πολιτεία and *policeme* for πολίτευμα. 'Le Livre de Politiques d'Aristote. Published from the Text of the Avranches Manuscript 223', Albert Douglas Menut (ed.), *Transactions of the American Philosophical Society* N. S. 60 (1970), pp. 126, 128.

intended began to be undermined, however, by the first humanist translation of the *Politics*, by Leonardo Bruni, who translated πολίτευμα as *regimen*, and rendered Aristotle's remark at Book III, chapter 7 that the πολίτευμα 'is the dominant part of a city' as the *'regimen* is the power and judgement [*potestas et arbitrium*] of a *civitas*'.[17] The standard modern translation of πολίτευμα then appeared for the first time in Jacques d'Estrebay's new translation of the *Politics* in 1542, which was prefaced by a violent denunciation of the poor Latinity of both the Moerbeke and the Bruni translations. In his new version he consistently translated πολιτεία as *respublica* and πολίτευμα as *administratio*, for example, saying in Book III, chapter 6 that 'Whatever has supreme authority [*summam authoritatem*] everywhere governs [*administrat*] the *civitas*, and the government [*administratio*] is the *respublica*'.[18] *Administratio* or 'government' then

---

[17.] *Politica Aristotelis a Leonardo Aretino e greco in latinum traducta* (Leipzig, 1502) f. 36v. At 1278b10, III.6, Bruni simply omitted any mention of πολίτευμα, saying that a *respublica* is 'an organisation of the *civitas* concerning magistrates, and principally concerning that which has supreme authority [*summam auctoritatem*] in the *civitas*, and is to be the most high [*principalissimum*]. The most high is that which everywhere governs and rules the *civitas*, as in a popular *civitas* the people [etc.]' (f. 35r.). (For Bruni's use of *respublica*, see James Hankins, 'Exclusivist Republicanism and the non-monarchical republic', *Political Theory* 38 (2010), pp. 452–82). Jacques Lefèvre D'Etaples, in his emendations to Bruni's translation, in an attempt to restore Aristotle's text added here that *quod autem gubernat, respublica est* (*Politicorum Libri Octo . . .* (Paris: Henricus Stephanus, 1506), ff 49r–49v).

[18.] *Aristotelis Politica ab Iacobo Lodoico Strebae . . . conversa* (Paris, 1542), p. 98.

became by far the most common translation of πολίτευμα, from the 1540s down to the present day.[19]

But as Bodin pointed out, in a modern state, administration, including the functions that Aristotle listed as the elements

[19.] See in particular Juan Sepulveda (trans.), *Aristotelis de Republica Libri VIII* (Paris, 1548), pp. 79r, 80v (*administratio*); Louis Le Roy (trans.), *Les Politiques d'Aristote* (Paris, 1576), p. 165 (*gouvernement politique*, contrasted with *la police* for πολιτεία; in the English translation of this edition, *Aristotles politiques, or Discourses of gouernment* (London, 1598) p. 150), the equivalent terminology is 'civile government' and 'commonweale'); William Ellis (trans.), *A Treatise on Government. Translated from the Greek of Aristotle* (London, 1776), p. 129 (πολιτεία 'form of government', πολίτευμα 'administration'); Benjamin Jowett (trans.), *The Politics of Aristotle* (Oxford University Press, 1885), vol. i, p. 79 (πολιτεία 'constitution', πολίτευμα 'government'). An attempt to make some distinction between πολίτευμα and 'government' is found in Joachim Périon's rival translation to Estrebay's (*Aristotelis De Republica, Qui Politicorum dicuntur, Libri VIII* (Basle, 1549) (first pub. Paris, 1543), where he used the term *reipublicae gerendae ratio*, i.e. what determined the form the government took, as his translation of πολίτευμα (e.g. p. 86). He was followed by Denis Lambin in his *Aristotelis De Reip. Bene Administandae Ratione, Libri Octo* (Paris, 1567), who translated πολιτεία as *civitatis administrandae forma* and πολίτευμα as *civitatis administrandae ratio* (e.g. p. 95). Pietro Vettori in his 1576 translation and commentary used *respublica* for πολιτεία and *arbitrium urbis* for πολίτευμα, thereby returning to some extent to Bruni's terminology, in *Commentarii* in vol. VIII *Libros Aristotelis De Optimo Statu Civitatis* (Florence, 1576), p. 215. Not until the late eighteenth century do we find any serious attempt to recast Aristotle's terminology along the lines of Bodin or Rousseau; the most interesting example of this is the first French translation of the *Politics* since Le Roy, Jean-François Champagne's avowedly Rousseauian (see vol. I, p. lxii), *La Politique d'Aristote, ou La Science des Gouvernemens. Ouvrage traduit dur Grec ... Par le Citoyen Champagne* (Paris: An V [1797]), in which

of a constitution, was very largely left in the hands of people or institutions who were clearly not sovereign. In particular, 'the right of deliberation about the state is conceded even to private citizens [as in a Parliament], and the administration of justice [*iurisdictio*] to the humblest man [as in a jury]. These, then, do not pertain to sovereignty [*summum imperium*]'.[20] Government (*gubernatio*), he said, was anything concerned with 'decrees, edicts and their execution'. For example, the Senate decides on war: the *princeps* proclaims it: the soldiers execute it. In trials, judges and arbitrators who are private citizens also decide: the magistrate gives a command: the *apparitor* executes it. (Bodin was thinking about a Roman jury trial.)[21]

πολιτεία appears as *gouvernement* and πολίτευμα as *le souverain*; though Champagne observed in a note referring to Book III of the *Social Contract* that Aristotle 'confond ici le souverain et le prince', i.e. 'puissance législative' with 'puissance exécutive' (I, p. 188). The same year the Scotsman John Gillies's (loose) translation, *Aristotle's Ethics and Politics, comprising his practical philosophy, translated from the Greek* (London, 1797) used 'form of government' for πολιτεία and 'sovereignty' for πολίτευμα (II, p. 175), though the intention of his translation, unlike Champagne's, was to show the errors of Locke and Rousseau (II, p. 3). Ernest Barker's 1946 translation of the *Politics* suggested, as usual in the English tradition, 'constitution' for πολιτεία, but 'the civic body' for πολίτευμα, or 'the body of persons established as sovereign by the constitution', *The Politics of Aristotle* (Oxford University Press, 1946), p. 106. Sophie Smith's Cambridge PhD thesis on John Case contains a full discussion of the sixteenth-century Aristotelian vocabulary in this area.

[20.] Page 356 of Miglietti, p. 181 of the 1566 edition, p. 234 of the second edition and p. 156 of Reynolds.

[21.] Page 358 of Miglietti, pp. 181–2 of the 1566 edition, p. 235 of the 1572 edition and p. 156 of Reynolds.

But none of these activities constituted the exercise of specifically *sovereign* power. That, Bodin argued in the second edition of the *Methodus*, consisted in *the right to choose* magistrates and other members of a government, together with the power of ultimate legislation. 'In every state one ought to investigate who can give authority to magistrates, who can take it away, who can make or repeal laws – whether one citizen or a small part of the citizens or a greater part. When this has been ascertained, the type of government is easily understood'.[22] Though it is often said that the *Methodus* did not display the same concentration on legislative sovereignty as the *Republic*[23]

[22.] '*[Q]uis imperium magistratibus dare & adimere, quis leges iubere aut abrogare possit*', p. 400 of Miglietti, p. 271 of the 1572 edition and pp. 178–9 of Reynolds. The 1566 edition (p. 207) has simply '*quis imperium magistratibus dare & adimere possit*' – a good example of the way he seems to have brought the 1572 edition fully in line with what he was going to say in the *Republic* (see the Note at the end of this chapter). A few lines later in both editions he referred to people 'who, while they have no powers but the creation of magistrates, still have the sovereignty'; this seems to have been an uncorrected passage left over from the first edition. We can assume that in 1566 Bodin was concentrating on the right to appoint magistrates, but by 1572 he had decided that legislation was equally important. Melissa Lane, in a forthcoming essay in a volume on *Popular Sovereignty* edited by Richard Bourke and Quentin Skinner, has argued that for Aristotle, too, the selection of magistrates was the key power that determined where τὸ κύριον lay, and that Bodin was much closer to Aristotle than he allowed. This may be true, but it was not unreasonable for Bodin to miss it, particularly as the passages in Book IV previously quoted do seem to point in a different direction.

[23.] I use this translation of the title of Bodin's great work to cover both the French version, published under the name *Les six Livres de la Republique* (first edition 1576, revised editions issued at intervals down to 1587), and

ten years later, in fact both works treated the principal powers of a sovereign as the right to legislate *and* the right to choose magistrates. Bodin indeed more or less repeated *verbatim* this definition in Book II, chapter 7 of the *Republic*: 'to decide on the type of state [*iuger un estat*], the question is not to know who have the magistracies or offices: but solely who has the sovereignty, and all the power to appoint and dismiss the officers, and to give laws to every one'.[24]

the (often quite different) Latin version, published under the name *De Republica libri sex* in 1586, and not significantly revised in subsequent editions. The only complete English translation, of a conflation of the two texts (see McRae's 'Introduction' to his edition, p. A38) appeared in 1606 as *The Six Bookes of a Commonweale*, translated by Richard Knolles; a photographic reprint of this with scholarly introduction and apparatus which K. D. McRae produced in 1962 (Harvard University Press) is still the standard English edition. There is no edition that tracks the many variants in the texts. But there is an excellent critical bibliography of Bodin's works by Roland Crahay, Marie-Thérèse Isaac and Marie-Thérèse Lenger, *Bibliographie critique des éditions anciennes de Jean Bodin* (Académie Royale de Belgique, 1992). I have chosen to give page references to the French editions of 1576 (Paris: Jacques du Puys), the first edition, and 1579 (Lyons: Jacques du Puys), the sixth edition, of which Crahay, Isaac and Lenger say that *pratiquement, le texte atteint ici son stade définitif* (p. 111); I also give references to the 1586 Latin edition (Paris: Jacques de Puy) and the McRae edition. All translations from Bodin are my own unless otherwise stated.

24. *Republique* 1576, p. 281; 1579, p. 235. The last phrase is a translation of *donner loy à chacun*, which Knolles (McRae, ed., p. 249) translated 'give lawes unto every man'; but it is noteworthy that the Latin version does not include this phrase, reading simply that we should establish the type of state *ex eorum persona, qui iura maiestatis habent*, and not from the distribution of its magistracies (*Republica* 1586, p. 233). So intriguingly the Latin version is closer here to the 1566 edition of the *Methodus*, and the French to the 1572 edition (see earlier n. 12).

In the *Republic* he also made clear that he believed this to be an entirely original discovery in political science. 'There is a clear distinction between the state and the government, a principle of politics [*secret de police* in French] which no one [the Latin adds, 'as far as I can tell', *quantum intelligere potuimus*] has hitherto observed'.[25] Some pages later he returned to the same theme and enlarged on his originality:

> Perhaps someone will say that I am the only person who thinks this, and that none of the ancients, and definitely none of the moderns, who have dealt with Republics have voiced this opinion. I will not deny it: but this distinction seems to me more than necessary to understand the state of each Republic, if one does not want to find oneself in a labyrinth of infinite errors, into which we see Aristotle fell, taking a democratic state for an aristocratic one and vice versa; contrary to common opinion, and even to common sense. It is impossible to build securely on such ill-founded principles ... From this error similarly has arisen the idea of those who have fashioned a Republic mixed of all three types, which I have refuted earlier.[26]

Given Bodin's use of the terms *status Reipublicae* and *estat* in these passages of the *Republic*, one might suppose (if one took the passages by themselves, or if one ignored the similar discussion in a different terminology in the *Methodus*) that he was distinguishing between the state in a modern sense – the abstract

[25] *Republique* 1576, p. 233; 1579, p. 189; *Republica* 1586, p. 189; McRae, ed., p. 199.
[26] *Republique* 1576, p. 282; 1579, p. 236; *Republica* 1586, p. 234; McRae, pp. 249–50.

entity behind or above the government – and the government itself, and was not making the same distinction that Rousseau was to make between a sovereign legislator and a government. But after first making the distinction, he went on to say that

> the state can be a monarchy, and nevertheless be governed as a democracy [*gouverné populairement*] if the prince opens up the Estates, magistracies, offices and rewards equally to everyone, without regard to their nobility, wealth or virtue. A monarchy can also be governed aristocratically, when the prince restricts the Estates and benefices to the nobles, or to the more virtuous, or to the richest. Similarly an aristocratic state [*seigneurie*] can be governed democratically, distributing honours and rewards to all the subjects equally, or aristocratically, restricting them to the nobility or the wealthy. This variation in government has misled those who have thought Republics can be mixed, without seeing that the state of a Republic is different from its government and administration.[27]

And later in his discussion he added democratic sovereignty to the scheme:

> If the majority of citizens [*pluspart des citoyens*] hold the sovereignty, and if the people give the honorable offices, the rewards and the benefices only to noblemen, as they did at Rome until the *Lex Canuleia*, the state will be democratic, but governed aristocratically.[28]

[27.] *Republique* 1576, pp. 233–4; 1579, pp. 189–90; *Republica* 1586, p. 189; McRae, pp. 199–200.
[28.] *Republique* 1576, p. 282; 1579, p. 235; *Republica* 1586, pp. 233–4; McRae, p. 249.

So it is clear that the distinction he was interested in was exactly Rousseau's, between a sovereign legislator of the familiar Bodinian type and an administration or government put in place by the sovereign. To put it another way, the sovereign he was thinking about had a specific institutional character and was either a single individual or a group of individuals; it was no more the state in the modern abstract sense than Charles IX of France was the state.

This innovative distinction between the sovereign and the government was of course intimately related to what Bodin claimed to be his equally innovative idea of sovereignty itself. As we just saw, Bodin claimed that 'From this error [of not understanding the distinction] . . . has arisen the idea of those who have fashioned a Republic mixed of all three types' – that is, that the central theme of Bodin's discussion of sovereignty, the impossibility of mixed government, depended in his eyes on understanding the distinction. So did another critical feature of his concept of sovereignty, its *perpetual* character. Right at the start of his discussion of sovereignty, in the famous Book i, chapter 8,[29] he was concerned to define it as *perpetual,* and consequently to distinguish between the underlying location of sovereignty and the form that

[29.] This was in fact chapter 9 in the first French edition; it became chapter 8 in the second authorised edition (Paris: du Puys, 1577), when Bodin moved the former chapter 8 to become chapter 6 of Book v, and remained in that position for subsequent editions (Roland Crahay, Marie-Thérèse Isaac and Marie-Thérèse Lenger, *Bibliographie critique des éditions anciennes de Jean Bodin* [Académie Royale de Belgique, 1992], pp. 101–2). In the Latin version it was chapter 8 from the beginning.

governmental power might take at any particular moment. As he said there,

> I have said that this power is perpetual, because it can happen that one or more people have absolute power given to them for some certain period of time, upon the expiration of which they are no more than private subjects. And even while they are in power, they cannot call themselves sovereign princes. They are but trustees and custodians [*depositaires, & gardes*] of that power until such time as it pleases the people or the prince to take it back, for the latter always remains in lawful possession.[30]

The most eye-catching example of this, and the one to which Bodin immediately moved, was the Roman dictator.

> Having laid down these maxims as the foundations of sovereignty, we may conclude that neither the Roman dictator, nor the Spartan harmoste, nor the aesymnetes at Salonica, nor he whom they call the archus in Malta, nor the balia of old in Florence – all of whom had the same duties – nor the regents in kingdoms, nor any other commissioner or magistrate who had absolute power for a limited time to dispose of the affairs of the commonwealth, had sovereignty. This holds even though the early dictators had full power [*toute puissance, summum ius*] and had it in the best possible form, or *optima lege* as the ancient Latins called it. For there was no appeal [from a dictator] in those days, and all the other offices were

---

30. Translation from Julian Franklin (ed.), *Bodin: On Sovereignty* (Cambridge University Press, 1992), pp. 1–2. *Republique* 1576, p. 152 (*recte* 125); 1579, p. 85; *Republica* 1586, p. 79; McRae, p. 84.

suspended ... It thus appears that the dictator was
neither a prince nor a sovereign magistrate [*Magistrat
souverain, summum magistratum*], as many have
thought [*comme plusieurs ont escrit, ut plerique putarunt*].[31]

The *pleri* included most importantly Pomponius in
the Digest itself, who said that the dictator possessed *summa
potestas*,[32] but also many Renaissance writers – for example,
Sir Thomas Elyot in *The Governour* described the dictator
as 'sovereign' and as possessing 'the pristine authority and
majesty of a king', and (no doubt uppermost in Bodin's
mind) Josse Clichtove in a commentary on Lefèvre's
In Politica Aristotelis Introductio listed the dictatorship as
one of the five *modi regni*, possessing *totius rei summam
authoritatem* and differing from the other kinds of kingship
only in that it was temporary.[33] From the perspective of the
later use of the sovereignty – government distinction, Bodin's
argument about the dictator was particularly ominous, for it

[31.] Translation from Julian Franklin (ed.), *Bodin: On Sovereignty*
(Cambridge University Press, 1992), pp. 1–2. *Republique* 1576, pp. 125–6;
1579, p. 85–6; *Republica* 1586, p. 79; McRae, p. 85. This is a list based
initially on the observations about the dictatorship and the *aisymnetai* in
Dionysius of Halicarnassus v.73, though Dionysius treats them both as
'elective tyrants'. See also Bodin's remarks in II.3, attacking Aristotle for
calling those magistrates 'kings' who were the equivalent of this
Dionysian list (*Republique* 1576, pp. 242–3; 1579, pp. 197–8; *Republica*
1586, pp. 196–7; McRae, p. 207).

[32.] *Hunc magistratum, quoniam summam potestatem habebat, non erat fas
ultra sextum mensem retineri. Digest* I.2.2.18.

[33.] *In Politica Aristotelis, introductio Iacobi Fabri Stapulensis: adiecto
commentario declarata per Iudocum Clichtoveum Neoportuensem* (Paris,
1535), p. 12r. The commentary was originally published in 1516.

raised the possibility that a ruler possessing untrammelled monarchical power – precisely 'the pristine authority and majesty of a king' – might not in fact be the sovereign, but instead might be subordinate to a democratic power. And as we shall see in Chapter 2, the nature of the dictator quickly became a central theme in the discussion of the possibility of modern democratic politics.

Moreover, Bodin's own defence of monarchy in this context was clearly hard to maintain. He was committed to the proposition that sovereignty had to be perpetual, and that a time-limited ruler such as the dictator could not be sovereign, however extensive his powers, and however minimal the temporal limits were on his office – so that even the archons of the early Athenian republic, who held 'absolute power' for nine or ten years, could not be called sovereign.[34] But Bodin had to recognise that this left monarchy in an awkward position. On the account he gave in chapter 8 a democratic or aristocratic sovereign was indeed perpetual, in the full sense of the term, as assemblies do not die; but a monarch was perpetual only in the sense that he held power for the term of his life – otherwise, as Bodin acknowledged, 'there would ... be few sovereign monarchs inasmuch as there are very few that are hereditary. Those especially would not be sovereign who come to the throne by election'.[35] So the difference between an

---

[34] Franklin, *Bodin: On Sovereignty*, p. 4; *Republique* 1576, p. 127; 1579, p. 87; *Republica* 1586, p. 80; *Six Bookes*, p. 86.

[35] He believed (correctly) that only the French and English monarchies were strictly speaking hereditary. Translation from Julian Franklin (ed.), *Bodin: On Sovereignty* (Cambridge University Press, 1992), p. 6. *Republique* 1576, p. 128; 1579, p. 88; McRae, p. 87. In the Latin version

elective dictator and an elective monarch became merely that the expiration date of the former's term of office was known in advance, and that of the latter was not. Moreover, though Bodin might say that there would otherwise be few perpetual sovereign monarchs, he also repeatedly said that elective monarchies had historically the tendency to turn into aristocracies, as in the cases of Poland and – above all – the Holy Roman Empire, precisely because the sovereignty was reclaimed by the electors on the death of each king.[36] We shall see in Chapter 2 that later readers of Bodin pounced on the unsatisfactory character of his account of perpetuity, and either questioned the whole Bodinian distinction between sovereign and government (as Grotius did) or reworked it to make it more satisfactory, but at the same time more threatening to elective monarchy (as Hobbes did).

Both these aspects of Bodin's theory of sovereignty – that is, the connection between the sovereignty–government distinction and the impossibility of mixed government, and the insistence that sovereignty must be understood as perpetual – had the same effect, to prise apart 'sovereignty' from the actual operation of governmental power. What we had hitherto supposed was political power, Bodin tells us, is not *really* where power lies: it might be the case that on a day-to-day basis we are ordered around by a king or an assembly of some kind, and there may be no recourse to any other institution to protect us

Bodin removed the remark that there are 'few that are hereditary': *Republica* 1586, p. 81.

[36.] *Republique* 1576, pp. 427–8; 1579, pp. 375–6; *Republica* 1586, pp. 390–1; McRae, pp. 434–5.

from those orders, but hidden underneath those structures and possibly apparent only at very long intervals was a different kind of power which gave *legitimacy* to these other institutions. He made this point in a long discussion in the *Republic* about the difference between 'laws' (*leges, lois*) and 'edicts' (*edicta, edits*);[37] 'laws' were the acts of the sovereign, but 'edicts' (though law-like in form) were the acts of magistrates and were necessarily subordinate to the sovereign's laws – they might, for example, be in force only during the time in office of the magistrate, or they might be like laws in all respects except that they were issued by bodies controllable by the sovereign, such as the Senate at Rome or Venice.

The most powerful example he gave of this, an example which (again) was to be widely used in defence of democracy, was the Roman constitution both in its republican heyday and under the principate. It was of course a standard part of the humanist political theory of the earlier sixteenth century that Rome had had a mixed constitution, and it was the Roman constitution that was repeatedly cited in the political debates of the post-Reformation period as the model for the (supposedly) mixed constitutions of modern Europe. Independently of Bodin in the 1550s, this idea had already begun to be questioned; in particular Nicholas Grouchy, in his great book on the Roman *comitia*, argued that

> [w]hile a kind of royal power can be seen in the consulate, and aristocratic power in the Senate, the people had such

---

[37.] *Republique* 1576, pp. 193ff; 1579, pp. 150ff; *Republica* 1586, pp. 150ff; McRae, pp. 156ff.

authority over all the magistrates, and the Senate, that it is not unjustified to say that all the sovereignty of the Republic [*omne imperium, omnem maiestatem illius Reip.*] was with the people.[38]

But Bodin was the person who linked this piece of historical scholarship with general political theory, and who made the democratic character of the Roman state a central part of his narrative – going so far as to say at one point that Rome under the principate down to the time of Vespasian was still a democracy, for 'a principate is nothing other than a democracy or aristocracy in which there is a chief who can give commands to every individual'.[39] Augustus seized the real power in the state, but – Bodin observed in a striking passage:

Here we must inquire into the thing itself [*reipsa*] and not the pretence [*simulatio*]: for he who has most power in the

[38.] *De Comitiis Romanorum Libri Tres* (Paris, 1555) p. 3r. It should be said that in the *Methodus* Bodin was understandably rather critical of Grouchy's view that the magistrates had no independent authority. Miglietti, p. 384; 1566 edition, p. 197; 1572 edition, p. 257; Reynolds, p. 170.

[39.] Translation from Julian Franklin (ed.), *Bodin: On Sovereignty* (Cambridge University Press, 1992), p. 107. *Republique* 1576, p. 231; 1579, p. 187; *Republica* 1586, p. 186; McRae, p. 196. Vespasian is mentioned in the Latin version, and in the English translation, but not in the French versions, which instead talk about the 'long temps après' Augustus during which Rome was really a republic. Vespasian was relevant because of the famous *lex de imperio Vespasiani*, an inscription from Rome known since at least the fourteenth century and now in the Capitoline museum, which appears to confer legislative authority on Vespasian; though what it clearly says is that Vespasian was to have the same authority as had been conferred on Augustus, Tiberius and Claudius, so it is not obvious that it made any difference to the legal

Republic [*plus in Republica potest*] is thought to
possess the sovereignty [*summum Imperium*], but if we are
concerned with rights [*de iure*], we should look not to
what is, but to what ought to be. And therefore a
principate is nothing other than an Aristocracy or a
Democracy in which one among many is preeminent in
dignity; but sovereignty [*maiestas*] is with the people or
the optimates.[40]

So the emperor too, like the dictator, could not be seen as a
sovereign: Rome remained a democracy in which – in
principle – the old legal order could at any time have
reasserted itself.

However, though these remarks about the dictator
and the emperor proved explosive in the context of the late
sixteenth- and seventeenth-century debates about European
monarchy, and though Bodin's attitude to democracy was
more subtle than might have been supposed – like Hobbes
(and, indeed, Rousseau himself), his principal objection was

status of the Emperors. Modern scholarship to some extent confirms
Bodin's general view of the legal basis of the principate: see P. A. Brunt,
'Lex de Imperio Vespasiani', *Journal of Roman Studies* 67 (1977), pp. 95–
116 and F. Millar, 'Imperial Ideology in the *Tabula Siarensis*' in J.
González and J. Arce (eds.), *Estudios sobre la Tabula Siarensis* (Madrid:
C.S.I.C., Centrro de Estudios Históricos, 1988), pp. 11–19.

40. My translation is from the Latin: *Republica* 1586, p. 187, which was
followed by the English translation, McRae, p. 197. The French is slightly
different: 'in matters of state [*en matiere d'estat*], he who is master of
force, is the master of men, of laws, and of the whole republic: but in
terms of right [*en termes de droit*], it is not necessary, says Papinian, to
pay attention to what is done at Rome, but properly [*bien*] to what ought
to be done'. *Republique* 1576, p. 231; 1579, pp. 187–8.

to democratic *government* with its instability and dema-
goguery, and not to democratic *sovereignty*[41] – it would be
perverse to deny that Bodin's object in writing both the
Methodus and the *Republic* was to produce a defence of
the modern French monarchy against its enemies. So the
natural question that arises is, why should a project of that
kind have led Bodin to invent this distinction and put so
much weight on it?

The conventional interpretation of Bodin's political
theory is still, I think, dominated by the work of Julian
Franklin in various books and articles thirty or forty

[41.] See for example his remarks about democracies in *Republic* VI.4 –
'the Swiss Republics have the highest reputation for their understanding
of how to regulate a state, and although they display the form of
popular Sovereignty [*popularis Imperii*] they are in fact governed
[*gubernantur*] aristocratically: they have two or three Councils, so that
the common people are exposed to state secrets [*arcana Imperii*] as
little as possible, and are kept well away from government
[*gubernaculis*]'. My translation from the Latin, *Republica* 1586, p. 703,
which the English translation followed (McRae, p. 708). The French text
does not mention the Swiss, referring instead to 'entre les seigneurs des
ligues, ceux qui mieux sont policez' *(Republique* 1576, p. 683; 1579,
p. 662). Prophetically, as far as Rousseau was concerned, Bodin said of
Geneva in particular that after the expulsion of the Bishop in 1536
'la Republique de Geneve fut changee de Monarchie Pontificale en estat
populaire gouvernee Aristocratiquement' (II.6, *Republique* 1579, p. 220).
This was a passage changed by Bodin to meet Simon Goulart's
objections (see p. 45): the first edition described Geneva purely as an
aristocracy (*Republique* 1576, p. 267: 'la Republique de Genesve fut aussi
changee de Monarchie Pontificale en Aristocratie'). Interestingly, the
Latin edition simply says that Geneva was changed *in popularem
statum eiecto pontifice* (*Republica* 1586, p. 220).

years ago.[42] In them he argued that Bodin in the *Republic* sought to construct a theory of legislative absolutism that would deny any role to the traditional sources of 'constitutional' authority, which had been used in France to restrain royal power, such as the Estates General or the courts. As Franklin saw it, by insisting on the supremacy of a single source of legislation over all other elements in a constitution, Bodin succeeded in asserting royal power against its enemies in the Wars of Religion, but at the cost of developing a deeply unconvincing dogma that sovereign power could not be divided. This is a very American – or I should say, modern American – view: in many of his works Franklin in effect simply pointed to the US Constitution as an adequate rebuttal of what he took to be Bodin's central claim,[43] and he paid surprisingly little attention to the other aspects of Bodin's theory.[44] An important part of

---

[42.] In particular *Jean Bodin and the Sixteenth-Century Revolution in the Methodology of Law and History* (New York: Columbia University Press, 1963); *Jean Bodin and the Rise of Absolutist Theory* (Cambridge University Press, 1973); 'Jean Bodin and the end of medieval constitutionalism' Horst Denzer (ed.), *Verhandlungen der Internationalen Bodin Tagung in München* (Munich: C. H. Beck, 1973), pp. 167–86; 'Sovereignty and the mixed constitution: Bodin and his Critics' in J. H. Burns (ed.), with the assistance of Mark Goldie, *The Cambridge History of Political Thought 1450–1700* (Cambridge University Press, 1991), pp. 298–328; and the introduction to his edition of *Bodin: On Sovereignty* (Cambridge University Press, 1992).

[43.] See his 'Sovereignty and the mixed constitution', p. 303.

[44.] For example, he relegated the subject of perpetuity to an appendix of his *Jean Bodin and the Rise of Absolutist Theory* with the remark that 'since the issue of perpetuity had practically no importance in the constitutional controversies of the time, and since it is only loosely

this interpretation was the claim that the *Methodus* was strongly constitutionalist,[45] and that

> ten years later, with the publication of his *République*,
> this position was abandoned. But the absolutism of the
> later work was so confused and strained that it cannot
> be taken as the natural outcome of the older view.
> It was rather an abrupt, and largely ill-founded,
> departure not only in Bodin's intellectual career but
> in the general movement of French and European
> thought.[46]

related to other elements in Bodin's doctrine, there was no convenient place to introduce it in the text' (p. 109). He also remarked at the end of the same work that 'Bodin's more enduring contribution is significant if indirect. His theory of sovereignty was the proximate source of the idea that there must exist in every legal system an ultimate legal norm or set of procedures by which all decisions are coordinated. Put in older language, a sovereign power must exist in every commonwealth, and must always be located in the norms accepted by the general community. Bodin wrongly thought that this authority must be vested in what we would call the government. But it is with Bodin's work that discussion of the issue was effectively initiated' (p. 108). Bodin would have been startled to read that he thought sovereignty 'must be vested in what we would call the government'.

45. 'Prior to the 1570s the mainstream of the French tradition had been tentatively constitutionalist, and Bodin himself had given strong expression to that tendency in his *Methodus* of 1566. His earlier theory of sovereignty, elaborated in that work, was implicitly adapted to a notion of limited supremacy'. *Jean Bodin and the Rise of Absolutist Theory*, p. vii. See also p. 23.

46. *Jean Bodin and the Rise of Absolutist Theory*, p. vii. Franklin's view of the relationship between the two works was shared to some extent by Beatrice Reynolds in her 1945 translation of the *Methodus*, describing it

So it was the innovatory aspects of the *Republic* that constituted the 'absolutist' theory, and their distinctiveness is to be found by comparing the *Republic* with the *Methodus*.

These, as I said, are broadly the assumptions about Bodin's political ideas which one still encounters, insofar as one does encounter them; for it is fair to say that most attention in the last twenty years has been lavished on Bodin's other works such as the *Theatrum Universae Vitae* and above all the *Heptaplomeres*, leaving the *Methodus* and the *Republic* to one side. But if we shift our gaze from legislative absolutism to Bodin's theory as a whole, and in particular to the sovereignty–government distinction, the standard interpretation begins to look much less plausible.

In the first place, the contrast between the *Methodus* and the *Republic* appears less clear-cut, because the sovereignty–government distinction and the stress on perpetuity are in fact both to be found first in the *Methodus*. And only four years before the *Republic* appeared, Bodin published a new edition of the *Methodus*, with what may

as his 'earlier and more liberal work' (p. x), but it was not present in the first, and most careful analysis of the *Methodus*, by John L. Brown in his *The Methodus ad facilem historiarum cognitionem of John Bodin: A Critical Study* (Washington, DC: Catholic University of America Press, 1939), and it does not seem to have been a common view earlier. There are sensible remarks about the relationship in Ralph E. Giesey, 'Medieval jurisprudence in Bodin's concept of sovereignty' in Horst Denzer (ed.), *Verhandlungen der Internationalen Bodin Tagung in München* (Munich: C. H. Beck, 1973), pp. 178–9, and Sara Miglietti in her edition of the text agrees that there is not a clear distinction between the *Methodus* and the *Republic* (pp. 31–48).

be cross-references to the new work in which he was engaged,[47] while what seem to be authorised editions of the *Methodus* continued to appear for the rest of Bodin's lifetime. The Latin *Republic* also contains cross-references to the

[47.] The 1572 edition of the *Methodus* has three references to other works in which Bodin says he has discussed various topics more fully, all of which are absent from the 1566 edition. At p. 249 he says about the Muscovites and Abyssians holding foreigners against their wills that 'these things we have discussed more at length in the book *De decretis*' (Reynolds, trans., p. 165). This is missing from the 1566 edition, p. 191. At p. 255 of the 1572 edition (compare p. 195 of the 1566 edition) he added a passage about the argument between Aeschines and Demosthenes over magisterial power, ending 'But these things are discussed more thoroughly in the book *De imperio* (Reynolds, p. 169). And at pp. 261–2 of the 1572 edition (compare p. 200 of the 1566 edition) he added to his account of the marks of sovereignty: 'They have been discussed more fully by us, however, in the book *De jure imperio* [sic], in the chapter about the right of majesty'. (Reynolds picked up that this last reference was an addition to the 1566 edition, but she missed that the other two also were). The fact that these references all appear for the first time in 1572, with the implication that Bodin expected his readers to be able at least in the near future to consult them, suggests that they refer to work he was currently engaged on, and not (as Myron Gilmore supposed, following Moreau-Reibel) some treatises from his youth (see Myron P. Gilmore, *Argument from Roman Law in Political Thought 1200–1600* (Harvard University Press, 1941), p. 94 and Jean Moreau-Reibel, *Jean Bodin et le droit public comparé* (Paris: Vrin, 1933), p. 24. The natural interpretation is that they were drafts of the *Republic*; the Muscovites and Ethiopians holding foreigners is indeed discussed at length in Book I, chapter 6 of the *Republic* (McRae, pp. 60ff), the dispute between Aeschines and Demosthenes is treated 'thoroughly' in Book III, chapter 2 (McRae, p. 283), and the marks of sovereignty are the subject-matter of Book I, chapter 10, entitled in the Latin version 'Quaenam propria sunt iura maiestatis?' Gilles Menage in a biographical note on Bodin appended to his *Vitae Petri Aerodii Quaesitoris Andegavensis et Guillelmi*

Methodus.[48] (The situation is rather similar to the relationship between Hobbes's *De Cive* and his *Leviathan.*) Moreover, as I suggested previously, even the account of legislative sovereignty in the *Republic* does not differ markedly from the account in the *Methodus,* if one reads them both without any prior expectations. The *Methodus*'s discussion is much briefer, but in addition to its stress on the sovereign's role in choosing magistrates (to which I shall turn in a moment) Bodin, as we have seen, acknowledged that the sovereign must be the ultimate source of law, whereas in the *Republic* he equally gave a central role to the choice of magistrates. Although he said that in some sense all sovereign power could be understood as legislative in character, he also accepted that 'the word law is too general' and other 'rights of Sovereignty' should be separately specified, particularly the right to select magistrates.[49] I could say much more about the broad similarities between the two works, but a full account of that would take me too far from my present theme (see the Note at the end of this chapter).

Menagii Advocati Regii Andegavensis (Paris, 1675), p. 143, recorded that 'Il ordonna par son Testament, dont j'ay vu l'original, que ses livres *de Imperio, & Jurisdictione, & Legis actionibus, & Decretis, & Judiciis,* seroient brulez: ce qui fut fait avant sa mort en sa présance'. But there is no reason to conclude from this that they were early works rather than drafts which he wished to destroy. Miglietti has come to the same conclusion (Miglietti (ed.), *Methodus,* pp. 44–7).

[48.] For example, *Republica,* pp. 46, 402, 421, 422 and 513. This was observed by Brown.

[49.] Translation from Franklin, *Bodin: On Sovereignty,* p. 59. *Republique* 1576, p. 199 (*droits de souveraineté*); 1579, p. 159; *Republica* 1586, p. 155 (*propria maiestatis capita*); McRae, p. 163.

The dominating concern of the political parts of the *Methodus*, and the reason why it has been read as 'constitutionalist', was an argument in defence of the special role of the parlements in the government of France. Bodin was accredited as an advocate of the Parlement of Paris in 1561 to 1562, and as he said in the dedication to his *Demonomanie* of 1580 he spent 'the best part of my life' in 'that sovereign school of justice' with 'unbelievable pleasure and profit'.[50] The relationship between the kings of France and their parlements was notoriously complex and subtle: royal acts had (normally) to be registered by the parlement to be treated as valid in the courts, and the registration process could involve a series of remonstrances by the parlement back to the king trying to get changes in acts of which they disapproved, remonstrances that characteristically cited general principles of justice but could also draw attention to 'inconveniens', which might arise as a consequence of the royal proposal.[51] The king could in the end force registration against the wishes of the parlement through a *lettre de jussion*, but too frequent a use of this power would have led to the breakdown of the system. Kings were reluctant to do this as they benefitted from the level of legal expertise and (to some extent) political consent that the process offered them. They also had somewhat limited powers over the membership of the parlement, which to a significant extent

---

[50.] *De la Demononamie des Sorciers* (Paris: Jacque du Puys, 1580), sig. á2r.

[51.] A good example is provided by the May 1563 remonstrance on the attempt to abandon the requirement for officers of the Crown to profess the Catholic faith. See Sylvie Daubresse, *Le Parlement de Paris ou La Voix de la Raison (1559–1589)*, Travaux d'Humanisme et Renaissance cccxcviii (Geneva: Librairie Droz, 2005), pp. 490–4.

consisted of members co-opted by the existing officers. But the parlement was, in the last analysis, the royal council, and the parlementaires (who standardly described themselves as 'representing' the *maiestas* (i.e. the sovereignty, in Bodin's terminology) of the king[52] – not, strikingly, as in England, the people, saw their task as protecting the interests of the monarchy even against the wishes of a particular king. This was most notably expressed in their constant struggle to halt the alienation of the royal domain and to preserve it intact for future monarchs.

Right at the beginning of the *Methodus*, and long before he actually turned to the history of states, Bodin announced that 'it is one thing to declare laws, another to take counsel concerning legislation. The latter is for the senate, the former for the people or the prince or whoever has the sovereignty'.[53] (The Parlement of Paris was standardly described by its admirers as the Senate of France.) And when he did turn to the history of France, in chapter 6, his constant theme was the importance and independence of the Parlement. Thus, he said that the reputation of 'our form of royal power' was best illustrated in civil affairs by the fact that 'foreign kings and princes from the extremities of Germany, Italy, and the shores of Spain flocked in a great throng to the senate of the French, as to a sacred asylum of justice'.[54]

[52.] Daubresse, *Le Parlement de Paris*, pp. 46ff.
[53.] Page 124 of Miglietti, pp. 29–30 of the 1566 edition, p. 37 of the 1572 edition and p. 32 of Reynolds.
[54.] Translation from Reynolds, p. 252, slightly emended; p. 536 of Miglietti, p. 300 of the 1566 edition and p. 395 of the second edition.

An example is when the Parlement of Paris adjudicated the dispute between Frederick II and Innocent IV over Naples. 'Furthermore', he claimed, 'the king, as well as private citizens, agrees to its laws and decrees', and he praised Louis XI and Charles VII for conceding that the Parlement could overrule their wishes.

> Indeed, it is the great secret [*magnum arcanum*] of this monarchy that the prince is arbiter of all rewards in the state, yet he cannot inflict any punishments, but relinquishes this unpleasant duty to the magistrates. Whereby it happens that he is held worthy of the love of all, the hate of none, and powerful men, condemned by the judges, have no cause to be angry at him, because he is not responsible. The superior courts, which in great part are drawn from the third estate, coerce the might of the nobles and more powerful subjects by impartial decrees and, as it were, maintain the highest and lowest in unbelievable harmony. Those who have been trying to overthrow the dignity of these courts seek the ruin of the state [*respublica*], since in these is placed the safety of civil order, of laws, of customs, and of the entire state [*respublica*].[55]

And his principal objection to the course that popular government took in Florence was that (in general) it did not have

---

[55.] Translation from Reynolds, p. 257, emended; p. 544 of Miglietti, p. 306 of the 1566 edition and p. 403 of the second edition. The passage continues: 'There are seven courts of this sort; the greatest consists of one hundred and forty judges, from whom there is no appeal'. This lack of appellate jurisdiction was of course an important reason why Bodin was concerned to deny that the court was simply the delegate of the king.

a senate: 'this is equivalent to a body that lacks a mind. For the safety of a state rests with the senate'.[56]

We find just the same defence of the authority and practical independence of the parlements in the *Republic*. There are many examples of this, but the most striking and revealing comes in his argument (against the late-medieval canonists, in particular) that there is an important difference between *law* and *contract*, and that

> a sovereign prince is bound [in the courts, i.e. not merely morally] by the contracts he has made, whether with his subject or with a foreigner. For since he is the guarantor to his subjects of the agreements and mutual obligations that they have entered with one another, there is all the more reason why he must render justice for his own act. Thus the Parlement of Paris wrote to King Charles IX in March 1563 that his majesty could not unilaterally break the contract between himself and the clergy without the clergy's consent, inasmuch as he had a duty to give justice.[57]

This refers to a remonstrance that the Parlement delivered on 11 March 1564,[58] protesting that a payment forced from the

[56.] Translation from Reynolds, p. 249; p. 530 of Miglietti, p. 297 of the 1566 edition and p. 390 of the second edition.

[57.] Translation from Franklin, *Bodin: On Sovereignty*, p. 35. *Republique* 1576, pp. 147–8; 1579, p. 106; *Republica* 1586, p. 99; McRae, p. 106.

[58.] Though Bodin was notoriously casual about dates, references, etc. (for his casualness, see e.g. the remarks in Giesey, 'Medieval jurisprudence', *Verhandlungen*, p. 168, n. 3 and p. 176), his dating of this remonstrance to 1563 is probably not an error. France began to date the new year from 1 January instead of 25 March in 1564 (Charles IX's Edict of Roussillon, issued in January 1563 O.S., registered by the Parlement of Paris,

Church by Charles IX had not been used for redeeming the royal domain, contrary to the agreement with the Church about its taxation made at Poissy in 1561 (the 'Contrat de Poissy'). But what Bodin did not tell his readers was that a royal *lettre de jussion* of July 1564 replied that the payment had been necessary to maintain the Swiss alliance, and that the Parlement gave way and authorised the payment.[59] So in fact the moral of the episode was that the royal will *could* override a contract, a moral Bodin conveniently forbore to draw.

Given Bodin's strenuous defence of parlements, which continued even into the period of his adherence to the Catholic League,[60] we can understand the real point of

December 1564 O.S and N.S.). Although the Edict intended that January 1563 O.S. should be regarded as January 1564 N.S., in practice the new dating did not come in until the following year. So when Bodin said March 1563, he will have meant March 1564 N.S. Daubresse comments that there is no record of a remonstrance of the kind Bodin describes in March 1563 (*Le Parlement de Paris*, p. 123, n. 12), but she does not consider the question raised by the change in dating the year, nor link Bodin's remark with the remonstrance of 11 March 1564 that she describes on p. 127, which is plainly what Bodin had in mind.

[59.] Daubresse, *Le Parlement de Paris*, p. 127.

[60.] See Paul Lawrence Rose, 'The politique and the prophet: Bodin and the Catholic League 1589–1594', *The Historical Journal* 21 (1978), pp. 783–808. In the letter (probably to the President of the Paris Parlement, Barnabé Brisson), which Bodin wrote in March 1589 justifying his switch to the League, and which was published anonymously as *Lettre d'un Lieutenant-Général de Province á un des premiers magistrats de France* (Paris, 1589), Bodin argued that 'une rébellion universelle ne se doyt appeler rébellion. L'union de tant de citez et de peuples que j'ay remarqué ne pouvant être chastiée: veu principalement que tout premieêrement tous les parlemens de ce Royaume qui sont les fortes barrières de la France sont uniz' (Moreau-Reibel, *Jean Bodin et le droit*

his distinction between sovereign and government, and why
it emerged from the distinctive constitutional arrangements of
ancien régime France. Unlike England, where it might be
possible to assert that Parliament (including the queen
or king) was both sovereign and government, in France there
could be no real plausibility in any claim about the supremacy
of the parlements – they were patently not sovereign bodies.
But, on the other hand, they were not mere agents of the
sovereign monarch, simply implementing his commands,
but were able (on Bodin's account) to have a very high degree
of autonomy in their decisions – in particular, there was no
appeal from their judgements sitting as a high court. The
delicate balance between king and parlements could not be
expressed by saying that the parlements were the *agents* of
the king, because the whole point of the system was that they
were not; at the same time, however, they could not be
regarded as *equal* to the king, nor as sharers in some sense
in his sovereignty. Bodin's great idea was that they were
engaged in something different from the activity of the sovereign monarch, and that their relative independence in practice
did not call into question the suzerainty of the king. The king's
function was to authorise or render legitimate law whose
content was (ideally) determined by the parlements, and to
authorise the punishment of offenders whose guilt had been
determined by the judges. The *Methodus*, read in this way,
then looks straightforwardly like a response by Bodin to the

public comparé, p. 426). In other words, he moved to the League once the
Parlement of Paris, and the other *parlements*, split, with most of their
members turning to the League.

hostility expressed towards the parlements in the 1550s and 1560s by the royal court, and in particular to a set of addresses to the parlements by the Chancellor Michel de l'Hopital in the early 1560s.[61]

Bodin also applied this reasoning to a famous debate in Roman law, the significance of which in his work has often been misunderstood. In both the *Methodus* and the *Republic* he turned his attention to the well-known dispute between the twelfth-century jurists Azo and Lothair over the meaning of the Roman legal term *merum imperium*, and whether magistrates possessed some kind of *imperium* in their own right, or merely a delegated power from the prince. The history of this argument formed the subject matter of Myron Gilmore's *Argument from Roman Law in Political Thought 1200–1600* (Harvard University Press 1941). I do not want to repeat it here, but the point I want to stress is that the distinctive feature of Bodin's approach was a hostility to *both* sides of the controversy. Bodin's position was that governmental structures are not mere agents of the sovereign; they are authorised by the sovereign precisely not to execute the law mechanically but instead to use their own discretion. However

---

[61]. For these addresses see Michel de l'Hôpital, *Oeuvres complètes* II (Paris, 1824), especially pp. 12ff for his argument that the Parlement should be concerned only with making judgements between parties according to law, and p. 17 for the response by the President of the Parlement insisting that it had to consider whether proposed laws were 'justes, utiles, possible et raisonnables'. See Nancy Lyman Roelker, *One King, One Faith: The Parlement of Paris and the Religious Reformations of the Sixteenth Century* (University of California Press, 1996), pp. 297 and 311 for a brief discussion of l'Hôpital's *harangues*.

on Bodin's account of sovereignty, this could not logically be a participation in *imperium*, because *imperium* did not include such things as jurisdiction or deliberation – it was the *choice* of magistrate that was the sovereign power, not what the magistrate *did*. His position on the old debate thus simply followed from his new idea about sovereignty, and he understood that the debate had made sense only to people who shared a broadly Aristotelian approach to sovereign powers in which everything a magistrate did was the kind of thing a sovereign would do.

Bodin discussed this Roman law question in broadly similar terms in both the *Methodus* (where it is in a central place in his section on sovereignty) and in the *Republic*, though I think the argument is clearer in the later work;[62] and he observed rather interestingly (in a passage added to the Latin version) that the issue had been confused by the fact that

> in democratic and aristocratic states [*imperii*], such as those of the Greeks and the Italians, they sought one thing above all others, that their magistrates should as far as possible be bound by the laws, so that they could not even if they wished diverge from their allotted role in the slightest degree. The ancients did this much more than men of our own time; in a royal monarchy [*potestas*] [like France] it is

---

[62.] Gilmore (in line with the desire to separate the two works) wanted to see more difference between the *merum imperium* passages than I think is warranted – the *Republica* reads more like an attempt to put the basic idea in a slightly new form, no doubt because it had already been criticised by professional jurists along the lines Cujas expressed when he read the first edition of the *Republique*.

often the opposite, for in criminal courts all kinds of punishment, and in civil courts the decisions about liability [*in privatis id quod ciuique interest*], are left up to the judgement of the magistrates.[63]

So modern states, unlike ancient republics, accepted that magistrates could have extensive discretion without being sovereigns or sharing in the sovereignty, and were therefore particularly vivid examples of the separation of government from sovereign power. Here, Bodin is even edging towards Rousseau's thought about the key difference between ancient and modern states.

A theory of this kind is in many ways more genuinely 'constitutionalist' than the conventional idea of mixed government, which Franklin took to be the paradigm of constitutionalism. In Bodin's account, there is a fundamental site of sovereignty, which is responsible for the major features of a society's political structures, and which gives legitimacy to the society's political activity. However, this is not itself necessarily a site of day-to-day power or decision-making. As Rousseau was to perceive, and as Bodin himself seems to have been well aware, this is a theory that is peculiarly appropriate for a modern democratic state, but it can also be employed, as Bodin wished, to analyse a monarchy of a broadly constitutionalist kind, in which the important political decisions are not taken by the monarch himself or herself. Indeed that was the reaction of most of his early readers: his analysis of

[63.] III.5. *Republica* 1586, p. 306; McRae, p. 335. The relevant page in the French versions (without this passage) are *Republique* 1576, p. 359; 1579, p. 308.

sovereignty was – contrary to what one would have expected
on the 'absolutist' interpretation of his work – quickly wel-
comed by readers uneasy about the growth of monarchical
power. Such a reaction was helped by the fact that – apart
from Aristotle – the main targets to be named in both the
Methodus and the *Republic* were Italian republicans, particularly Machiavelli, and not contemporary resistance theorists;
though in both Book I, chapter 8 on sovereignty and in his
chapter on tyrannicide in the *Republic* (Book II, chapter 5)
Bodin did condemn certain unspecified books that defended
resistance against a tyrant.[64]

The first response we know of came from Simon
Goulart, the Calvinist minister of Geneva, who arranged for
a French edition of the *Republic* to be produced in Geneva in
1577, a project he would not have undertaken had he not
fundamentally approved of the work.[65] Goulart added a

[64.] Machiavelli is expressly attacked in the preface to the first French
edition. The references to resistance theorists are 'ceux qui ont escrit du
devoir des Magistrats, & autres livres semblables' I.8 (*Republique* 1576,
p. 137; 1579, p. 96; McRae, p. 95) which must be a reference to Beza's *De
Iure Magistratuum in subditos* (though in the Latin version he merely
refers to *libris pervulgatis* (*Republica*, p. 89); and 'livres imprimez' II.5
(*Republique* 1576, p. 259; 1579, p. 212; McRae, p. 224) (in the Latin,
perniciosissimis scriptis, p. 212). Goulart complained of Bodin's lack of
specificity in this area – see his remarks in his preface, *Les Six Livres de la
Republique* (n.p. [Geneva] 1577) sigs *1-*1v. The remark about the 'devoir
des Magistrats' is on p. 205 of this edition, and that about 'livres
imprimez' is on p. 389.

[65.] He said that 'pour autant qu'en ces discours de Bodin il y a beaucoup de
choses dites librement & qui peuvent servir, on a pensé faire plaisir aux
François de les leur communiquer en petit volume, tant pour soulager
leur main & leur bourse, que dautant qu'ils eussent estre frustrez de la

preface praising Bodin as a 'man who is right in very many places',[66] but correcting Bodin's view of the Genevan constitution and observing that Bodin had been mistaken in saying (as he did in the first edition) that both Luther and Calvin had been opposed to rebellion against a tyrannical monarch; Goulart quoted *in extenso* Calvin's famous remarks about Ephors to show that he had supported constitutional resistance of this kind against tyrants. In a prefatory letter to the 1578 Paris edition of the French *Republic* Bodin responded to this in hurt tones, stressing that he had opposed 'the opinions of those who write on enlarging the rights of the treasury and the royal prerogative' and was simply hostile to the more radical claims that sovereign kings must be elected and can be deposed by their people.[67] He also added a discussion of Calvin to the relevant passage in later editions of the French *Republic*, saying that Calvin in his observations about ephors 'shows sufficiently that it is never lawful in a legitimate Monarchy [*en la droite Monarchie*] to attack or defend oneself against one's sovereign King, nor to make an attempt on his life or honour; for he was not talking about anything other than democratic [*populaires*] or

---

lecture d'iceux, á cause qu'apres la premiere edition mise en lumiere lon avoit defendu au libraire de la faire imprimer' (sig *5r - *5v). For a discussion of this edition, see Corinne Müller, 'L'edition subreptice des *Six Livres de la République* de Jean Bodin [Genève, 1577]. Sa génèse et son influence', *Quaerendo* 10 (1980), pp. 211–36.

66. 'homme qui a beaucoup leu á la verité' (sig. ¶8v).

67. *Republique* 1579, sig. á5; McRae, p. A71. Though in Latin, this letter is not appended to the *Republica*.

Aristocratic Republics'.[68] Of course, Calvin had added to his list of ephoral institutions, modern Estates Generals – something Bodin simply (and characteristically) omitted.

As Bodin's response to Goulart makes clear, he believed that his defence of parlements and his insistence that kings could be held to their contracts comprised a defence of 'the interest of the people' in 'these perilous times', and that he and the Genevan were essentially on the same side, for each would be opposed to the kind of extreme resistance theory he condemned. That this was not a misreading of the situation is confirmed by other early uses of the *Republic*. Most strikingly (and something I commented on in my *Philosophy and Government*) Aggaeus van Albada, a Frisian jurist who was a member of the Dutch delegation at the Peace Conference of Cologne in 1579, quoted freely from the French *Republic* in the annotations to the edition of the papers exchanged at the conference which he published at the end of 1579, alongside quotations from the *Vindiciae contra tyrannos*, Beza's *De Iure Magistratuum* (in the version issued by the Catholic radical Johann Baptist Fickler) and other 'monarchomach' texts.[69]

[68.] *Republique* 1579, p. 213; McRae, pp. 224–5. In the Latin *Republic* Bodin added a marginal note making a similar point (*Republica*, p. 212). See the *Republique* 1576, p. 259 and the Geneva edition, p. 389 for the original text (marked in the margin of the Geneva edition with 'Voyez l'advertissement au lecteur', i.e. Goulart's preface).

[69.] *Acta pacificationis quae coram Sac. Caesareae Maiest. Commissariies, inter Seren. Regis Hispaniarum ... Ordinumque Belgii legatos, Coloniae habita sunt* (Leiden, 1580), pp. 53 and 283 on intervention, pp. 97 and 99 on contracts. Van Albada's page citations of the French *Republic* make clear that he was reading it in the Genevan edition, no doubt as part of a set of works approved by the Calvinists; this may also confirm

Van Albada was particularly interested in Bodin's defence of armed intervention by neighbouring princes in civil war, an aspect of his thought which has received little modern attention,[70] and in his claim that princes are civilly bound by their contracts. We can find the same in other early uses of the work, and in general, I think it is fair to say, Bodin is not treated as a theorist of 'absolutism' until well into the seventeenth century.[71]

> that Goulart was correct in saying that it was hard to get hold of the first Paris edition. There is a discussion of the Dutch use of Bodin by Jan Machielsen, 'Bodin in the Netherlands', in Howell A. Lloyd (ed.), *The Reception of Bodin* (Leiden: Brill, 2013), pp. 157–92, though he does not mention Albada.
>
> [70.] In arguing this, Bodin was in line with mainstream radical Protestantism; see my 'Alliances with infidels in the European imperial expansion' in Sankar Muthu (ed.), *Empire and Modern Political Thought* (Cambridge University Press, 2012), pp. 61–83.
>
> [71.] See François Grimaudet's discussion of the distinction between *lettres de justice* and *commandements Opuscules politiques* (Paris, 1580), pp. 6 r and v, and, rather remarkably, Jean Boucher, the 'monarchomach' Leaguer, who quoted Bodin in defence of tyrannicide in his *De iusta abdicatione Henrici III* of 1589, at a moment when Bodin himself was openly on the side of the League. He cited Buchanan on the subject, and then said that 'nec longe discrepat Bodini opinio' when he said (11.5) that a tyrant who occupies the *praesidia, arces*, etc. can be treated as a public enemy (sig. Y1v). William Barclay in his *De regno et regali potestate* (1600) pointed out the error in this reading of Bodin, 'viri certe in Politicis acuti' (p. 359), an interesting example of both sides seeking to use Bodin's authority. Though it has often been said (including by me in *Philosophy and Government 1572–1651* (Cambridge University Press, 1993), p. 28), that defenders of the French monarchy in the late sixteenth and early seventeenth century such as William Barclay and Pierre Gregoire were followers of Bodin, it is striking how little they actually refer to him; though Gregoire did use the sovereign–government distinction in his

The last question to raise about Bodin's theory has to do with his claim of originality. As we saw, he asserted in the *Republic* that 'no one has hitherto observed' the distinction between sovereign and government, and 'I am the only person who thinks this'. How far was this really true? Bodin was after all rather prone to make sweeping claims of this kind. But in this instance it seems that he was substantially justified. Certainly, he was correct in asserting that the humanist Aristotelians of his own day did not make such a distinction, and in fact explicitly treated all political authority as 'government', in Bodin's sense of the term.[72] The one tradition in which writers did say something similar at first glance to Bodin was the tradition of late medieval and early modern scholasticism, in which it was commonplace to say that 'the people' created their political institutions, including monarchical structures, but were separate from them, and it might be thought that this was the same idea as Bodin's distinction. 'The people' would be a Bodinian sovereign, and the political institutions would be a Bodinian government. But this was not at all the distinction that Bodin had in mind. First, his distinction was formally speaking neutral between the three types of sovereign: a monarch could be the

highly Bodinian denial of the possibility of mixed government (without citing Bodin). See his *De Republica Libri Sex et Viginti* (Lyons, 1596) I, p. 236 It is also worth noting that the Protestant La Popelinière's contemporary history of the French wars of religion records the stand of 'Bodin jurisconsulte' at the Estates General (*L' histoire de France enrichie des plus notables occurrences* (La Rochelle, 1581) II, pp. 341, 351). For the seventeenth-century English reading of Bodin, see Chapter 2.

[72] See p. 17 and n. 15.

underlying sovereign just as much as a people could be, and indeed – as we have seen – that was for him in practice the most important case. This was not true for the scholastics: they took it to be a fundamental fact about all political associations that they were in some sense the creation of their members, so that a king or an aristocracy could not lurk underneath the government in the way Bodin conceived.

This formal neutrality was linked to the second difference between Bodin and the scholastics, the fact that his sovereign had to be an actual and determinate legislator with a recognised capacity to issue law and to appoint the government. Few of the scholastics were willing to say this: there was a pervasive vagueness in almost all of their accounts of how 'the people' created the institutions and whether they were themselves part of the institutional structure. A common view is illustrated by the early sixteenth-century Spanish scholastic Francisco de Vitoria in his *Relectio De Potestate Civili*, who said 'the material cause in which power of this kind resides is by natural, and divine law the *respublica* itself', though the power 'is principally in kings, to whom the *respublica* commits it as its agents' since 'this power cannot be exercised by the multitude itself ... [and] it is therefore necessary that the exercise of the power [*potestatis administratio*] be conferred on some man or men who can administer it [*curam gererent*]'.[73] On this account, all political societies, of whatever

---

[73.] See the similar idea expressed by some conciliarists in 1444, quoted by A. J. Black, *Monarchy and Community in the Later Middle Ages: Political Ideas in the Later Conciliar Controversy 1430–1450* (Cambridge University Press, 1970), p. 17: 'the power of the universal church is

constitutional structure, were brought into being by the *populus* or the *respublica*, but the *populus* or *respublica* did so precisely because it could not itself constitute a determinate locus of political authority; it lay behind all determinate structures but was not itself one. This was, of course, a very difficult picture to make sense of, for if the 'multitude' could not exercise power, how could it 'commit' the power to a monarch? And writers such as Vitoria were unwilling or unable to spell out just what kind of institutional process was involved.[74]

brought into activity through the existence of the general council. Such power exists in the dispersed church in the same way that the seed exists in the grass, or wine in the grape; but, in the general council, it exists in its formal and complete essence'. The grape is, in Aristotelian terms, the material cause of the wine.

[74.] Suarez, writing in 1612, but apparently little interested in what Bodin had done, made very similar remarks in his *De Legibus ac Deo Legislatore*, saying that 'men as individuals possess to a partial extent (so to speak) the faculty for establishing, or creating, a perfect community; and by virtue of the very fact that they establish it, the power in question does come to exist in this community as a whole. Nevertheless, natural law does not require either that the power should be exercised directly by the agency of the whole community, or that it should always continue to reside therein. On the contrary, it would be most difficult, from a practical point of view, to satisfy such requirements, for infinite confusion and trouble would result if laws were established by the vote of every person; and therefore, men straightway determine the said power by vesting it in one of the above-mentioned forms of government [i.e. the standard regimes, including democracy, rather inconsistently, given what Suarez had just said], since no other form can be conceived' (*De Legibus*, Book III, chapter 4.1, in James Scott Brown (ed.), *Selections from Three Works of Francisco Suárez, S. J.* (Oxford University Press, 1944 for the Carnegie Endowment Classics of International Law), vol. I, p. 206 of the reproduction; II (translation) p. 383). And he felt quite free to describe

They were also quite prepared to say that the king or other governor possessed *summum imperium* or *summa potestas*, in the sense that no other institution in the society was superior to them, even while they attributed this residual power to the people as a whole.

One natural way of expressing this kind of thought was that the institutions of power 'represented' the people; this was the language used especially by the fifteenth-century conciliarists whom Antony Black has studied, but it was widespread in the late Middle Ages. Thus, Pierre D'Ailly said that *plenitudo potestatis* in the universal church was in the church in the sense that an effect is in its cause, that is, the church brought the institutions into being; but it was in the council as the church's representative, *ut res visa dicitur esse in speculo.*[75] The most remarkable and modern-sounding of these conciliarists was John of Segovia, who analysed the pope as the church's representative.

> He ceases to be a private and is made a public person; he loses in a sense his isolated unity, and puts on [*induit*] the united people, so that he may be said to bear or represent the person not of one but of many [*gestare sive representare personam multorum*] ... Whoever is made ruler or president of any people puts aside his private and takes on

civil rulers such as kings or even *duces* as possessing *supremam potestatem* (*De Triplici Virtute Theologica, Selections from Three Works* I, p. 800 of the reproduction, II [translation], p. 808).

[75.] In Jean Gerson, *Opera Omnia*, Louis Ellies Dupin (ed.), (Antwerp, 1706) vol. II, col. 950; Antony Black, *Council and Commune: The Conciliar Movement and the Fifteenth-Century Heritage* (London: Burns & Oates, 1979), p. 23.

a public person, in that he must seek not, as before, what is useful to himself, but what is useful to all. He carries [*gerit*] two persons; he is a private person, and by legal fiction a public person.[76]

As long as representation involved a rather vague sense that the people were embodied in their ruler without actually choosing him, what we normally term 'virtual' representation, it was quite different from the relationship between a Bodinian sovereign and its government. As we shall see in Chapter 2, this idea was destined to be revived and would play a major part in the political thought of the seventeenth and eighteenth centuries; indeed in a somewhat different form, it persists down to our own time.

It was also possible, however, for writers in the scholastic tradition to talk about 'actual' representation: the idea that any legitimate civil society must contain something such as an institutionalised means whereby the people could choose their legislators. As a number of people have observed, virtual representation was discussed in late-medieval texts much more than actual representation, but there are exceptions – notably Nicholas of Cusa in his well-known *De Concordantia Catholica* (1433), who argued that all church rulers had to be elected to have legitimacy.[77] This is then not so unlike the claim in Bodin that a sovereign must be able to choose the government or magistrates; but (leaving aside the issue of neutrality) it still differs vitally from Bodin's developed

[76.] Black, *Monarchy and Community*, pp. 25, 143, 148.
[77.] Paul E. Sigmund (ed. and trans.), *The Catholic Concordance* (Cambridge University Press, 1991), pp. 98–9.

position (clearly set out in the *Republic*, as we have seen, and equally clear in at least the 1572 edition of the *Methodus*) that a sovereign must not only choose the magistrates but must also have the power of ultimate legislation. These medieval writers, like the later critics of democracy, simply assumed that a modern state (or a complex modern institution such as the Church) could not involve popular legislation, and that even if legislators could be elected that was as far as the involvement of 'the people' in their politics could go. Either way, it then became possible for writers such as Rousseau, Constant and Sieyès looking back to say that representation had been the great modern (that is, post-classical) invention.[78]

There were instances in the Middle Ages, of course, of communities that were small enough to operate like ancient city-states, particularly in Italy, and the theorists who focused on those communities were able to envisage legislative power being vested in the popular assembly, and (correctly) to see

[78.] 'This [representative] system is a discovery of the moderns ...
[T]he condition of the human race in antiquity did not allow for the introduction or establishment of an institution of this nature ... Their social organization led them to desire an entirely different freedom from the one which this system grants to us'. Benjamin Constant, *Political Writings*, Biancamaria Fontana (ed.), (Cambridge University Press, 1988), p. 310 (*The Liberty of the Ancients Compared with that of the Moderns*, 1819). For Rousseau, see his remarks in Book III, chapter 15 of the *Social Contract* (*Social Contract and Discourses*), p. 240; Launay (ed.), *Oeuvres complètes*, p. 558. The clearest statement by Sieyès about the modernity of representation is in one of his manuscripts; see Pasquale Pasquino, *Sieyès et l'invention de la constitution en France* (Paris: Edition Odile Jacob, 1998), p. 163, but the whole tenor of his remarks on the subject points in that direction. See p. 170.

this as close to the ideas of Aristotle. The most famous case of this is Marsiglio of Padua, with his theory of the people as *legislator humanus*, possessing what amounts to sovereign legislative power as well as choosing the *principatus* who acted purely as an administrator of the law. Marsiglio, accordingly, barely used the language of representation, and his closest follower (a century later), John of Segovia, made explicit that representation would break down if the people could physically congregate together.

> If it occurs that the whole people assembles itself together, and asserts or desires something contrary to what the president himself says; then the people will deservedly prevail, since truth itself is preferred to fiction. For the truth is that this people is many persons; while the fiction is that the president himself, who in truth is a single person, is said to be many by representation.[79]

Black has indeed claimed that Segovia anticipated Rousseau in his idealisation of the small democratic community, though Segovia (unlike Marsiglio and Rousseau) seems to have believed that in the absence of such an assembly representation would have to be the means whereby political decisions are made. It is true that Marsiglio and Segovia did come closer to the ideas of the modern democrats with whom I am concerned than most earlier writers did (though it should be said that there is no evidence that either Bodin or Rousseau had ever read them). But, once again, neither of them made the kind of distinction which Bodin or Rousseau did between

[79.] Black, *Monarchy and Community*, pp. 27, 143.

a fundamental and a less fundamental level of legislation or political decision-making. As far as Marsiglio was concerned, the *legislator humanus* monopolised legislation, and the *principatus* was merely a judge (though he put hereditary monarchs into the category of *princeps*, without acknowledging that they standardly possessed legislative powers). So his political theory, as he himself stressed, stayed very close to Aristotle's, and was in a sense an idyll of an ancient or a modern Italian city-state ruled by what would later be termed a democratic *government* – whereas Bodin presented his new distinction between sovereign and government precisely as part of a critique of Aristotle and this kind of republican vision, and in the context of a discussion of (mostly) large states of a standard modern kind. From Bodin's perspective, all these earlier writers had unsurprisingly made the same error as their master Aristotle, and a proper understanding of the modern state could begin only with his new analysis.

Note

As I said in the chapter, I think that there is much less difference between the *Methodus*, especially in its 1572 version, and the *Republic* than has been supposed, at least during the last fifty years or so. If we consider the features of the *Methodus* which have been taken to be distinctively 'constitutionalist', in a way the *Republic* is presumed not to be, they boil down to four claims (in addition to the rather different point that in the *Republic* there may be only one mark of sovereignty, namely legislative supremacy. This, if it is a significant change from the *Methodus* (and I have given reasons previously for thinking that it is not), would not in itself make the *Republic* more 'absolutist' than the *Methodus*. The first claim is that in the *Methodus* Bodin believed that coronation oaths bind non-tyrannical kings to govern in accordance with law; the second that the king of France could not overturn fundamental laws, what he termed '*leges totius imperii proprias*'[80] without the consent of the Three Estates; the third that the king has no general rights over the private property of the citizens; and the fourth that he is bound by his own laws.[81]

To deal with these in turn: first, the account of the oath which the French kings took in the *Republic* says nothing significantly different from the account in the *Methodus*;[82] in the *Republic* Bodin was concerned to refute the idea (which he had not considered in the *Methodus*) that kings might be bound by their oaths to keep the laws *of their predecessors*, and he easily showed that the French oath involved no such thing. It was instead a general promise to govern by law and justice, and Bodin applauded it in very similar terms to those he used in the *Methodus*. Second, Bodin continued to believe that the fundamental laws of France could not be changed except with the consent of the Estates; he made that clear in

---

[80.] Miglietti, p. 448; 1566 edition, p. 239; 1572 edition, p. 314. Reynolds (p. 204) translates this as 'laws peculiar to the whole kingdom', though given the use of the term *leges imperii* to describe these laws in the *Republic* we should think of them as something more than merely laws of general (rather than regional) application in France.

[81.] These are all drawn from Franklin, *Jean Bodin and the Rise of Absolutist Theory*.

[82.] *Republique* 1576, pp. 135–6; 1579, pp. 94–5; *Republica*, p. 88; McRae, p. 94. Miglietti, p. 448; 1566 ed., p. 239; 1572 edition, p. 314: Reynolds, p. 204.

the most concrete of circumstances the year after the *Republic* was published, when as a delegate at the Estates General at Blois in 1577 he spoke out against the alienation of the royal domain (a constant theme of his writing and activity). 'As for the basic property of the said Domain, it belongs to the people, and consequently they can consent to its perpetual alienation if the Provinces have mandated their delegates expressly for this purpose, and not otherwise'.[83]

Third, it is generally recognised that this particular constitutional limitation is the same in both works. And fourth, Bodin says in the *Methodus* that a king is bound by his own law only if it continues to be *aequus*; otherwise, those who decree the laws have to be above them.[84] But this is no more than he says in the *Republic*, that the sovereign prince 'may derogate from the laws that he has promised and sworn to keep, if they cease to be just [*si la iustice d'icelle cesse*], without the consent of his subjects'.[85]

And above all, the *Republic* contains the same committed defence of the role of parlements in the French

---

[83.] '[Q]uand au fond et propriété dudit [sic] Domaine, qu'il appartenoit au peuple, et par conséquent pourroit bien consentir l'aliénation perpétuelle dudit Domaine, si les Provinces avoient baillé procuration expresse á cette fin; et non autrement'. *Recueil de pièces originales et authentiques' concernant la tenue des . . . Etats-généraux d'Orléans en 1560* (Paris, 1789), vol. III, p. 347.

[84.] This is described as an *honesta oratio* in the *Methodus* (Miglietti, p. 444; 1566 edition, p. 237; 1572 edition, p. 311) – which Reynolds translates rather misleadingly (p. 203) as 'a fine sentiment' (with an untoward implication of naïveté).

[85.] *Republique* 1576, p. 134; 1579, p. 93; *Republica*, p. 87; McRae, p. 93.

monarchy that Bodin had put forward ten years earlier. Bodin repeated that there were certain fundamental laws, what he now in the Latin version called simply *leges imperii*, 'which concern the state of the Kingdom, and its foundation [*establissement*]', and 'since they are annexed and united to the crown, the Prince cannot derogate from them'.[86] These *leges imperii* included in particular Salic law and the integrity of the royal domain – though, as he now made clear, the domain included not simply crown lands but also the offices of state. In Book III, chapter 5 he raised the question of whether (at least in a non-despotic monarchy) a magisterial office, *munus magistratuum*, belonged (*proprium sit*) to the *Respublica* or to the prince, or even to the magistrate himself.[87] His answer was that it belonged to the *Respublica*, though the *creatio* of the magistrate (in French, *la provision*) belonged to the prince, and any alienation of office (i.e. giving a hereditary right over it) had to be approved by the estates, just as alienation of crown land required their approval. In the absence of consent by the estates, the parlement could obstruct alienations (see in particular the discussion in Book VI, chapter 2).

The status of these fundamental laws has often puzzled readers of Bodin, for one might imagine that they imply some kind of über-sovereignty lodged with the Estates. But the best way of thinking about them is to link them to the fundamental distinction Bodin drew between 'royal' and 'seigneurial' monarchy (*monarchia regalis* and *unius dominatus*). Under a 'seigneurial' monarchy, the subjects were

---

[86.] *Republique* 1576, p. 136; 1579, p. 95; *Republica*, p. 88; McRae, p. 95.
[87.] *Republic*, p. 303; McRae, p. 330; *Republique* 1576, p. 354; 1579, p. 303.

the slaves of the king, but a 'royal' monarchy appeared when a king 'renders himself as obedient to the laws of nature, as he wishes his subjects to be towards himself, leaving each man his natural liberty, and the ownership of his goods' - which might happen if a lordly monarch 'having justly conquered his enemies' country gives them back their liberty, and the ownership of themselves and their goods'.[88] It is the fact that subjects have *property rights* in their possessions which is crucial;[89] Bodin repeatedly explained, for example, the inalienability of the royal domain as a consequence of the imperative need to respect individual property.

> So that Princes should not be forced to tax their subjects, or to search for means to confiscate their goods, all peoples, & Monarchs have taken it to be a general, and indubitable law, that the public domain ought to be holy, sacred, and inalienable, whether by contracts, or by prescription.[90]

Salic law, on the other hand, was presented simply as a consequence of the law of nature which gave rulership to men.[91] So a king who undertook to govern in accordance with

[88.] *Republique* 1576, pp. 238–9; 1579, p. 194; *Republica*, pp. 193–4; McRae, p. 204.

[89.] See also for this the *Methodus*. Miglietti, p. 448; 1566 edition, p. 240; 1572 edition, p. 315; Reynolds, p. 205.

[90.] *Republique* 1576, pp. 618–9; 1579, p. 597; McRae, p. 651. The Latin text is different: Bodin simply said there that the inalienability of the domain was in order that 'there should be something fixed [*firmamentum*] which can act as a foundation on which the state [*publica res*] can rest' (*Republica*, p. 639).

[91.] See the remarks in the *Methodus*, Miglietti, pp. 536–8; 1566 edition, pp. 301–2, 1572 edition, p. 397; Reynolds, p. 253. For the *Republic*, see

the law of nature and to respect his subjects' property rights (as the Kings of France had done, among other things by sanctioning a system of civil actions that would be meaningless if their subjects were slaves)[92] was, Bodin argued, necessarily limited in what he could do, without it being the case that he had any *institutional* superior over him. The Estates were relevant because the subjects' property rights required that consent be given before kings could take their possessions (except, Bodin argued, in time of war or great necessity, when taxation without consent was legitimate – indeed, he appears to have thought that this was the only time when taxes should be levied).[93]

It should be added that (contrary again to what has often been said) Bodin was inclined to argue even in the *Republic* that violent resistance against a prince who sought to reduce his free citizens to the status of slaves could be justified. In Book III, chapter 7 he told the story of Louis II Count of Flanders, whose harsh government (according to Bodin) induced the citizens of Ghent to rebel in 1379. After the rebellion was crushed, the citizens 'were glad to crave of him grace and pardon', but Louis 'would not so receive them, but propounded unto them most hard conditions, and not beseeming a free people to accept of: as that they should all come unto him out of the citie to crave pardon

especially *Republique* 1576, pp. 718ff; 1579 edition, pp. 698ff; *Republica*, pp. 738ff; McRae, pp. 746ff, with notes pp. A168–A169 correcting Knolles's translation (Knolles naturally watered down Bodin's remarks about female rule).

[92.] Miglietti, p. 448; 1566 edition, p. 240; 1572 edition, p. 315: Reynolds p.

[93.] *Republique* 1576, p. 633; 1579, p. 611; *Republica*, p. 654; McRae, p. 663.

with halters about their neckes'. The citizens refused and overthrew the Count in a new uprising:

> It was then recognised that there is no one more courageous against his lord, than a desperate subject: and no war more just, than that which is necessary, as an ancient Roman senator said. These citizens, in addition to their inevitable punishment, were reduced to suffering a shame worse than death. Shame is always feared more by honourable men than death itself.[94]

A conviction of this kind underlay his switch to support the Catholic League in the late 1580s, when he argued that 'a universal rebellion should not be called a rebellion'.[95] In addition to these fundamental constraints on monarchical power, Bodin in the *Republic* made a distinction he had not suggested in the *Methodus*, between 'law' and 'contract'. Contracts dealt with property, and any contracts made between the king and his subjects could not be voided by royal *fiat*, but had to be handled by the courts in the same way as contracts between subjects – leading him (as we have seen) to praise, and to misrepresent, the short-lived resistance on this issue by the Parlement to Charles IX. In the end, it should be acknowledged, it is hard to extract a wholly consistent answer from Bodin on the question of legal limits on a monarch, although the answer appears to be broadly the same in both his works.

[94] *Republique* 1576, p. 393; 1579, pp. 342–3; *Republica*, pp. 339–40; McRae, p. 376.
[95] See earlier p. 40 n. 60.

2

Grotius, Hobbes and Pufendorf

Although one might have supposed that the new distinction between sovereign and government would be relatively uncontroversial, the opposite in fact proved to be the case. Throughout the seventeenth and eighteenth centuries the distinction was the focus of debate, with only the most radical writers being willing to align themselves with Bodin. What troubled Bodin's critics, it is clear, was primarily the implication of his views for the understanding of monarchy, and in particular his account of the Roman Republic and Principate: for in this account seventeenth-century readers found the political structures which had always been the greatest source of fascination and emulation for modern states interpreted disconcertingly as democracies. The one group of theorists that was able to use the distinction without raising this awkward question was the group of German constitutional writers studied by Franklin, who used it to analyse the German Empire along the lines Bodin had proposed for France, namely a monarchical sovereign and an aristocratic or even (for Bartholomew Keckerman) a democratic government.[1]

---

[1] See Julian Franklin, 'Sovereignty and the mixed constitution: Bodin and his critics' in J. H. Burns (ed.) with the assistance of Mark Goldie, *The Cambridge History of Political Thought 1450–1700* (Cambridge University Press, 1992), pp. 298–328.

But outside Germany, to espouse the distinction was in general to put forward a radical political position.

This is strikingly illustrated by the fact that, as Jason Maloy has shown, the early English Independents or 'Brownists' seized on Bodin's ideas in this area to clarify their revolutionary ecclesiological ideas.[2] Arguing against (mostly) Presbyterian critics who accused the Brownists of introducing democracy to church government, John Robinson, the principal Independent theorist, asserted (citing 'Bodin of Commonw. book 1, chap. last') that

> we beleev, that the externall Church-government under Christ the onely mediatour, and monarch thereof is plainly aristocraticall, and to be administred by some certain choice men, although the state, which manie unskilfully confound with the government, be after a sort popular, and democraticall. By this it apperteyns to the people freely to vote in elections and judgments of the church: in respect of the other we make account, it behoves the *Elders* to *govern* the people even in their voting in just libertie, given by Christ whatsoever.[3]

That is, the *state* in Bodinian terminology, or the sovereign, was a democracy in the sense that the congregation

---

[2] Jason Maloy, *The Colonial American Origins of Modern Democratic Thought* (Cambridge University Press, 2010), pp. 100–6.

[3] *A iust and necessarie apologie of certain Christians* (n.p., 1625), p. 38, published first in Latin 1619. See also his 'Admonitio ad lectorem' in Robert Parker's *De politeia ecclesiastica Christi* (Frankfort, 1616) sig. (:)5r: 'Statum quidem Ecclesiae nos aliquatenus Democraticum esse credimus, at regimen neutiquam: sed contra, ut Christi capitis respectu, Monarchicum; sic & administrorum ratione, prorsus Aristocraticum'.

determined doctrine and elected the ministers, but the government was an aristocracy in the sense that it was a board of elders who made administrative decisions – though Robinson insisted that those decisions should be made 'in the face of the congregation' and not privately.[4] What this illustrates is that the Bodinian distinction mapped very neatly onto a system in which not only were magistrates elected but fundamental matters decided by popular assemblies, just as it had done in Bodin's discussion of the Roman constitution. Robinson's ideas were very influential on the Congregationalist settlers of New England, and the system of government the settlers used both in their churches and in their town meetings was precisely what he described – and may have contributed to how the American revolutionaries thought about their constitution, a theme I will take up in the last chapter.

When the English Revolution broke out, Bodin continued to be consulted by the radicals. For instance, Henry

---

[4] It should be said that the Presbyterian opponents of the Independents did not necessarily disagree with this as a picture of church government; thus the Presbyterian George Gillespie, attacking an anonymous reprint of chapter 4 of Robinson's *Apologie*, said, 'I remember I have read in sundry places of *Bodin de repub.* that the state is oft times different from the governement', but complained that in practice Robinson had tilted the balance of government towards democracy through his requirement that the elders deliberate and vote in public. *An Assertion of the Government of the Church of Scotland* (Edinburgh, 1641), pp. 24–5. The reprint was entitled *The Presbyteriall Government Examined* (1641). Chapter 4 is reprinted down to sig. D2v, and is then followed by another text. (This has, I think, not been noticed by bibliographers.) The *Apologie* was also fully reissued in 1644.

Parker, the chief spokesman for the Parliamentarians, responded to a sermon by Archbishop Ussher in Oxford in 1643 on Romans 13.1 ('Let every soule bee subject to the higher powers') in which Ussher observed in passing that 'Nero was the *power*, to whom these Romans were subject'.[5] Parker replied by citing Bodin on the underlying character of the principate: 'for that he was not onely a grave Statesman, but a learned Lawyer also' to show that 'our great Irish Prelate, when he sends us for St. Pauls meaning to the Romane Empire before Vespasians dayes, there to find out what soveraigne power is irresistible ... sends us not to regall power, more then to Aristocraticall, or Democraticall'.[6] Similarly the official defence of Parliament's action against the King, William Prynne's *Soveraigne Power of Parliaments and Kingdomes*, seized on this aspect of Bodin:

> John Bodin a learned Civilian clearly proves:
> That the Roman Emperors were at the first; nothing else but Princes of the Commonweale, The SOVERAIGNTY NEVERTHELESSE STILL RESTING IN THE PEOPLE, and THE SENATE: So that this Common-wealth was then to have beene called a Principality.[7]

[5] The *soveraignes power, and the subiects duty* (Oxford, 1643), sig. C1.

[6] *Jus populi; or, A discourse wherein clear satisfaction is given as well concerning the right of subjects as the right of princes* (London, 1644), sig. I3v. There is a discussion of Prynne's use of Bodin in Glenn Burgess, 'Bodin in the English Revolution', in Howell A. Lloyd (ed.), *The Reception of Bodin* (Leiden: Brill, 2013), pp. 387–408.

[7] *The third part of The soveraigne povver of parliaments and kingdomes* (London, 1643) sig. O3. See also *The fourth part* (London, 1643), sigs. Aa2v, Bb1v.

And *A moderate and most proper reply to a declaration* (1642) quoted Bodin on Louis II of Flanders, and declared that 'if the Parliaments War be necessary, and a necessary War is just, certainly a just War, cannot justly be called a Rebellion' (sig A4v).

Royalists pushed back against this use of Bodin, emphasising instead his hostility to armed resistance to hereditary monarchs.[8] This culminated in Robert Filmer's *The necessity of the absolute power of all kings: and in particular, of the King of England* (1648), which was a set of quotations from the Knolles's translation of the *Republic* (originally published anonymously and without acknowledgement, though one variant does have on its title page 'by John Bodin, a Protestant according to the Church of Geneva'). But even Filmer was troubled by Bodin's ideas on the Roman Republic, and went to some pains to refute them in his *Observations on Aristotles Politiques* (1652), with an explicit denial of the sovereignty/government distinction:

> [I]t is *Bodins* opinion, that *in the Roman state, the government was in the magistrates, the Authority and counsell in the Senate, but the Soveraign Power and Majesty in the People.* Lib.2.c.1. So in his first book, his doctrine is, that *the ancient Romans said, Imperium in magistratibus, Authoritatem in Senatu, Potestatem in plebe, Majestatem in Populo jure esse dicebant.* These four words *Command, Authority, Power,* and *Majesty* signifie ordinarily, one and the same thing, to wit, the Soveraignty, or supreme Power;

---

8. John Spelman, *A View of a Printed Book* (1643) sigs. B2v, C4, D3, D3v; Laud in his *History* written in the Tower (1695, p. 130).

> I cannot finde that *Bodin* knowes how to distinguish them;
> for they were not distinct faculties placed in severall
> subjects, but one and the same thing diversly qualified, for
> *Imperium, Authoritas, Potestas,* and *Majestas* were all
> originally in the Consuls... [T]he command of the people
> which *Bodin* so much magnifies, was properly *jussus
> Consulum* the command of the Consuls by the advise or
> consent of the assembly of the Centuries.[9]

So the Consuls, the monarchical element in the Republic,
ruled like the Kings of England (on Filmer's account), taking
advice but not instructions from their Parliament.

The most important and theoretically far-reaching
criticisms of Bodin's distinction, however, came not from the
relatively obscure Filmer but from the most influential theorist
of the early seventeenth century, Hugo Grotius. Grotius
always had a rather low opinion of Bodin's work: he described
him (in conversation in 1643 with Gui Patin) as someone who
'knew a great deal but was very confused. His book *De republica* is a great heap of a work, full of falsities', and in a letter to
his friend Jean De Cordes in 1634 he said that he had always
thought of Bodin as 'a man more devoted to things than to
words' and as someone 'barely instructed in Greek'.[10] As early

---

[9.] [Robert Filmer], *Observations upon Aristotles Politiques, touching forms
of government* (London, 1652) sigs. D4, D4v; Johann Sommerville (ed.),
Patriarcha and Other Writings (Cambridge University Press, 1991),
pp. 261–2.

[10.] René Pintard, *La Mothe le Vayer – Gassendi – Guy Patin. Études de
bibliographie et de critique suivies de textes inédits de Guy Patin* (Paris:
Boivin, 1943), p. 81; B. L. Meulenbroek (ed.), *Briefwisseling van Hugo
Grotius* (The Hague: Martinus Nijhoff, 1966), vol. v, p. 279. (See also

as 1602 he was already questioning Bodin's views about the location of sovereignty in the Roman republic: responding to a friend's comments on a (now lost) part of his *Parallelon Rerumpublicarum*, in which he had discussed the government of Rome, he said that

> As for the Roman Republic, like you I disagree with Bodin ... I believe that the Roman Republic when it was at its best was an example of those types of aristocracy which Aristotle defines as 'constitutions which incline more than the so-called polity towards oligarchy' ... For although the highest authority which Bodin calls sovereignty [*ius Maiestatis*] may have been in the people in time of war, there's plenty of evidence to show where the administration of government [*rerum administratio*] was to be found ordinarily and – as one might say – on a day-to-day basis, καὶ πάντων τῶν τυχόντων διακονία. I do not think anyone denies that at Rome that power was with the *optimates*.[11]

So Grotius was already questioning the worth of Bodin's idea that a sovereign might lurk under the superficial apparatus of the day-to-day government and be distinguishable from it; as far as he was concerned the actual administration *was* the sovereign.

Noel Malcolm, 'Jean Bodin and the authorship of the "Colloquium Heptaplomeres"', *Journal of the Warburg and Courtauld Institutes* 69 (2006), p. 120.) Grotius was being rather unfair about Bodin's Greek: Bodin's first publication was a scholarly edition in Greek of Oppian's *De Venatione* (Paris, 1555).

[11.] P. C. Molhuysen (ed.), *Briefwisseling* (The Hague: Martinus Nijhoff, 1928), vol. I, p. 29.

In his *De Iure Belli ac Pacis* of 1625 he applied this reasoning to the most difficult case, the Roman dictator. As I showed in the first chapter, Bodin had used the dictator as a prime example of a ruler who apparently had total power but was not sovereign. Grotius met this example head on.

> We must distinguish between the Thing itself, and the
> Manner of enjoying it; which takes Place not only in
> Things corporeal, but also in incorporeal: For a Right of
> Passage, or Carriage through a Ground, is no less a Thing
> than the Ground itself. But these some have by a full Right
> of Property, some by an usufructuary Right, and others by
> a temporary Right. Thus, amongst the *Romans*, the
> Dictator was Sovereign for a Time. The Generality of
> Kings, as well those who are first elected, as these who
> succeed to them in the Order established by the Laws,
> enjoy the Sovereign Power by an usufructuary Right. But
> there are some Kings, who possess the Crown by a full
> Right of Property, as those who have acquired the
> Sovereignty by Right of Conquest, or those to whom a
> People, in order to prevent greater Mischief, have
> submitted without Conditions. Neither can I agree with
> those, who say the *Roman* Dictator had not the Sovereign
> Power, because it was not perpetual: For the Nature of
> moral Things is known by their Operations, wherefore
> those Powers, which have the same Effects, should be called
> by the same Name. Now the Dictator, during the whole
> Time of his Office, exercised all the Acts of civil
> Government, with as much Authority as the most absolute
> King; and nothing he had done could be annulled by any
> other Power. And the Continuance of a Thing alters not the
> Nature of it, though if the Question be concerning Dignity,

which is generally called Majesty, doubtless, he that has a
perpetual Right, has a greater Majesty, than he that
enjoys it but for a Time, because the Manner of holding
adds to the Dignity. The same Thing may likewise be said
of such, as during the Minority, Lunacy, or Captivity of
their Kings, are appointed Regents of the Kingdom, so that
they depend not on the People, and cannot be deprived
of their Authority before the Time fixed by Law.

But it is otherwise with those who are invested with a
precarious Power, and which may be at any Time recalled,
as were the Kings of the ancient *Vandals* in *Africk*, and of
the *Goths* in *Spain*, whom the People might depose, upon
any Dislike. Whatever such a Prince does, may be
abrogated by those who vested him with a Power so liable
to Revocation; and consequently as the Exercise of his
Authority has not the same Effects as the Acts of a true
Sovereign, so neither is the Authority the same. (1.3.11.1;
see also 1.3.8.1)[12]

Grotius was able to defend this pre-Bodinian view of the
dictator because his own theory of sovereignty resembled in
a number of respects the ideas of Bodin's predecessors, though

[12.] The convention in citing passages from *De Iure Belli ac Pacis* is to use the
paragraph numbers. For the English text, I use my edition of the
eighteenth-century English translation of Jean Barbeyrac's edition,
Richard Tuck (ed.), *The Rights of War and Peace* (Indianapolis: Liberty
Fund, 2005); the original was *The Rights of War and Peace* (London,
1738). For the Latin text, the authoritative edition is the reprint by
Scientia Verlag (Aalen, 1993) of the 1939 Leiden edition by B. J. A. de
Kanter-van Hettinga Tromp, with additional notes by R. Feenstra,
C. E. Persenaire and E. Arps-de Wilde. This is the only critical edition,
showing the variants between the first and later editions.

he gave them a new theoretical sophistication. He set out his theory in a succinct passage at I.3.7, in which he gave a definition of *summa potestas*.

> That is called Supreme, whose Acts are not subject to another's Power, so that they cannot be made void by any other human Will. When I say, by any other, I exclude the Sovereign himself, who may change his own Will, as also his Successor, who enjoys the same Right, and consequently, has the same Power, and no other. Let us then see what this Sovereign Power [*summa potestas*] may have for its Subject. The Subject then is either common or proper: As the Body is the common Subject of Sight, the Eye the proper; so the common Subject of Supreme Power is the State [*civitas*]; which I have before called a perfect Society [*perfectum coetum*] of Men ... The proper Subject is one or more Persons, according to the Laws and Customs of each Nation [*gens*].

As he said, he had earlier defined a *civitas* as 'a compleat Body of free Persons [*coetus perfectus liberorum hominum*], associated together [*sociatus*] to enjoy peaceably their Rights, and for their common Benefit' (1.1.14). He termed this *coetus perfectus* indifferently a *civitas*, a *gens* and (most commonly) a *populus*.

This short passage proved to be highly influential over the next hundred years or so; its argument was adopted in its essentials by Samuel Pufendorf, as we shall see, and given a more systematic form with Pufendorf's idea of the double contract, in which the first contract was between individuals to form a civil society, and the second contract determined the type of rule they would be under (I discuss this fully later in this chapter). Pufendorf's idea was in turn to be one of Rousseau's prime targets in the *Social Contract*. Unlike Pufendorf, Grotius did not go into detail about the process whereby a *coetus perfectus* came into being, but he too seems to have thought that it was produced by an agreement between the people who composed it; thus, he remarked in a discussion of whether it was possible for a sovereign to alienate part of his state that

> in transferring a Part of the State there is something else required; it must be done with the Consent of that Part also, which is to be thus transferred. For when Men form themselves into a State, they make together a Sort of perpetual and eternal Society, in respect of those Parts, which are called *integral*; from whence it follows, that these Parts are not so subjected to the Body, as the Limbs of a natural Body are, which entirely depend on the Life of that Body, and therefore may be justly cut off for the Service of it; for this Body that we are now speaking of, is of a very different Nature from that, it being formed by Compact and Agreement only, and therefore the Right that it has over its particular Members, is to be determined by the Intentions of those who originally framed it; which can never be reasonably imagined to be such, as to invest the Body with a Power to cut off its own Members whenever it pleases, and to subject them to the Dominion of another. (II.6.4)

And according to Grotius, the society formed in this way would naturally determine its affairs by majority voting. As he said at II.14.12, discussing the way in which a wide variety of governmental structures were possible,

> [e]very Society, as well as every particular Person, has a Power to oblige itself either by itself, or by its major Part.

73

> This Right they may transfer, either expresly, or by
> necessary Consequence, by transferring, for Instance, the
> Sovereignty: For in Morals, he who gives the End, gives all
> Things that conduce to the End ... But this is not without
> its Bounds and Limitations, nor indeed is an unlimited
> Power of obliging absolutely necessary to the good
> Government of a Nation, no more than it is to the
> Advantage of a Trust; but only as far as the Nature of that
> Power requires

He had explained the naturalness of majoritarianism at 11.5.17:
'it is altogether unreasonable, that a greater Number should be
governed by a less; and therefore, tho' there were no Contracts
or Laws that regulate the Manner of determining Affairs,
the Majority would naturally have the Right and Authority
of the Whole'.

So Grotius presumed that a 'common subject' would
decide matters by majority voting; but at the same time he
wanted to distinguish it from a 'proper subject' of a democratic kind. When the common subject acted, it did not
behave as a democratic legislative sovereign. If there were to
be such a sovereign, there would first have to be a majority
decision within the *coetus* that it should make the proper
subject of its sovereignty a democracy, and Grotius took this
to be neither necessary nor desirable. This is a hard idea to
understand, and as we shall see, Pufendorf went to some pains
to correct Grotius's formulation, so that the initial *coetus*
would explicitly not be a democracy. But we can get some
sense of the point of Grotius's distinction if we follow his
attempts to explain how a people or nation has an identity
separable from its sovereign. He grappled with this

throughout Book II of *De Iure Belli ac Pacis*, coming closest
to making it clear in Book II, chapter 9, a chapter that has
been oddly neglected by most recent writers on Grotius, with
the notable exception of Annabel Brett in her recent book.[13]
The title of the chapter is 'When jurisdiction and property
cease', and in it Grotius set out his ideas about the circumstances in which a people could cease to exist. He described
a people as

> one of those Kind of Bodies that consist indeed of
> separate and distant Members, but are, however, united
> in Name, as having ἕξιν μίαν, *one Constitution* only,
> according to *Plutarch*; *Spiritum unum, one Spirit*, as
> *Paulus* speaks. Now this Spirit or Constitution in the
> People, is a full and compleat Association [*consociatio
> plena atque perfecta*] for a political Life; and the first and
> immediate Effect of it is the sovereign Power [*summum
> imperium*], the Bond that holds the State together, the
> Breath of Life, which so many thousands breath, as *Seneca*
> expresses it ... (II.9.3)

One Constitution is an addition by the eighteenth-century
translator of the Grotian text; in this part of the original,
Grotius left the Greek untranslated into Latin, as he did also
in the next line – 'Spirit or Constitution' is *spiritus sive* ἕξις.
But in a footnote added to the 1642 edition with a lengthy
quotation from the Hellenistic mathematician Conon of
Samos on the subject of identity, Grotius translated Conon's

[13.] Annabel S. Brett, *Changes of State: Nature and the Limits of the City in
Early Modern Natural Law* (Princeton University Press, 2011), pp. 136–8.

ἕξις as *tenor*, in other words, continuity.[14] A people possess identity over time, like a river or the Argonauts' ship, two standard examples in the ancient philosophical literature, by virtue of this *spiritus* or this *tenor*, despite the fact that the individuals who constituted the people died off and were replaced, though Grotius left unexplained in his blizzard of quotations precisely how this was so.

A people united by this 'spirit' could only be extinguished, he argued, by its literal destruction, in which the individual citizens were killed or driven far away from one another, or by the loss of *aut omni, aut perfecta iuris communitate*, which we can take to mean the loss of an entire legal order or of so much of one that the people ceased to be independent.

> So *Livy* tells us, that the *Romans* were willing that *Capua* should be inhabited as a Town, but that there should be no Corporation, no Senate, no Common-Council, no Magistrates, no Jurisdiction, but a dependent Multitude [*sine imperio multitudinem*],[15] and that a Governor

---

[14.] This is Grotius's own translation; Denis Pétau in his edition and translation of Achilles Tatius, from which the quotation from Conon comes, used the customary Latin *habitus* to translate ἕξις (Dionysius Petavius (ed.), *Uranologion sive systema variorum authorum* (Paris, 1630), p. 134).

[15.] It is interesting that Grotius used this term here in contrast to *populus*. Two sections later he used *multitudinis imperium* to mean democracy; on the other hand in one of his Biblical commentaries he distinguished between a *multitudo* and a *populus* in rather Hobbes-like terms. On *Deut* xxxii.21, *in eo qui non est populus*, Grotius said *Iuris consociatio populum facit. Eo nomine indigna multitudo, quae aut nullas aut malas habet leges.*

should be sent from *Rome*, to dispense Justice among them. And therefore *Cicero*, in his first Oration to the People against *Trullus*, says, that *Capua* had 'not so much as the Shadow of a State [*reipublicae*] left'. (II.9.6)

Even if the people subsequently gathered again in the same place, the breach in continuity was sufficient to render them a new people:

> a People, like a Ship, by a Dissolution of the Parts, is entirely destroyed, because its whole Nature consists in that perpetual Conjunction [*perpetua coniunctione*]. Therefore the City of *Saguntum* was not the same, when it was restored to the antient Inhabitants, eight Years after they had been driven out of it. (III.9.9)

The spirit binding a people together was entirely independent of the form of government that constituted the 'proper' site of sovereignty.

> [T]he *Romans* were the same People under Kings, Consuls, and Emperors. Nay, tho' the Government be never so absolute [*etiamsi plenissimo iure regnetur*], yet the People are the same they were, as when they were free, whilst he who rules, rules as the Head of that People, and not as the Head of another. For that sovereign Power [*imperium*] which is in the King as Head, rests still in the People as in the Whole, whereof the Head is a Part: So that if the King,

Opera omnia theologica in tres tomos divisa (London, 1679), vol. I, p.102. (I owe this reference to Noah Dauber.) The commentary on Deuteronomy was published in 1644, a year after Grotius had read *De Cive*.

> being elective, should die; or if the Royal Family be
> extinct, the Sovereignty [*ius imperandi*] reverts to the
> People. (11.9.8)

It was even the case (he thought) that different peoples could
share the same sovereign without necessarily becoming a
single entity:

> It is not in the moral Body [*morale corpus*], as 'tis in the
> natural, where one Head cannot belong to several Bodies;
> for there the same Person may be head, under a different
> Consideration, to several distinct Bodies; of which this is a
> certain Proof, that upon the Extinction of the reigning
> Family, the Sovereign Power reverts to each People. (1.3.7)

And a people could be ruled by a foreign *civitas* without losing
its separate character.

But in the absence of events such as the extinction of
a ruling family, the sovereign power was (we might say)
only virtually in the people: there was no institutional means
by which it could express itself. He repeatedly insisted, especially in his famous discussion at 1.3.8,[16] that it was entirely
possible for a people to have no rights vis-à-vis their
ruler, and to be the equivalent of a slave, without ceasing to
exist as a people and therefore without ceasing to possess
sovereignty as a 'common' subject. And he was happy to use

[16.] 'Here we must first reject their Opinion, who will have the Supreme Power
to be always, and without Exception, in the People; so that they may
restrain or punish their Kings, as often as they abuse their Power. What
Mischiefs this Opinion has occasioned, and may yet occasion, if once the
Minds of People are fully possessed with it, every wise Man sees'.

the medieval language of (virtual) representation to express
the relationship between the people and its ruler: thus at
11.20.24 he said that a

> Law-Maker is in some Measure bound by his own Laws;
> but this only holds ... as far as the Law-Maker is looked
> upon as a Member of the Community, not as he is the
> Representative, and carries with him the Power and
> Authority of the State [*quatenus auctor legis ut pars civitatis*
> *spectatur, non qua civitatis ipsius personam atque*
> *auctoritatem tollere*].

And elsewhere he said that when Louis the Pious ceded the
city of Rome to Pope Paschal, he was in fact returning it to the
Roman people:

> [T]he *French* having received the Sovereignty over the
> City from the People of *Rome*, might well restore it to
> the same People, in the *Person* of him, who *represented*
> them, as being *Chief* of the first Order of the State
> [*cujus populi quasi personam sustinebat, qui primi ordinis*
> *princeps est*]. (1.3.13)

The practical conclusions that Grotius drew from these prem-
ises make clear what he was thinking. First, unlike Bodin,
he believed that rulers were in general fully bound by the
debts of their predecessors, since it was the people as a juridical entity that incurred the debt vis-à-vis other states. So, for
example, 'a Debt contracted by a free People, ceases not to
be a Debt, because they are at present under a King; for
the People are the same, and they still retain a Property in
those Things that belonged to them as a People, and hold the
Sovereignty too, tho' it be not exercised now by the Body,

but the Head' (11.9.8).[17] Second, there were significant restrictions on what sovereigns (in the sense of the proper subjects of
sovereignty) could do when it came to uniting or dividing
peoples. A people could share a sovereign with another people
without becoming united with it:

> It is not in the moral Body [*morale corpus*], as 'tis in the
> natural, where one Head cannot belong to several Bodies;
> for there the same Person may be head, under a different
> Consideration, to several distinct Bodies; of which this is a
> certain Proof, that upon the Extinction of the reigning
> Family, the Sovereign Power reverts to each People. (1.3.7)

This was vital for a patriotic Dutchman such as Grotius, since
before the Revolt the Netherlands had shared a sovereign with
Spain without (or so the Dutch believed) having lost their
separate national identity.[18] Furthermore, a king or other ruler

---

[17.] On the other hand, Thebes was not liable for debts after the former
inhabitants of Thebes had all been sold into slavery and replaced – the
city lacked the continuity necessary for identity (III.9.9). See II.14.10–12
for his full discussion of the question of the debts owed by succeeding
sovereigns, and the various qualifications he introduced. Bodin's
discussion of the issue is in a famous passage at the end of Book I,
chapter 8 where he asserted that a king who had come to the throne not
by hereditary right but by law – that is, not in a kingdom which was
treated as private property, but in a monarchy of the French type – was
not necessarily bound by the debts incurred by his predecessors.
Franklin, *Bodin: On Sovereignty*, pp. 41–5; *Republique* 1576, pp. 152–3;
1579, pp. 110–11; *Republica* 1586, pp. 137–40; McRae (ed.), pp. 111–13.

[18.] See my 'The making and unmaking of boundaries from a natural law
perspective' in Allen Buchanan and Margaret Moore (eds.), *States,
Nations, and Borders: The Ethics of Making Boundaries* (Cambridge
University Press, 2003), pp. 146–8 for a discussion of the extent to which

was entitled to alienate his sovereignty over the whole society
to another ruler – unilaterally if it was a 'patrimonial' kingdom; otherwise, with some form of popular consent. But even
a patrimonial king could not alienate *part* of his kingdom
without consent.

> [I]n transferring a Part of the State there is something else
> required; it must be done with the Consent of that Part
> also, which is to be thus transferred. For when Men form
> themselves into a State [*civitas*], they make together a
> Sort of perpetual and eternal Society, in respect of those
> Parts, which are called *integral*; from whence it follows, that

medieval and early modern states did indeed seek to preserve their
separate identities in cases of dynastic union. Grotius also said that while
a shared sovereign did not imply union, it was in principle possible for
separate peoples to merge without ceasing to exist – 'if two Nations be
united, the Rights of neither of them shall be lost, but become common,
as the *Sabins* first, and afterwards the *Albans*, were incorporated with the
Romans, and so were they made one State, as *Livy* (Lib. 1.) expresses it'
(ii.9.9). (We might think here of the idea of 'pooled sovereignty', which
has often been proposed to justify the EU.) Pufendorf questioned the
logic of this, and argued that either a new state was created by such a
union, or one state became subordinate to another: 'there are no Ways of
uniting distinct Commonwealths, so that each shall preserve its own
separate Constitutions, and be as it was before; but by strict Alliance and
Confederacy, which rather gives Rise to a System than a Commonwealth,
properly so called'. Basil Kennet (trans.), *The Law of Nature and Nations*
(London, 1749), viii.12.6. Like Grotius's *De Iure Belli ac Pacis*, Pufendorf's
De Iure Naturae et Gentium is conventionally cited by paragraph
numbers. For the original text, see *De Jure Naturae et Gentium Libri Octo*
(Lund, 1672) for the first edition, ibid. (Frankfurt, 1684) for the second
edition. The notes are translated in Jean Barbeyrac (trans.), *Le Droit de la
Nature et des Gens* (Amsterdam, 1706).

> these Parts are not so subjected to the Body, as the Limbs of
> a natural Body are, which entirely depend on the Life of
> that Body, and therefore may be justly cut off for the
> Service of it; for this Body that we are now speaking of, is of
> a very different Nature from that, it being formed by
> Compact and Agreement only, and therefore the Right
> that it has over its particular Members, is to be determined
> by the Intentions of those who originally framed it
> [*ex primaeva voluntate*]; which can never be reasonably
> imagined to be such, as to invest the Body with a Power to
> cut off its own Members whenever it pleases, and to
> subject them to the Dominion of another. (1.6.4)

In this one respect, when their continued existence was
threatened, the people continued to possess a collective
authority over even the most absolute ruler.

Heroically, Grotius was prepared to accept the full
implications of his ideas about the identity of a people even
in the case of modern Rome, arguing in a notorious section of
Book II, chapter 9:

> I say, that the *Roman* People are now the same they were
> heretofore, tho' mixed with Foreigners; and that the
> Empire still remains in them, as in a Body, where it resided
> and subsisted. For whatever the *Roman* People had a Right
> to do formerly, before they had Emperors, they had a
> Right to do the same upon the Demise of any Emperor,
> before the Successor was established. (II.9.11)

Consequently,

> tho' he who is elected by the seven Electoral Princes,
> who represent the whole Body of the *Germans*, has an

undoubted Right to reign over the *Germans*, according
to their own Customs; yet is he not but by the Approbation
of the *Roman* People made King or Emperor of the
Romans, or as Historians often call him, King of *Italy*;
and by Vertue of that Title, he becomes Lord of all that did
formerly belong to the *Roman* People, and has not passed
from them to the Jurisdiction of any others, either by
Treaties, or by Seizure, upon the Presumption of its
being abandoned, or by Conquest. From whence we may
easily apprehend by what Right the Bishop of *Rome*, when
the Throne becomes vacant, grants the Investiture of the
Fiefs of the *Roman* Empire, because he holds the prime
Rank among the *Roman* People, who are at that Time
intirely free and independent. For it is usual to have
what relates to a whole Body, executed by the principal
Person, in the Name of [*nomine*] that Body.

Barbeyrac, like many contemporary readers of Grotius, could
not stomach this, remarking that 'Our Author has been very
much criticized on this Article; and it must be confessed not
without Reason', though he sought to defend him against the
charge of pure subservience to the Pope: 'I am persuaded that
my Author has sincerely and honestly followed the Consequences of certain Principles, false indeed, but specious, and
which he permitted to dazzle him'.

We can now, finally, see why Grotius thought it reasonable to say that the Roman dictator was a temporary sovereign,
and not merely the agent of the sovereign people. The identity of
the Roman people as the common subject of sovereignty was
preserved intact under the dictator, as indeed it was through all
the twists and turns of Roman history, even down to the present

day. But the proper subject, the source of law, could be found anywhere, inside or outside the *civitas*, and perpetual or temporary – indeed, on Grotius's account it would be rather unreasonable to expect a perpetual proper subject, as, while the perpetuity of the people was given by their continuous identity as the common subject along the lines of the Argonauts' ship, the identity of the proper subject might vary from year to year or even for a shorter period, and it might well be that a sovereign democratic assembly could be superseded for six months by an equally sovereign dictator.[19] Wherever a site of unquestionable legislation or jurisdiction could be located and for however long a period, there was the proper subject of sovereignty.[20]

But – and this is the critical point for my general theme – Grotius's common subject of sovereignty was not a Bodinian sovereign; it would be closer to the truth to say that it was the community inside which legislation had force, rather than the site of legislation. Only in a quasi-revolutionary moment, prompted either by an attack on the people by its sovereign or by the extinction of its government, could it act collectively, and even then its actions were limited to a decision over a new proper subject. So within Grotius's theory it could not function like a Bodinian sovereign vis-à-vis the day-to-day legislators, but was instead in some ways like the people in

---

[19] In the same way he argued that there could be divided sovereignty in the sense that joint sovereigns could take it in turns to issue laws or could share legislation between them (1.3.17).

[20] 'In Civil Governments, because there must be some dernier Resort [*quia progressus in infinitum non datur*], it must be fixed either in one Person, or in an Assembly; whose Faults, because they have no superior Judge, GOD declares, that he takes Cognizance of' (1.3.8.2).

pre-Bodinian political theory, capable (in most instances) only of virtual representation. This, after all, was the force of his analogy with the eye: while in some sense the *person* sees, he or she can do so only with his or her eye. One of Grotius's most important legacies was that he restated this medieval idea in a modern form, cutting the link between it and a strongly Aristotelian theory and allowing his successors – down, it is possible to say, to the present day – to think of a people as a sovereign entity which has in general no capacity to exercise sovereign power. There was accordingly no distinction between sovereign legislator and government in Grotius's theory, because only a 'government' exercised sovereignty in practice, and the analysis of politics – as he had argued in 1602 – had to concentrate on the actual sources of power and law in the society, as they were experienced by the citizens in their daily lives. It was not sovereignty but government, in Bodin's sense of the terms, that in Grotius's view was critical to an understanding of politics.

We might also say that Grotius's idea of sovereignty (and this should not surprise us) was closest to the modern idea of sovereignty in international relations, in which states are 'sovereign' in the sense that there is no juridical superior over them, but in which the question of *internal* sovereignty is undetermined. A sovereign state internationally may even (according to many modern writers) have no site of sovereignty at all internally – the classic example would be the United States (though as we shall see in Chapter 4, that has always been a contentious example). Grotius did not quite believe this, as he thought that there must always be a site of internal sovereignty, but he did believe that we think about the autonomous status of a nation and its role as a bearer of sovereignty in a different way from the way we think about the absolute power of a ruler. His chief interest, as I have said, was in the autonomy and independence of nations, especially that of Holland,[21] and in their capacity to exist over a very long period irrespective of the forms of government – which in the Dutch case had linked Holland over many centuries to many different external political authorities.

Given this understanding of Grotius's theory, we can now begin to see that in this area his major critic was Thomas Hobbes – and that it may even be that Hobbes worked out his constitutional ideas expressly in opposition to those of Grotius, even at the same time (as I have argued in various places) that he accepted some of Grotius's fundamental ideas about natural rights and laws. He set out his case against Grotius's theory of sovereignty in chapter 7 of *De Cive* and the related chapter 2 of Part II of the *Elements of Law*, two chapters that in many ways contain the heart of his political theory but which have been relatively neglected in modern discussions of Hobbes.[22] Chapter 7 contains a remarkable account of

---

[21.] I say Holland rather than the United Provinces, because Grotius himself referred to the provinces as *nationes*, and wrote the history of his own *gens* or *natio* and the various sovereigns it had come under in his *De Antiquitate Reipublicae Batavicae* (Leiden, 1610).

[22.] As always, the relationship between *De Cive* and the *Elements of Law* is unclear. They either draw on a recent common ancestor or one is a loose translation of the other (except for *De Cive*'s chapters on religion). In the case of chapters VII and II.2, it may be significant that Hobbes discusses 'usufructuary' monarchy in *De Cive* but not (under that designation) in the *Elements of Law*. This suggests that he had Grotius in view when he wrote this part of *De Cive*, and as a critique of Grotius would be the natural form which the development of his ideas in

democracy as the first and most basic form of a commonwealth, as well as an extensive discussion of the various forms a democracy can take. Among those forms, Hobbes argued, were all kinds of time-limited monarchies, and he set out his ideas in a long paragraph from which I will quote extensively, as it makes his views entirely clear, and inter alia provides the vivid analogy that gives my book its title.[23] He presumed, as everyone in his time did, that a democracy must involve an actual assembly of citizens, and he considered four possible cases in which a time-limited monarch might be created. The first was the case when the assembly elected a king without any provision for reassembling on his death; in such a case the democracy had ipso facto dissolved itself and transferred sovereignty to the king. The second was when

> the *people* leave the assembly after the election of a *time-limited Monarch* with the decision already made to meet at a certain time and place after his death; in this case, on the Monarch's death, power resides firmly in the *people* by their previous right, without any new act on the part of the citizens; for in the whole intervening period *sovereign power* [*summum imperium*] (like *Ownership* [*Dominium*])

this area would take, the implication is that they were first worked out fully in *De Cive* (or in a similar, lost work) and then presented in an abridged English-language form in the *Elements*. On the other hand, the *Elements* seems to lack important features of the discussion in *De Cive*, and looks like a relatively rough draft (see footnote 24).

[23.] VII.16. Richard Tuck and Michael Silverthorne (eds.), *On the Citizen* (Cambridge University Press, 1998), pp. 98–100. For the Latin text see Howard Warrender (ed.), *De Cive: The Latin Version* (Oxford University Press, 1983), pp. 156–8.

remained with the *people*; only its *use* or *exercise* was enjoyed by the time-limited *Monarch*, as a *usufructuary*.

The third case was

> if after the election of a *time-limited Monarch*, the *people* has departed from the council with the understanding that it would hold meetings at fixed times and places while the term set for the Monarch is still running, (as *Dictators* were appointed among the Romans), such a one is not to be regarded as a *Monarch* but as the first minister [*primo ministro*] of the *people*, and the *people* can, if it shall see fit, deprive him of his office [*administratio*] even before his term is finished, as the Roman *people* did when they gave Master of the Horse *Minutius* equal power with *Quintus Fabius Maximus* whom they had previously made *Dictator*.

And the fourth was

> if the *people* leaves their council after appointing a *time-limited Monarch* without leave to meet again except on the orders of the appointee, the *people* is understood to be thereupon dissolved; and power belongs absolutely to anyone appointed on these terms. The reason is that it is not in the citizens' power to revive the commonwealth except at the will of the sole holder of power. And it does not matter that he may have promised to summon the citizens at certain times, since the *person* to whom the promise was made no longer exists except at his discretion.[24]

[24.] In the *Elements of Law* the distinction between the four cases is less crisp. The dictator is the same as an elected king: 'if this power of the people were not dissolved, at the choosing of their king for life; then is the people sovereign still, and the king a minister thereof only, but so, as to

Having set out the four cases, Hobbes enlarged his discussion with the analogy which, as I have mentioned, has provided me with the title for this text.

> What we have said about these four cases of the *people*
> electing a *time-limited Monarch* will be more fully
> developed by a comparison with an *absolute Monarch* who
> has no heir apparent; for the *people* is a *Lord* [*Dominus*] of
> the citizens in such a way that it cannot have an heir unless
> it nominates one itself. Besides, the intervals between
> meetings of the citizens may be compared to the times
> when a *Monarch* is asleep; for the power is retained though
> there are no acts of commanding. Finally, the dissolution of
> a meeting on the terms that it may not reconvene is the
> death of a *people*, just as sleeping without waking is the
> death of a man. If a King without an heir is about to go to
> sleep and not wake up again (i.e., is about to die), and
> hands sovereign power to someone to exercise until he

put the whole sovereignty in execution; a great minister, but no otherwise for his time, than a dictator was at Rome' (II.2.9). And the right of the people to assemble during the monarch's or dictator's term of office (*De Cive*'s third case) is treated as a general right: 'though in the election of a king for life, the people grant him the exercise of their sovereignty for that time; yet if they see cause, they may recall the same before the time. As a prince that conferreth an office for life, may nevertheless, upon suspicion of abuse thereof, recall it at his pleasure'. This suggests that at the time Hobbes wrote the *Elements*, while he certainly believed that the critical question with regard to elective kingship was whether the democratic assembly had 'the right of assembling at certain times and places limited and made known' or not (II.2.10), he had not fully focused on the fact that there might be different specifications of the times, some of which would not permit the assembly to exercise its sovereign rights until the death of the incumbent ruler.

awakes, he is handing him also the succession; likewise if
[a] *people* in choosing a temporary Monarch, at the same
time abolishes its own power of reconvening, it is passing
dominion over the commonwealth to him. Further, a king
who is going to sleep for a while gives sovereign power to
someone else to exercise, and takes it back when he wakes
up; just so *a people, on the election of a temporary Monarch,*
retains the right of meeting again at a certain time and
place, and on that day resumes its power. A king who has
given his power to someone else to exercise, while he
himself stays awake, can resume it again when he wishes;
just so a *people* which duly meets throughout the term set
for a *time-limited Monarch* can strip him of power if it so
wishes. Finally a king who gives the exercise of his power to
another person while he sleeps, and can wake up again only
with the consent of that person, has lost his life and his
power together; just so a *people* which has committed
power to a *time-limited Monarch* on the terms that it
cannot meet again without his command, is radically
dissolved, and its power rests with the person it has elected.

The thoroughness with which Hobbes worked through these
possibilities is itself a testimony to the importance he placed
on the subject. It is clear that he was tracking Grotius's
discussion at *De Iure Belli ac Pacis* I.3.11 which I quoted earlier,
with its analysis of the sovereignty of elected monarchs which
'some have by a full Right of Property, some by an usufructuary Right, and others by a temporary Right'. And it is
also clear that he wished to attack Grotius's view that the
dictator – and *a fortiori* other elective rulers – was a sovereign.
Essentially, Hobbes restated the Bodinian distinction between
sovereign and government, even using the same terminology

of *summum imperium* or *summa potestas* and *administratio*.[25]
But he was willing to go much further. As we saw in Chapter 1,
Bodin was concerned to insist that monarchs elected for life
were significantly different from the dictator – for otherwise,
as he said, 'there would ... be few sovereign monarchs inasmuch as there are very few that are hereditary. Those especially would not be sovereign who come to the throne by
election'. Hobbes, however, ruthlessly followed through the
logic of the distinction and concluded that elective monarchs
were indeed not sovereign: all the elective monarchies
of Europe were (by implication) really either aristocracies or
democracies. Not even the monarchomachs had gone so far as
to say this.

It is worth considering the far-reaching implications
of these ideas. On Hobbes's account, a sovereign can be very
thoroughly asleep: in the case of an elected monarchy, it might
in principle be asleep for sixty or seventy years, or even more.
Moreover, when awake the sovereign might do nothing more
than select a new monarch, and promptly fall asleep again.
So all actual legislation to do with the ordinary lives of the
citizens, and all actual power exercised over them, would be in
the hands of the monarch; yet the monarch would not
be sovereign. At the very least this calls into question a naively
Austinian view of Hobbes's theory of sovereignty, for it is very
clearly not a theory of habitual obedience to a site of *power* in
the sense of physical strength (control of an army, say).

[25.] As always, Hobbes was highly reticent about his sources. But he had read
Bodin and quotes him (as one would expect) approvingly on sovereignty
in the *Elements of Law* II.8.7.

This point was made by Hobbes himself very clearly in chapter 10 of *De Cive*, writing about an infant monarch:

> The comparative advantages or disadvantages of
> different types of commonwealth [do not] result from the
> fact that sovereignty [*imperium*] itself or the
> administration of government business [*imperii negotia
> administranda*] is better entrusted to one man rather than
> to more than one, or on the other hand to a larger rather
> than a smaller number. For sovereignty [*imperium*] is a
> *power* [*potentia*], administration of government
> [*administratio gubernandi*] is an *act*. *Power* is equal in
> every kind of commonwealth; what differs are the acts,
> i.e. the *motions* and *actions* of the commonwealth,
> depending on whether they originate from the
> deliberations of many or of a few, of the competent or of
> the incompetent. This implies that the advantages and
> disadvantages of a régime do not depend upon him in
> whom the authority of the commonwealth resides,
> but upon the ministers of the sovereignty [*ministros
> imperii*]. Hence it is no obstacle to the good government
> of a commonwealth if the *Monarch* is a woman, a boy
> or an infant, provided that the holders of the ministries
> and public offices are competent to handle the
> business. (x.16)[26]

[26.] Our edition of *De Cive* for Cambridge University Press translates *imperium* in this passage as 'government', but I have now come to realise that this is misleading and that it should be contrasted with *gubernatio*, *administratio* or the other terms which in this tradition meant government as distinct from sovereignty. I have slightly modified the translation in some other respects.

(Kinch Hoekstra has very recently stressed the importance of this feature of Hobbes's theory.)[27] Hobbes expressed it in dramatic fashion in *Leviathan* when he asserted (in a passage that has often surprised his readers) that

> If a Monarch subdued by war, render himself Subject to the Victor; his Subjects are delivered from their former obligation, and become obliged to the Victor. But if he be held prisoner, or have not the liberty of his own Body; he is not understood to have given away the Right of Soveraigntie; and therefore his Subjects are obliged to yield obedience to the Magistrates formerly placed, governing not in their own name, but in his. For, his Right remaining, the question is only of the Administration; that is to say, of the Magistrates and Officers; which, if he have not means to name, he is supposed to approve those, which he himself had formerly appointed.[28]

This was an important practical issue when Hobbes was writing, for the King was (or had recently been) in prison, but royal governors were still in office in many places of great strategic significance for the royalists, including the Channel Islands, Virginia and – above all – Ireland. And on Hobbes's account it was entirely reasonable to suppose that the imprisoned King was still sovereign, as he remained sovereign until his death even if he could do nothing – just as he would if he were similarly inert while asleep. What both the imaginary

[27.] Kinch Hoekstra, 'Early modern absolutism and constitutionalism', *Cardozo Law Review* 34 (2012–13), pp. 1095–8.

[28.] Richard Tuck (ed.), *Leviathan* (rev. edn, 1996) p. 154; original edn, chapter 21, pp. 114–15.

case of the sleeping king and the real case of the imprisoned king illustrate is that the power of the sovereign was not conditional upon his *choosing* to use it, as in neither case would the sovereign effectively be able to make a choice to exercise power over the citizens. Instead it was conditional on the *possibility* (the *potentia*) of the sovereign being able at some point to assert his superiority to his ministers, or to his captors; and for the imprisoned ruler that remained a possibility right down to the moment before the executioner's axe fell.

Hobbes provided an even more startling example in chapter 13 of *De Cive*:

> We must distinguish between the *right* and the *exercise* of sovereign power; for they can be separated; for instance, he who has the *right* may be unwilling or unable to play a personal role in conducting trials or deliberating issues. For there are occasions when kings cannot manage affairs because of their age, or when even though they can, they judge it more correct to content themselves with choosing ministers and counsellors, and to exercise their power through them. When *right* and *exercise* [*jus & exercitium*] are separated, the government of the commonwealth is like the ordinary government of the world, in which God the first mover of all things, produces natural effects through the order of secondary causes. But when he who has the right to reign wishes to participate himself in all judgements, consultations and public actions, it is a way of running things comparable to God's attending directly to every thing himself, contrary to the order of nature. (XIII.1)

God, too, is a sleeping sovereign.

Moreover, the structure of government put in place by the sovereign could be complex and contain elements of all three traditional regimes – in this sense, like Bodin, Hobbes was not necessarily opposed to mixed *government*. He spelt this out particularly clearly in the *Elements of Law* II.1.17.

> But though the sovereignty be not mixed, but be always either simple democracy, or simple aristocracy, or pure monarchy; nevertheless in the administration thereof, all those sorts of government may have place subordinate. For suppose the sovereign power be democracy, as it was sometimes in Rome, yet at the same time they may have a council aristocratical, such as was the senate; and at the same time they may have a subordinate monarch, such as was their dictator, who had for a time the exercise of the whole sovereignty, and such as are all generals in war. So also in a monarchy there may be a council aristocratical of men chosen by the monarch; or democratical of men chosen by the consent (the monarch permitting) of all the particular men of the commonwealth. And this mixture is it that imposeth; as if it were the mixture of sovereignty. As if a man should think, because the great council of Venice doth nothing ordinarily but choose magistrates, ministers of state, captains, and governors of towns, ambassadors, counsellors, and the like; that therefore their part of the sovereignty is only choosing of magistrates; and that the making of war, and peace, and laws, were not theirs, but the part of such councillors as they appointed thereto; whereas it is the part of these to do it but subordinately,

the supreme authority thereof being in the great council that choose them.[29]

It is worth noting that Hobbes included here as a possible part of the functions of government 'the making of war, and peace, and laws' – powers which of course an elective monarch also had to possess, and which Rousseau was also to assign to government rather than to sovereignty.[30]

Hobbes's repudiation of Grotius on the dictator and the elected monarch was at the same time, as one would expect, a repudiation of Grotius's whole theory of sovereignty. For Hobbes, there could be no common subject of sovereignty: the only subject of sovereignty was Grotius's proper subject, the actual source of law. Above all, a people did not possess even conceptually a distinct identity from their sovereign. This is also set out most clearly in *De Cive*, where his whole argument began from an analysis of democracy (which is why the discussion of elective monarchy and dictatorship is so extensive in that work). Indeed, Samuel Pufendorf was to observe, rather acutely, that '*Mr. Hobbes* imposeth upon less intelligent Readers, by the ambiguous Signification of the Word *People*', in appealing to an intuitive notion of democratic sovereignty and then extending the same notion to monarchy:

[29.] Ferdinand Toennies (ed.), *The Elements of Law Natural and Politic* (London: Simpkin, Marshall and Co., 1889) (reprinted with new introduction by Maurice Goldsmith, London: Frank Cass and Co., 1969), pp. 115–16.

[30.] At least, he assigned the making of war and peace to the government, and in effect a large part of legislation – see my discussion pp. 132–133.

> Should a Man contend with so much Earnestness, that
> he cannot, in democratical Governments, conceive such
> a Compact in his Mind [i.e. a compact between
> sovereign and people], or that he judgeth it utterly
> useless; yet he cannot fairly take Occasion thence to
> exclude it from other Forms, where those who command,
> and those who obey, are really and naturally different
> Persons. (*The Law of Nature and Nations* VII.2.12)

Hobbes agreed with Grotius that the formation of a people immediately and necessarily implied a commitment to majoritarianism. As he said at *De Cive* VI.2,

> [I]f the move towards formation of a commonwealth is to
> get started, each man of the multitude must agree with the
> others that on any issue anyone brings forward in the
> group, the wish of the majority shall be taken as the will of
> all; for otherwise, a multitude will never have any will at all,
> since their attitudes and aspirations differ so markedly
> from one another. If anyone refuses consent, the rest will
> notwithstanding form a commonwealth without him.[31]

In the following chapter he expressed the thought in this way:

> When men have met to erect a commonwealth, they are,
> almost by the very fact that they have met, a *Democracy*.
> From the fact that they have gathered voluntarily, they are
> understood to be bound by the decisions made by
> agreement of the majority. And that is a *Democracy*, as long

---

[31.] I have replaced the term *crowd* in our translation with *multitude*, to
bring it clearly into line with the terminology used elsewhere by Hobbes
and Pufendorf, and possibly by Grotius (see earlier p. 76 n. 15).

as the convention [*conventus*] lasts, or is set to reconvene at certain times and places. For a convention whose will is the will of all the citizens has *sovereign power*. And because it is assumed that each man in this convention has the right to vote, it follows that it is a *Democracy*. (VII.5)

This democracy has straight away a determinate institutional character:

> *Democracy* is not constituted by agreements which individuals make with the *People*, but by mutual agreements of individuals with other individuals. The first part of the statement is evident from the fact that in every agreement the persons making the agreement must exist before the agreement itself. But prior to the formation of a commonwealth a *People* does not exist, since it was not then a person but a number of individual persons. Hence no agreement could be made between the *people* and a *citizen*. But after a commonwealth has been formed, any agreement by a citizen with the *People* is without effect, because the *People* absorbs into its own will the will of the citizen [*voluntate sua voluntatem civis illius ... complectitur*] (to whom it is supposed to be obligated);[32] it can therefore release itself at its own discretion; and consequently is in fact free of obligation. (VII.7)

---

[32] (To whom it is supposed to be obligated) is a translation of (*cui supponitur obligari*), with *cui* apparently referring to the citizen and the subject of the verb being the People, although one would have supposed that the citizen is obligated to the People and not vice versa. This may simply have been carelessness on Hobbes's part.

This was precisely what Grotius had not been willing to say. For Hobbes, a 'people' formed by the civil covenant simply *is* the democratic assembly – only it (we may say) has the institutional specificity which was the key thing that Hobbes wished to attribute to the people, and thereby block all attempts by self-appointed spokesmen to speak on the people's behalf (or, we would say today, to claim knowledge of 'public opinion').[33] The idea of a common subject of sovereignty distinguishable in some fashion from the institution of a democracy thus made, on Hobbes's argument, no sense at all.

In chapter 12 of *De Cive* Hobbes accordingly proceeded to make exactly the move that Pufendorf criticised.

> Men do not make a clear enough distinction between a *people* and a *multitude*. A *people* is a *single* entity, with *a single will*; you can attribute *an act* to it. None of this can be said of a multitude. In every commonwealth the *People* Reigns; for even in *Monarchies* the *People* exercises power [*imperat*]; for the *people* wills through the will [*per voluntatem*] of *one man*. But the citizens, i.e. the subjects, are a *multitude*. In a *Democracy* and in an *Aristocracy* the citizens are a multitude, but the *council* [*curia*] is the *people*; in a *Monarchy* the subjects are a *multitude*, and (paradoxically) the *King* is the *people*. (XII.8)[34]

---

[33] Compare his remarks about majority opinion, *De Cive* VI.20: 'it is not a natural rule that the consent of the majority should be taken for the consent of all', that is, it requires a specific institutional context for a majority to be authoritative.

[34] As before, I have replaced 'crowd' with 'multitude'.

If the assembly is the people in a democracy, then it must simply follow (on Hobbes's analysis) that the monarch is the people in a monarchy. The extraordinary character of this claim is in itself testimony to the fact that his theory emerged from reflections on democracy, together with the conviction that there could be no formal distinction between a democratic sovereign and a monarchical one. He made this even clearer in an important and interesting note added to the 1647 edition of *De Cive*:

> A popular state obviously requires absolute power, and the citizens do not object. For even the politically unaware see the face of the commonwealth [civitatis faciem] in the popular assembly and recognise that affairs are being managed by its deliberations. A Monarchy is no less a commonwealth than a Democracy ... But to most people it is less obvious that the commonwealth is contained in the person of the King [civitatem in persona Regis contineri]. (VI.13.n)[35]

To some extent Hobbes was using these arguments to undermine the claim that democracy had some superior status to

---

[35.] In his *De Homine* (1658) Hobbes began his discussion of 'fictitious men' in chapter 15 with the remark, 'What the Greeks call πρόσωπον, Latin speakers sometimes call the *face* or *countenance* of a man [*faciem* sive *os*], and sometimes the *person*: the *face* if they wish to be understood as referring to a real man, and the *person* if they are referring to a fictitious one'. (*Opera Philosophica, quae Latine scripsit, Omnia* (Amsterdam, 1668), p. 84 of William Molesworth (ed.), *De Homine*; *Opera Philosophica, quae Latine scripsit, Omnia* (London: John Bohn, 1839), vol. II, p. 130, my translation). So the 'face of the commonwealth' in this passage can be taken to be the same as its 'person'.

monarchy: whatever could be said about democracy could be said equally truthfully about monarchy. And it is true that his later works are full of sneers about the 'democratical gentlemen' who had overthrown the English monarchy.[36] But his earlier works are far more measured, and reveal that his hostility was (as we might have expected) to *deliberative assemblies*, and not to democratic power exercised *without* deliberation. This comes out particularly clearly from his discussion of the subject in chapter 10 of *De Cive*, in which he said (as Rousseau was also to say) that the danger of popular states was that 'there may be as many *Neros* as there are *Orators* who fawn on the *people*' (x.7).[37] But he went on to say,

> These disadvantages found in the deliberations of large
> assemblies prove that *Monarchy* is better than *Democracy*

[36.] 'Why may not men be taught their duty, that is, the science of just and unjust, as divers other sciences have been taught, from true principles and evident demonstration; and much more easily than any of those preachers and democratical gentlemen could teach rebellion and treason?' Ferdinand Toennies (ed.), *Behemoth or The Long Parliament* (London: Simpkin, Marshall and Co., 1889) p. 39. See also ibid., pp. 20, 26–31, etc., for other similar passages (though mostly associating the democratical gentlemen with the Presbyterians and the prewar Parliamentarians). *Leviathan* contains similar abuse of 'those Democratical writers, that continually snarle at that estate [of monarchy]' (p. 226; original edn, chapter 29, p. 171).

[37.] See Rousseau in his *Economie Politique*: 'Athens was in fact not a Democracy, but a very tyrannical Aristocracy, governed by philosophers and orators' (p. 122). Hobbes in the *Elements of Law* had said precisely that 'a democracy, in effect, is no more than an aristocracy of orators, interrupted sometimes with the temporary monarchy of one orator' (II.2.5, pp. 120–1).

insofar as in *Democracy* questions of great importance
are more often passed to such assemblies for discussion
than in a *Monarchy*; it cannot easily be otherwise. There
is no reason why anyone would not prefer to spend his
time on his *private business* rather than on *public affairs*,
except that he sees scope for his eloquence, to acquire a
reputation for intelligence and good sense, and to return
home and enjoy the triumph for his great achievements
with friends, parents and wife ... But if in a *Democracy*
the *people* should choose to concentrate deliberations about
war and peace and legislation in the hands of just one man
or a very small number of men, and were happy to
appoint magistrates and public ministers, content, i.e. to
have authority without executive power [*authoritate sine
ministerio*], then it must be admitted that *Democracy* and
Monarchy would be equal in this matter. (x.15)

He had said something similar already in the *Elements of Law*,
where, discussing the 'aptitude' of a commonwealth 'to dissolve into civil war', he observed that

to this are monarchies much less subject, than any other
governments. For where the union, or band of a
commonwealth, is one man, there is no distraction;
whereas in assemblies, those that are of different opinions,
and give different counsel, are apt to fall out amongst
themselves, and to cross the designs of commonwealth for
one another's sake.

But

this aptitude to dissolution, is to be understood for an
inconvenience in such aristocracies only where the affairs
of state are debated in great and numerous assemblies,

as they were anciently in Athens, and in Rome; and not in
such as do nothing else in great assemblies, but choose
magistrates and counsellors, and commit the handling of
state affairs to a few; such as is the aristocracy of Venice
at this day. For these are no more apt to dissolve from this
occasion, than monarchies, the counsel of state being
both in the one and the other alike.[38]

Once deliberation had been removed from the business of a
democratic assembly, and once a distinction had been drawn
between sovereignty and government, the conventional objections to democracy (as I observed at the beginning of Chapter 1)
lost their force, and this was true even for Hobbes himself. His
hostility to the 'democraticall gentlemen' (from this perspective)
thus most resembled the hostility of the Girondins for the
Jacobins, which I discuss in the next chapter: the gentlemen's
most deceitful claim was that in some way the people could be
involved in the activity of *government*, as this concealed their
own bid for supreme power in a deliberative assembly, the
House of Commons. They were not truly 'democraticall'
but oligarchic, and Hobbes expressly said that England after
1649 was no more a democracy than it was a monarchy.[39]

[38.] II.5.8, p. 143. Hobbes in this passage assumed that, as he said (above p. 101
n. 37), democracies are 'in effect' aristocracies when they decide things in
deliberative assemblies, and carelessly continued to describe non-
deliberative democracies as aristocracies, something he corrected in the
equivalent passage of *De Cive*. I do not think that we should suppose that
his ideas about democracy underwent any major change between the
two works.

[39.] '[T]he supreme authority must needs be in one man or in more. If in
one, it is monarchy; the Rump therefore was no Monarch. If the

So already in Hobbes we find centrally the thoughts which we shall also find in Rousseau: an insistence that the people have no existence separate from the sovereign, and that the clearest example of this is to be found in the fact that the first and most fundamental way in which a people are formed is by the creation of a democratic assembly to which all may come and which is governed by majority voting and not by deliberation. Rousseau went further and argued that such an assembly could not dissolve itself and transfer its sovereignty to (for example) a king, but – at least in this area – that was the only significant difference between his theory and Hobbes's. It is true that in *Leviathan* and Hobbes's other late works the resemblance between Hobbes and Rousseau is not so clear, which is one reason why the conceptual importance of democracy to Hobbes has usually been overlooked;[40] and it is also

authority were in more than one, it was in all, or in fewer than all. When in all, it is democracy; for every man may enter into the assembly which makes the Sovereign Court; which they could not do here. It is therefore manifest, that the authority was in a few, and consequently the state was an oligarchy'. *Behemoth*, p. 156.

[40] At the beginning of *Leviathan*, chapter 18, he said that 'A *Commonwealth* is said to be *Instituted*, when a *Multitude* of men do Agree, and *Covenant, every one, with every one,* that to whatsoever *Man,* or *Assembly of Men,* shall be given by the major part, the *Right* to *Present* the Person of them all, (that is to say, to be their *Representative;*) every one, as well he that *Voted for it,* as he that *Voted against it,* shall *Authorise* all the Actions and Judgements, of that Man, or Assembly of men, in the same manner, as if they were his own' (p. 121; original edn p. 88). This is the closest he came in *Leviathan* to the explicit theory of the priority of democracy in *De Cive*: effectively, this passage continues to take democracy, in the form of a binding majority vote, to be primary, but avoids calling it by the name of democracy. It also takes the

true that even in *De Cive* Hobbes occasionally wavered from his clear-eyed position, and found himself talking about a people as if it might be distinguishable from the sovereign, as indeed he did in the passage in which he called the King the people – 'the *people* wills through the will [*per voluntatem*] of *one man*'. But in that passage above all it is plain that he meant what he said when he said that the King was the people, and it might correspond more to what he had in mind if we were to translate the phrase *per voluntatem* as '*in* the will of one man'. In all his writings Hobbes insisted that the sovereign represents or is the agent for the citizens *taken as individuals*,[41] and that it was only insofar as the sovereign had a

transition to monarchy to be potentially almost instantaneous. The difference from Pufendorf is contained in the clause 'every one, as well he that *Voted for it*, as he that *Voted against it*' – that is, each individual commits himself to be bound by the majority vote first, and only after that is he committed to monarchy. This is precisely what Pufendorf denied. See the remarks on Hobbes's ideas in this area by Maurice Goldsmith in his introduction to the reissue of Toennies's edition of the *Elements of Law*, pp. xix–xx. Presumably, given Hobbes's intention to present *Leviathan* to the King of Scots (see my edition p. lv and Noel Malcolm's edition (Oxford University Press, 2012), vol. i, pp. 51–60), he was at pains to avoid as far as possible the democratic implications of his theory, but he could not eliminate them entirely.

41. The term *representation*, as is well known, appears for the first time only in *Leviathan* (or, actually, in Samuel Sorbière's 1649 translation into French of *De Cive* (*Du Citoyen* v.9 and note to vi.1, Simone Goyard-Fabre (ed.), (Paris: Flammarion, 1982), pp. 145, 150). It was Lucien Jaume who originally pointed this out to me), but in both *De Cive* and *De Homine* Hobbes said in various places that the sovereign's will is 'taken to be' the will of each of the citizens – that is, *habenda est*, which we might translate 'is deemed'. He also used in both works the term *attribute* (*attribuere*), while at *De Cive* vii.7, saying that 'the *People*

unitary will (either the naturally single will of a monarch, or the agreed decision of an assembly) that these individuals were united. Nothing like the Grotian (or, later, the Pufendorfian) picture of a prior agreement among all the citizens to form a society independent of any governmental structure finds its way into Hobbes, and the practical conclusions that Grotius drew from his account were denied by Hobbes in all his works. Thus, on succession, while Grotius argued that in the event of the failure of a hereditary royal line power to choose a successor reverted to the body of the people (as, it should be said, Bodin also believed), Hobbes declared in *Leviathan* that 'If a Monarch shall relinquish the

absorbs into its own will the will of the citizen' (*populus voluntate sua voluntatem civis . . . complectitur*), he used the word *complector*, 'embrace' or 'absorb', which (as Lewis and Short observed) was used by both Cicero and Quintilian to mean 'to comprehend a multitude of objects in discourse or in a written representation'. In *De Homine* (published seven years after *Leviathan)* he used the verb *repraesentare* both to describe the representation by one man of many other men (the key representative relationship in Hobbes) – *ut ergo idem histrio potest diversas personas diversis tempoiribus induere, ita quilibet homo plures homines repraesentare potest* – and to describe the 'representation' of God (1668 *Opera*, pp. 84, 85; Molesworth, ed., pp. 130, 132); in *De Cive* when talking about the representation of God he used the term *vicem gerere* (II.12) and *proregia* (XI.1). *Repraesentare* in classical Latin does not quite mean 'represent' in the full English sense – in particular, it does not denote acting as someone's agent – and as a good Latinist Hobbes was presumably always somewhat wary of using it, until (as Quentin Skinner has suggested in 'Hobbes on Representation', *European Journal of Philosophy 13* (2005), pp 155–84) he was spurred into doing so by its prevalence among the pamphleteers of the English Revolution. But he was clearly groping for a terminology along these lines from the beginning.

Soveraignty, both for himself, and his heires; His Subjects
returne to the absolute Libertie of Nature, ... The case is the
same, if he dye without known Kindred, and without declaration of his Heyre'.[42] Similarly, Hobbes gave no credence
to the idea that different nations might preserve their separate identity under a common sovereign, arguing at some
length in *Behemoth* that after the union of the crowns
Scotland and England were no more foreign to one another
than the provinces of France: 'Have not many of the provinces of France their parliaments and several constitutions?
And yet they are all equally natural subjects of the King
of France'.[43]

All this makes even more striking the fact that, in
addition to weakening the case for democracy, in *Leviathan*
and some of his other late works, as Quentin Skinner and
David Runciman have argued, Hobbes seems to have veered
towards a terminology dangerously close to the Grotian or
Pufendorfian idea, in which the 'state' over which the ruler is
sovereign is personified as a single and separate entity,
though an entity with no capacity for action independent
of the sovereign.[44] *Leviathan* in this respect may indeed
be significantly different from *De Cive*, and certainly the

[42] Page 154; original p. 114; see also *De Cive* VII.18.
[43] *Behemoth*, pp. 34–5.
[44] David Runciman, *Pluralism and the Personality of the State* (Cambridge
University Press, 1997); Quentin Skinner, 'From the state of princes to
the person of the state' in his *Visions of Politics* (Cambridge University
Press, 2002), vol. II, pp. 368–413, 'Hobbes and the purely artificial person
of the state' in ibid., vol. III, pp. 177–208, and 'Hobbes on representation',
European Journal of Philosophy 13 (2005), pp. 155–84.

famous image of the state as an artificial man (found both in a well-known passage of the Introduction and in the frontispiece to the book) has no place in the earlier work; Pufendorf praised it in his *De Iure Naturae et Gentium* as a 'very ingenious Draught' (*ingeniose delineavit*), even at the same time as he was very critical of Hobbes's account of popular identity, ridiculing the claim that the King is the People.[45] On the story I am telling about this debate, a move of this sort by Hobbes has to be seen as surprising, and (it should be said) it was not often recognised by contemporaries. Pufendorf's own idea of a *civitas* or state was expressly presented in opposition to Hobbes's theory, at least as it had appeared in *De Cive*, and though Pufendorf used a paraphrase of Hobbes's definition of *Unio* in *De Cive* to describe the full civil union under a sovereign, he was attacked for doing so by both Gottlieb Gerhard Titius and Jean Barbeyrac on the grounds that (in Titius's words) Hobbes 'confounds the State and the Ruler' (*Civitatem & Imperantem confundat*).[46] Barbeyrac and Titius certainly did not take Hobbes to be the theorist of a state which is even notionally separable from the sovereign, and it seems to have been Pufendorf's

---

[45] *The Law of Nature and Nations* VII.2.13–14.

[46] Gottlieb Gerhard Titius, *Observationes in Samuelis L. B. de Pufendorf De Officio Hominis et Civis* (Leipzig, 1703), Observation 557 (p. 563); Barbeyrac's note to his translation of *De Iure Naturae et Gentium* VII.2.13. Different paraphrases of Hobbes's definition in *De Cive* V.9 appear in Pufendorf's *Elementorum Jurisprudentiae Universalis Libri II* (The Hague, 1660), Book II, Observation V.2 (p. 355) (written before he had read *Leviathan*), in his *De Iure Naturae et Gentium* VII.2.13 and in his *De Officio Hominis et Civis* II.6.10.

formulation and not Hobbes's which was most influential, at least on the Continent (where *De Cive* and not *Leviathan* was always the text of choice) during the next century, as we shall see in Chapter 3.[47]

The political implications of Hobbes's ideas, and in particular of his remarks about elective monarchy, were, on the other hand, very clear to contemporaries, and they occasioned some of the sharpest criticism that Pufendorf delivered to Hobbes in his *De Iure Naturae et Gentium* of 1672. Referring to the second of Hobbes's cases of time-limited monarchy, in which the people agreed to meet on the monarch's death, but in the meantime '*sovereign power* (like *Ownership*) remained with the *people*', Pufendorf expostulated that

> we utterly dislike the Assertion of Mr. *Hobbes*, which we meet with in his Book *De Cive*; ... This Notion, if taken in the gross Sense in which it is deliver'd, we cannot but look upon as highly dangerous and prejudicial to all those limited Princes, who are ordain'd by the voluntary Donation of the People, and bound up to certain fundamental Laws. And the rather, because, as he hath taken the Liberty to call a King for Life a *temporary Monarch*, others may, with as much Reason, extend the Name to those who receive the Sovereignty, with the Privilege of transmitting it by Inheritance, yet so as to keep it within their own Line and Family. Besides, since

[47.] This was recognised by Gierke in his discussion of Hobbes and Pufendorf – see e.g. his *Natural Law and the Theory of Society*, trans. Ernest Barker (Cambridge University Press, 1958), pp. 116–17.

> Mr. *Hobbes* hath not determin'd how far he would
> stretch the Parallel which he useth, he may easily be
> intangled in a Train of very pernicious Consequences.
> For since Property, consider'd in itself, is a much more
> noble Right, than that of temporary Use; some Men may,
> on these Principles, conclude that the People are superior
> to the Prince, and have a Power of bringing him to
> Correction, in case he doth not govern, according to their
> Pleasure and Humour. (vii.6.17)

(This was indeed Hobbes's third case – and Pufendorf was
right that the distinction between the second and third cases
was a fine one; it was after all not present in Hobbes's mind
when he wrote the *Elements of Law*). Pufendorf accused
Hobbes of 'breaking and dividing' sovereignty, so that
'the κτῆσις, the *Property* or real Possession resides in the
People, and the χρῆσις only, or the *Use* in the Prince',
and, like Grotius, he insisted that the power was the same
whatever the situation after the holder of the power left office
or died.

> [W]ho for Instance, will pretend, that a Father hath
> only the χρῆσις of paternal Authority, because upon his
> Death the Children are at their own Disposal? Or that a
> Master hath only the χρῆσις of the despotical Power,
> because, in case he die without Heirs, the Slave recovers
> his Liberty?

He was more hesitant about the dictator, but not on any
major theoretical grounds. Partly, he believed that the
dictator had not in fact had 'all, and each precise Part of
the Sovereignty so committed to him together, as that,

during the six Months Space, he might exercise it as he pleas'd',[48] and partly he thought that

> Tho' the Continuance of a Thing doth not change the Nature of it, yet there is no doubt to be made, but that a temporary Command is in Dignity much inferior to a perpetual one; since Men are wont to respect those with a much more solid Veneration, whom they apprehend to be incapable of returning to a private Condition, than those whom in a little time they are again like to see on the same Level with themselves.

He also admitted that it might be impossible to find an example of a truly time-limited sovereign of this kind. But it is clear that his general theory committed him, just as it had Grotius, to this being at least a conceptual possibility.

This is because, as I have said, his general theory of sovereignty was fundamentally the same as Grotius's, though he tried to clarify and make more precise something Grotius had left rather vague. Like Grotius, he believed in distinguishing between the common and the proper subject of sovereignty;[49] like Grotius, he took the proper subject to be

---

[48.] Barbeyrac noted on this passage, 'This is only true with respect to later Times, and we here speak of the Dictatorship, such as it was originally, and as it remain'd for several Ages, when there was any Necessity to have Recourse to it. See what I have said upon the same Place of *Grotius*', where he endorsed Grotius's view. So Barbeyrac reasonably enough took Pufendorf to be saying essentially the same as Grotius about the dictator, and he agreed with both of them.

[49.] 'The Sovereign Authority [*summum imperium*], besides that inheres in each State [*civitas*], as in a common or general *Subject*; so, farther, according as it resides either in one Person, or in a Council (consisting of

the usual three regimes; and like Grotius, he took the common subject to be an association of free men which constituted and gave identity to a 'people'. He endorsed entirely Grotius's conclusion that a people could not be dismembered, even by a patrimonial sovereign who had (in general) no obligation to consult his subjects, though, unlike Grotius, he was clear-headed about the fact that the same argument should apply to the *union* of different peoples.[50] Insofar as there was a divergence from Grotius, it came simply over Pufendorf's wish to spell out in detail the nature of the agreement between individuals, which created the association. As is well known, he argued that the formation of a *civitas* required two separate covenants or contracts – this was seen in the eighteenth century as Pufendorf's distinctive position. The first was between the individuals 'each with each in particular, to join into one lasting Society [*coetum*, Grotius's term], and to concert the Measures of their Welfare and Safety, by the publick Vote [*communi consilio ductuque*]' (VII.2.7). The second was the covenant

> when the Person or Persons, upon whom the Sovereignty is conferred, shall be actually constituted; by which the Rulers, on the one hand, engage themselves to take care of the common Peace and Security, and the Subjects, on the other, to yield them faithful Obedience; in which, likewise, is included that Submission and Union of Wills, by which

some, or all of the Members) as in a proper or particular *Subject*, it produceth different Forms of Commonwealths [*respublicae*]' (VII.5.1).
50. VIII.5.9 (repeating Grotius on dismemberment) and VIII.12.6 (on union).

we conceive a State to be but *one Person*. And from this
Covenant the State receives its final Completion and
Perfection. (VII.2.8)

This two-covenant theory, however, merely made explicit
what had been implicit in Grotius: that there were two separate agreements, one to create the *coetus* and the other to locate
sovereignty in its proper subject.

As I said earlier, Pufendorf used the Hobbesian language, that in principle civil society required this 'union of
wills', and that 'the only Method . . . by which many Wills may
be conceived as joined together' is

> that each Member of the Society submit his Will to the Will
> of one Person, or of one Council; so that whatsoever this
> Person or this Council shall resolve, in Matters which
> necessarily concern the common Safety, shall be deemed
> the Will of all in general, and of each in particular. (VII.2.5)

(In this passage, incidentally, he coined the phrases 'general'
and 'particular' will – see Barbeyrac's French translation,
'la volonté de tous en général & de chacun en particulier').
But the use to which he put this language was expressly
designed to avoid Hobbes's conclusions. Only the second
covenant, by which the 'proper' sovereign was created,
involved this Hobbesian cession of wills; the first, by which
the initial *coetus* was formed, was based on the kind of *con-
sensus* and continued separateness of individual wills which
from Hobbes's point of view made up a *multitude*. One might
think (and this has occasionally been suggested) that nevertheless Pufendorf's theory was little different from Hobbes's,
for Hobbes after all thought that we create a civil society by

covenanting with our fellow citizens that we should all have
the same sovereign, and this civil society acting as a democracy could then choose any other type of sovereign. Pufendorf's first covenant would then be Hobbes's civil covenant,
and the second covenant a decision of the primaeval democracy to transfer sovereignty to a king, or to retain it in its own
hand. Pufendorf was himself perfectly aware of this possibility,
and he was concerned to deny it; in the process he opened up
a space between his own view and that of Grotius, indicating
that he recognised the dangers to which Grotius's acceptance
of majoritarianism in the initial *coetus* had led. Pufendorf
conceded that

> [w]hen . . . a Number of free Persons assemble together,
> in order to enter upon a Covenant about uniting
> themselves in a civil Body, this preparative Assembly hath
> already some Appearance of a Democracy; properly in
> this Respect, that every Man hath the Privilege freely to
> deliver his Opinion concerning the common Affairs.

But it was not a true democracy, as

> he who dissents from the Vote of the Majority, shall not in
> the least be obliged by what they determine, till such time
> as, by means of a second Covenant, a popular Form shall be
> actually confirm'd and establish'd. Mr. *Hobbes*, for want of
> distinguishing these two Covenants, hath handled this
> Subject with great Confusion.

And he insisted that a

> Number of Men cannot become one Body, unless they
> have agreed upon a constant Method of transacting

114

> publick Business. If they break up without settling this
> Point, yet prefix a Time and Place for considering and
> debating the Matter farther, in order to a final Resolution;
> we have then no more than the Rudiments and first
> Principles of a State, which cannot be properly styl'd a
> Democracy . . . But we are then to call it a democraticall
> Government, when the Right of settling Matters, relating
> to the publick Safety, is conferr'd for ever on a general
> assembly. (VII.5.6)[51]

But Pufendorf also continued to claim that it was this agreement to meet in mutual discussion, rather than the agreement to submit their wills to a sovereign, which bound men
together into civil society and gave them an identity as a
people. The people, understood in this sense, remained
the common subject of sovereignty, even though they had
no formal and institutionalised legislative power, and the
distinction between sovereignty and government, understood in the Bodinian or the Hobbesian fashion, was, he
thought, merely scholastic. He had indeed already said precisely this in his work *De statu imperii Germanici* of 1667,

[51.] He gave a concrete illustration of the kind of debate he had in mind, in
'that Account, which *Dionysius Halicarnassaeus* gives us of the first
Settlement of the Monarchy in *Rome*. For here, first of all, a Number of
Men flock together, with Design to fix themselves in a new State; in order
to which Resolution a tacit Covenant, at least, must be supposed to have
passed amongst them. After this, they deliberate about the Form of
Government, and that, by Kings being preferred, they agree to invest
Romulus with the sovereign Authority. And this holds too in the Case of
an *Interregnum*, during which, the Society being held together only by
the prime Compact, it is frequent to enter the Debate about the Frame
and Model of the Commonwealth' (VII.2.8).

in which he attacked the use that had been made in the interpretation of the juridical character of the Holy Roman Empire of the idea 'that the form of any State [*Reipublicae*] ought to be distinguished from the manner of its Administration [*administrationis*]', and in particular the claim that the Empire must be an aristocracy as sovereignty was lodged with the Electors:

> (though these things may thus with Subtilty enough be disputed in the Schools, yet) no wise man will thereby be perswaded to think the *German* Empire is an *Aristocrasie*, especially if he has any competent degree of Civil or Politick Experience and Knowledge.[52]

This was because a genuine aristocracy required a Senate, that is, an aristocratic seat of government, and there was no such institution in the Empire; viewed objectively, the governmental structure of the Empire, Pufendorf famously concluded, was an 'irregular' or even 'monstrous' entity, closer to a federation than to anything else. Like Grotius, it was the actual governmental structure that interested Pufendorf, and not the constitutional authority which might lie behind government, and be used to change it.

The model of political association favoured by Grotius and Pufendorf appealed to a certain kind of English radical in the late seventeenth century. James Tyrrell, for example, devoted part of his *Patriarcha Non Monarcha* of 1681 to an enthusiastic summary of Pufendorf, saying that

---

[52] Michael J. Seidler (ed.), *The Present State of Germany*, trans. Edmund Bohun (Indianapolis: Liberty Fund, 2007), pp. 163–4.

> where divers Men have United together into a perfect
> Commonwealth, it is necessary for the ... liberty or faculty
> of appointing, resolving all means necessary for their own
> safety, should now exist in the Supreme Power, as in a
> common Subject ... Yet when this Supreme Authority is
> considered as it is conferred upon one Man, or one Council
> consisting of all, or few, as its proper subject, it is not
> always free, and absolute, but in some places limited by
> certain laws.[53]

And the same idea is found, in its essence, in Tyrrell's friend
and collaborator John Locke, though (as in many areas of his
thought) Locke defended the original, Grotian version of the
theory against Pufendorf's emendations. Locke did not use the
language of 'common' and 'proper' subjects of sovereignty;
indeed, a striking feature of the *Second Treatise* is that Locke
barely uses the language of sovereignty at all, and never
applies it to civil society.[54] Chapter 8 of the *Second Treatise*
contains an account of 'the Beginning of Political Societies'
which, on the face of it, rather resembles Hobbes.

> The only way whereby any one devests himself of his
> Natural Liberty, and *puts on the bonds of Civil Society* is by
> agreeing with other Men to joyn and unite into a
> Community... When any number of Men have so
> *consented to make one Community* or Government, they

[53.] *Patriarcha Non Monarcha* (London, 1681), pp. 240–1.

[54.] Unlike the *First Treatise*, where he is attacking the notion of Adam's
sovereignty – but there he is tracking the terminology employed by
Filmer. References to the *Two Treatises of Government* are to Peter
Laslett's edition (Cambridge University Press, 1960; new edn 1988).

> are thereby presently incorporated, and make *one Body
> Politick*, wherein the *Majority* have a Right to act and
> conclude the rest. (§95)

And indeed Locke specifically referred to 'the mighty *Leviathan*' in this chapter when emphasising the necessity of
majoritarianism.[55] Chapter 10 enlarges upon this, saying that
this majority

> may imploy all that power in making Laws for the
> Community from time to time, and Executing those Laws
> by Officers of their own appointing; and then the *Form* of
> the Government is a perfect *Democracy*: Or else may put
> the power of making Laws into the hands of a few select
> Men, . . . and then it is an *Oligarchy*: Or else into the hands
> of one Man, and then it is a *Monarchy* . . . And so
> accordingly of these the Community may make
> compounded and mixed Forms of Government, as they
> think good. (§132)

This 'Legislative Power' Locke described as 'Supream', though
in chapter 11 he listed the general moral constraints upon its
exercise – most familiarly, that it could not undermine private
property. This in itself was not enough to separate Locke from
Hobbes, however, as Hobbes too always acknowledged that
there would be natural law constraints on the sovereign,
though they were a different set from those Locke chose.

[55.] If 'the consent of every individual' were to be necessary for collective
decisions, 'Such a Constitution as this would make the mighty *Leviathan*
of a shorter duration, than the feeblest Creatures; and not let it outlast
the day it was born in' (§98).

But the key difference came in chapter 13, in practical political terms (as Laslett observed) one of the most important in the book,[56] where Locke explained how the 'Community' retained its separate identity and was not subsumed into the 'Supream Power'.

> Though ... there can be but *one Supream Power*, which is *the Legislative*, to which all the rest are and must be subordinate, yet the Legislative being only a Fiduciary Power to act for certain ends, there remains still *in the People a Supream Power* to remove or *alter the Legislative*, when they find the *Legislative* act contrary to the trust reposed in them ... And thus the *Community* may be said in this respect to be *always the Supream Power*, but not as considered under any Form of Government, because this Power of the People can never take place till the Government be dissolved. (§149)

So, though Locke did not use the terminology of 'common' and 'proper' sites of sovereignty, his actual account is very close to those of Grotius and Pufendorf, and in particular to Grotius's, given Locke's acceptance of majoritarian decision-making within the 'Community'.[57] The Lockean 'Community' continued to have an identity and a residual capacity to action despite having vested 'supream power' in a government, and having itself no continued legislative role, just as the 'common subject' did. Locke's use of the term *community* may indeed be an echo of the 'common subject' – it is a relatively unusual

---

[56.] See Laslett's footnote, p. 366.

[57.] The fiduciary element is present in the equivalent passage of Grotius, see above p. 74.

term within at least the modern natural law tradition of Grotius, Hobbes and Pufendorf.

A familiar tradition in the history of political thought put Locke and Rousseau (speaking very broadly) on one side, and Hobbes on the other (though an earlier tradition had been well aware of the similarities between Hobbes and Rousseau). But for the radicals of the eighteenth century, including above all Rousseau, it was the idea that the sovereign could have the power to shake off the old systems of government which, as we shall see in my next chapter, fascinated them. And in their eyes Grotius and Pufendorf represented the ideological under-pinnings of the old system, and insofar as Locke belonged in their camp, he too could provide little help for radical politics; as Mark Goldie has recently stressed,[58] and as I discuss in Chapter 4, Locke had to be read in a new and possibly tendentious way for the eighteenth-century radicals to call him in aid. For at least some of them, it was Hobbes who best represented the new possibilities; and I do not think they were wrong.

[58.] 'Situating Swift's politics in 1701' in Claude Rawson (ed.), *Politics and Literature in the Age of Swift* (Cambridge University Press, 2010), pp. 31–51.

3

The eighteenth century

The political positions taken up by Grotius, Pufendorf and Barbeyrac dominated the first half of the eighteenth century; their hegemony is illustrated by the distribution of Barbeyrac's great editions of *De Iure Belli ac Pacis* and *De Iure Naturae et Gentium*, in their Latin, French and English versions, which we can find in libraries from the Mississippi to the Urals. It will unquestionably have been Barbeyrac's French translation of Grotius which lay (as Rousseau later recalled) on his father's workbench.[1] Indeed, Helena Rosenblatt has drawn our attention to the importance of these texts, and the more popular version provided by Burlamaqui, in the political struggles at Geneva in Rousseau's youth. It is striking that in the arguments she has documented between the democrats and the patricians in Geneva over the rights of the popular General Council against the small governing councils of the city, the distinction between sovereign and government was a recurrent theme in the writings and speeches of the democrats, and a denial of the distinction was equally part of the patricians' repertoire. For example, the radical Jacques-Barthélemy Micheli du Crest described Geneva in a manuscript of the 1730s as a 'democratic republic', by which he meant 'a free state, in which the people

---

[1.] In Launay (ed.), the dedication to the *Discourse on the Origin of Inequality, Oeuvres complètes*, vol. II, p. 207; *The Social Contract and Discourses*, p. 34.

itself exercises the acts of sovereignty, without however exercising subordinate government'.[2] Barbeyrac himself responded to Micheli, insisting that 'the people of Geneva can be as sovereign as you please; it still does not exercise the acts of sovereignty itself' – that is, what Micheli called merely a government was, in Barbeyrac's eyes, to be treated as an effectual site of sovereignty, exactly the point which Grotius

[2.] Helena Rosenblatt, *Rousseau and Geneva* (Cambridge University Press, 1997), p. 143. See also the democrat Pierre Fatio's remarks in 1707, ibid., p. 104. Micheli had read Bodin, and his ideas seem to track Bodin's in a number of respects, notably his account of the marks of sovereignty and his denial of the possibility of a mixed sovereignty. See his 'Maximes d'un Républicain sur le Gouvernement Civil', *Revue Française d'Histoire des Idées Politiques*, 15 (2002), 155–82, in particular paragraphs 7, 24 and 52. A number of Genevan contemporaries drew parallels between Micheli's ideas and those of Rousseau, notably the author of *Lettre d'un citoyen de Genève à un autre citoyen* (Geneva, 1768), p. 72, possibly Rousseau's former friend Jacob Vernet, and Toussaint Pierre Lenieps, who compared Rousseau to Micheli in a letter of August 1764 from R. A. Leigh, et al. (eds.), *Correspondance complète de Jean Jacques Rousseau* (Banbury: Voltaire Foundation, 1965–98), p. 21. However, Rousseau criticised Micheli in the *Letters from the Mountain* for failing to see the merits of the Genevan constitution as established by the international 'Mediation' of 1738, and in particular for failing to see that the right of remonstrance by the citizens constituted the best means by which the citizens could exercise a loose day-to-day control over the government (Launay, ed., *Oeuvres complètes*, vol. III, p. 466; *Letter to Beaumont, Letters Written from the Mountain, and Related Writings*, p. 260). Essentially, the difference between them was that Micheli – while acknowledging the distinction between sovereign and government – wished for much more democratic involvement in government than Rousseau was willing to accept. On their relationship, see Richard Whatmore, *Against War and Empire: Geneva, Britain, and France in the Eighteenth Century* (Yale University Press, 2012), pp. 74–80.

and Pufendorf had made. But Micheli spent the last part of his life as a political prisoner in a Bernese gaol, whereas Barbeyrac died an honoured and successful jurist; as Rousseau observed, 'truth is no road to fortune, and the people dispenses neither ambassadorships, nor professorships, nor pensions'.[3] The commanding heights of the early eighteenth century belonged to Grotius and his followers, and their influence reached into all the prestigious areas of intellectual life – for example, contemporary classical scholarship was enlisted to endorse Grotius's and Barbeyrac's ideas about the sovereignty of the dictator in Johannes Jens's essay *De dictatoribus populi Romani* of 1698.[4]

Something like their assumptions even lurks behind Montesquieu's *L'Esprit des Lois*. Montesquieu remarked in his *Pensées* that 'I thank MM. Grotius and Pufendorf for having accomplished a large part of the work which has been required of me, and with a level of ability which I cannot match', and he seems to have been particularly impressed by Pufendorf's *De statu imperii Germanici*.[5] Pufendorf's scorn in that work for the 'scholastic' nature of any constitutional theory that disregarded the actual shape of politics in a given country would clearly have struck a chord with Montesquieu, and there is no suggestion in *L'Esprit des Lois* of anything

---

[3] Launay (ed.), *Oeuvres complètes*, vol. II, p. 527; *The Social Contract and Discourses*, p. 184.

[4] Cited by Barbeyrac in his note to Grotius, *The Rights of War and Peace* 1.3.11, n. 7. The essay is to be found in Jens's *Ferculum Literarium* (Leiden, 1717), pp. 89–130; it is dated 1698 on p. 130.

[5] Montesquieu, in D. Oster (ed.), *Oeuvres complètes* (Paris: Éditions du Seuil, 1964), p. 874 (my translation). See p. 211 for Montesquieu's enthusiasm for *De statu imperii Germanici*.

resembling the idea of a sleeping sovereign. Indeed, Montesquieu consistently (and perhaps quite deliberately) conflated the terms *sovereign* and *government*, as in the fundamental definitions of Book II, chapter 1: 'republican government [*gouvernement republicain*] is that in which the people as a body, or only a part of the people, have sovereign power [*la souveraine puissance*]'.[6] And in general throughout the work it was *gouvernement* with which he was concerned, and which, for example, he wished to divide into 'legislative' and 'executive' powers, without any suggestion that the legislative was sovereign and the executive was not.[7]

When Rousseau turned against this entire culture, which in his eyes had done nothing but rationalise the inequalities of eighteenth-century Europe, he expressly put a revival of the distinction between sovereign and government at the heart of his project; its salience for him was recognised by those close to him such as Toussaint Pierre Lenieps, who wrote to Rousseau shortly after reading the *Social Contract* that 'I finally managed to buy your *Social Contract*. I have understood sovereignty and Government in this way, but I have never seen it established with such truth and

---

[6.] Translation from Anne M. Cohler, Basia Carolyn Miller and Harold Samuel Stone (trans. and ed.), *The Spirit of the Laws* (Cambridge University Press, 1989), p. 10.

[7.] See, for example, his remarks on England in the famous chapter 6 of Book XI, in which he described the 'puissance exécutrice' as 'partie du gouvernement', and insisted that the executive must not be subordinate to the legislative but must (e.g.) possess a veto over it. See also his criticism of Hobbes in his *Pensées* for supposing that 'the actions of the Prince are the actions of the People' (*Oeuvres complètes*, pp. 938–9).

forcefulness'.[8] It was also something that his early critics contested, equally aware of its importance in his theory.[9] Rousseau seems first to have drawn the distinction in his article for the *Encyclopédie* entitled 'Economie', seven years before the *Social Contract*.[10] But Book III of the *Social Contract* gives the fullest account of his views. It is organised round the

[8.] 'J'avois ainsi conçu la souveraineté & le Gouvernement, mais je n'avois rien vû qui l'eut établi avec autant de verité & de force'. *Correspondance complète* 14, pp. 57–8.

[9.] See Paul-Louis de Bauclair's *Anti-Contrat Social* (The Hague, 1765), in which he said (in words reminiscent of pre-Bodinian Aristotelianism) that 'Government, in its most basic meaning, is nothing other than a *manner of being*, associated with a body politic, from which it is distinguished as an accident from a substance; it is nothing other than the *modus administrandi* ... I am very happy to personify the Government, but it will not be a body intermediate between the Subjects and the Sovereign [a reference to Rousseau's description of it in chapter 1, Book III]; it will be the body of Administrators of the State, of which the Sovereign is the Head [*Chef*]. The Government, in this sense, if it consists as he supposes of inferior and subordinate members, is not to be distinguished from the Sovereign, but rather regarded as its Co-operators and Co-Adjutors in the administration of the body politic' (pp. 113–4).

[10.] 'I must here ask my readers to distinguish also between *public economy*, which is my subject and which I call government, and the supreme authority, which I call *Sovereignty*; a distinction which consists in the fact that the latter has the right of legislation, and in certain cases binds the body of the nation itself, while the former has only the right of execution, and is binding only on individuals'. *The Social Contract and Discourses*, p. 120; Launay (ed.), *Oeuvres complètes*, vol. II, p. 278; see ibid., p. 294 for the early draft of this passage, to be found in MS R.16 of the Bibliothèque Publique et Universitaire of Neuchâtel. See also Bruno Bernardi's edition of the *Discours sur l'économie politique* (Paris: Vrin, 2002) and his remarks on the passage, p. 28. It may be significant that most of the references to Bodin in Rousseau's works are to be found in 'Economie'.

distinction, and begins with the remark 'Before speaking of the different forms of government [gouvernement], let us try to fix the exact sense of the word, which has not yet been very clearly explained' – which as we have seen was precisely the case in the tradition Rousseau was attacking. He continued by stating at the start of chapter 1 of *Government in General* that 'I warn the reader that this chapter requires careful reading, and that I am unable to make myself clear to those who refuse to be attentive', in recognition of the fact that what he was going to argue was widely unfamiliar. What he then proceeded to assert was much closer to Hobbes than anyone had been prepared to say for almost a century, though there were of course some significant differences, particularly in terminology.

> What then is government? An intermediate body set up between the subjects and the Sovereign, to secure their mutual correspondence, charged with the execution of the laws and the maintenance of liberty, both civil and political.
>
> The members of this body are called magistrates or kings, that is to say governors, and the whole body bears the name prince. Thus those who hold that the act, by which a people puts itself under a prince, is not a contract, are certainly right. It is simply and solely a commission, an employment, in which the rulers, mere officials of the Sovereign, exercise in their own name the power of which it makes them depositaries. This power it can limit, modify or recover at pleasure; for the alienation of such a right is incompatible with the nature of the social body, and contrary to the end of association.[11]

[11.] *Social Contract and Discourses*, pp. 208–9; Launay (ed.), *Oeuvres complètes*, vol. II, pp. 539–40.

In the *Social Contract* he had first made the distinction in Book II, chapter 2, 'That Sovereignty Is Indivisible':

> Sovereignty, for the same reason as makes it inalienable, is indivisible; for will either is, or is not, general; it is the will either of the body of the people, or only of a part of it. In the first case, the will, when declared, is an act of Sovereignty and constitutes law: in the second, it is merely a particular will, or act of magistracy—at the most a decree [*un décret*].
>
> But our political theorists, unable to divide Sovereignty in principle, divide it according to its object: into force and will; into legislative power and executive power; into rights of taxation, justice and war; into internal administration and power of foreign treaty. Sometimes they confuse all these sections, and sometimes they distinguish them; they turn the Sovereign into a fantastic being composed of several connected pieces: it is as if they were making man of several bodies, one with eyes, one with arms, another with feet, and each with nothing besides. We are told that the jugglers of Japan dismember a child before the eyes of the spectators; then they throw all the members into the air one after another, and the child falls down alive and whole. The conjuring tricks of our political theorists are very like that ... [W]henever Sovereignty seems to be divided, there is an illusion: the rights which are taken as being part of Sovereignty are really all subordinate, and always imply supreme wills of which they only sanction the execution.[12]

[12.] *Social Contract and Discourses*, pp. 183–84; Launay (ed.), *Oeuvres complètes*, vol. II, p. 526.

And he linked this polemic expressly to Grotius and Barbeyrac, ridiculing them for entangling 'themselves up in their own sophistries, for fear of saying too little or too much of what they think, and so offending the interests they have to conciliate'.

In place of these juggling tricks, Rousseau proposed a simple scheme. As in Hobbes, individuals in a state of nature agreed that henceforward their particular wills would be subsumed in a collective or general will. (It is incidentally, I think, fairly clear that the language of general and particular wills in Rousseau comes from Pufendorf's discussion of the civil covenant in *De Jure Naturae et Gentium* VII.2.5, and not – as Patrick Riley conjectured – from the theological discourse of Malebranche et al. It thus straightforwardly belonged to the discourse of the transformation of a multitude into a people.)[13] Also as in Hobbes, this general will formed the canon of moral as well as political rectitude, as Rousseau said in his *Encyclopédie* article.

> [T]his general will, which tends always to the preservation and welfare of the whole and of every part, and is the source of the laws, constitutes for all the members of the State, in their relations to one another and to it, the rule of what is just or unjust: a truth which shows, by the way, how idly some writers have treated as theft the subtlety prescribed to children at Sparta for obtaining

---

[13.] For Riley's view, see his *The General Will Before Rousseau* (Princeton University Press, 1986) and 'Rousseau's General Will' in Patrick Riley (ed.), *The Cambridge Companion to Rousseau* (Cambridge University Press, 2001), pp. 124–53.

their frugal repasts, as if everything ordained by the
law were not lawful.[14]

Which is precisely the example Hobbes used to make the same
far-reaching claim in *De Cive* XIV.10.[15]

Third, Rousseau entirely endorsed Hobbes's claim in
De Cive that the initial location of the general will must be in
a democratic assembly governed by majority voting. 'Apart
from this primitive contract, the vote of the majority
always binds all the rest. This follows from the contract itself'
(IV.2 p. 250).[16] And lastly, as he said in the passage from
Book III from which we began, he insisted that there could
be only one covenant or contract, that which forms the civil
society. In Book III, chapter 16 he expressly attacked the
double covenant theory which, as we saw, was at the heart of
the Grotian and Pufendorfian scheme, and which in the pages
of Pufendorf and Burlamaqui had explicitly been presented as

[14.] *Social Contract and Discourses*, pp. 120–1; Launay (ed.), *Oeuvres
complètes*, vol. II, p. 278.

[15.] 'When in the old days the Lacedaemonians gave permission to boys
by a specific enactment to pilfer other people's things, they laid it
down that those things were not other people's but belonged to the
pilferer; and so such pilferings were not thefts'. Significantly,
Pufendorf was explicitly critical of this passage of Hobbes. See his
Two Books of the Elements of Universal Jurisprudence, William Abbott
Oldfather (trans.), Thomas Behme (ed.), (Indianapolis: Liberty Fund,
2009), Definition XIII.6–7, pp. 206–10 (I owe this reference to David
Grewal).

[16.] Chapter 2, Book IV, *Social Contract and Discourses*, p. 250; Launay (ed.),
Oeuvres complètes, vol. II, p. 565.

a repudiation of Hobbes's single contract theory.[17] Speaking of the creation of a government, Rousseau remarked that

> It has been held that this act of establishment [of a government] was a contract between the people and the rulers it sets over itself – a contract in which conditions were laid down between the two parties binding the one to command and the other to obey. It will be admitted, I am sure, that this is an odd kind of contract to enter into . . .
>
> First, the supreme authority can no more be modified than it can be alienated; to limit it is to destroy it. It is absurd and contradictory for the Sovereign to set a superior over itself; to bind itself to obey a master would be to return to absolute liberty.
>
> Moreover, it is clear that this contract between the people and such and such persons would be a particular act; and from this it follows that it can be neither a law nor an act of Sovereignty, and that consequently it would be illegitimate . . .
>
> There is only one contract in the State, and that is the act of association, which in itself excludes the existence of a second.[18]

The resemblance between Rousseau's theory and Hobbes's in these respects (not to mention, I would say, in many other

[17.] For Pufendorf, see *The Law of Nature and Nations*, VII.2.9 (with Barbeyrac's notes), and for Burlamaqui, see Jean-Jacques Burlamaqui, *The Principles of Natural and Politic Law*, Thomas Nugent (trans.), Peter Korkman (ed.), (Indianapolis: Liberty Fund, 2006), p. 294.

[18.] *Social Contract and Discourses*, p. 243; Launay (ed.), *Oeuvres complètes*, vol. II, pp. 559–62.

respects) is so striking that it is not surprising that many early readers of Rousseau accused him of being a Hobbist. The *Lettre d'un citoyen de Genève à un autre citoyen* of 1768, probably by his former friend, the Genevan Jacob Vernet (an acute and not at all unsympathetic reader), expressly said of Rousseau that

> believing with *Hobbes* that men are born the enemies of one another, and that our worst enemies are our superiors, like him he remedies this by Despotism, though locating it in a different place. Whereas Hobbes gives arbitrary power to a Prince, Mr Rousseau (who knows no middle ground) instead gives a similar power to the multitude.[19]

While the Dutch conservative Elie Luzac asserted of Rousseau that 'to talk in this way is not only to outdo Hobbes, but to go beyond all the bounds of good sense'.[20]

Rousseau did indeed move beyond Hobbes in a number of ways, though not in the ways that Luzac supposed. One is that he was committed to the idea that the will of the sovereign is law, and *only* law. He frequently expressed this by defining the power of the sovereign as legislative and that of

[19.] 'Mr. Rousseau, qui croyant avec *Hobbes* que les hommes sont nés ennemis les uns des autres, & croyant de plus que nous n'avons pas de pires ennemis que nos supérieurs, y remédie comme lui par le Despotisme, mais en le plaçant differemment. Car au lieu que Hobbes donne le pouvoir arbitraire à un Prince, Mr. Rousseau qui ne connoit point les milieux, donne un semblable pouvoir à la multitude'. *Lettre d'un citoyen de Genève à un autre citoyen* (Geneva, 1768), pp. 72–3.

[20.] 'mais en parler commes vous faites, ce n'est pas seulement rencherir sur Hobbes, c'est passer toutes les bornes du bon sens'. [Elie Luzac], *Lettre d'un anonime à Monsieur J.J. Rousseau* (Paris, 1766), p. 70.

the government as executive, thereby moving back from Montesquieu's use of those terms, where neither was sovereign, to something closer to Locke's usage, where the legislative was 'supreme'. Though Hobbes believed that the will of the sovereign was law, he generally included in the category of law sovereign acts with a very specific focus, more like governmental measures – as in chapter 26 of *Leviathan*.

> [E]very man seeth, that some Lawes are addressed to all the Subjects in generall, some to particular Provinces; some to particular Vocations; and some to particular Men; and are therefore Lawes, to every one of those to whom the Command is directed.[21]

And he obviously included among the acts of sovereignty the declaration of war. Rousseau famously denied all this: as far as he was concerned, the democratic sovereign's acts could only be general in form, and the 'whole people' could only legislate for the 'whole people'. In the well-known words of Book II, chapter 6,

> law considers subjects en masse [*en corps*] and actions in the abstract, and never a particular person or action. Thus the law may indeed decree that there shall be privileges, but cannot confer them on anybody by name. It may set up several classes of citizens, and even lay down the qualifications for membership of these classes, but it cannot nominate such and such persons as belonging to them; it may establish a monarchical government and hereditary succession, but it cannot choose a king, or

[21] p. 183, original edn, p. 137.

nominate a royal family. In a word, no function which
has a particular object belongs to the legislative power.[22]

And as he said in Book II, chapter 2,

> the acts of declaring war and making peace have been
> regarded as acts of Sovereignty; but this is not the case, as
> these acts do not constitute law, but merely the application
> of a law, a particular act which decides how the law
> applies.[23]

But we should be a little cautious about how we interpret these
remarks. In the same chapter, in words I quoted earlier, he said
that the act of a government 'is merely a particular will, or act
of magistracy—at the most a decree [*un décret tout au plus*]',
thereby picking up the kind of contrast between a *law* and
an *edict* or decree that Bodin had drawn. The distinction
Rousseau made between sovereign acts which applied to the
whole people, and governmental acts which did not, did not
map straightforwardly onto the institutional structures of
any state in his own time, nor of most states since. It was,
for example, not like the distinction between acts of the US
Congress and orders of the president, nor was it like the
distinction between Acts of Parliament in England and Orders
in Council; those are distinguished not (on the whole) by
scope, but by source – that is, an act of Congress or Parliament
can overrule an executive order, but not vice versa. Modern

[22.] *Social Contract and Discourses*, p. 192; Launay (ed.), *Oeuvres complètes*,
vol. II, p. 530.

[23.] *Social Contract and Discourses*, p. 183; Launay (ed.), *Oeuvres complètes*,
vol. II, p. 526.

legislatures are quite prepared to pass legislation which, in Rousseau's terms, would count as 'particular'. The same could abundantly be said of the *ancien régime* French monarchy, most of whose legislative pronouncements were far from general in character, including such things as *édits* setting up monopolistic trading companies. It may be relevant that when Rousseau discussed the structure of governments, and the advantages and disadvantages of aristocratic, democratic and monarchical administration, he treated the English Parliament as an example of a possible mixed type (which – like Bodin and Hobbes – he endorsed as a conceivable form at the level of government, though not sovereignty); that is, on his analysis the English legislature was part of a government.

The principal force of Rousseau's remarks about the necessary generality of 'law' and the contrast with the particularity of government was to draw attention to the *fundamental* character of popular sovereignty. As he said in Book III, chapter 4,

> If we take the term in the strict sense, there never has been a real democracy, and there never will be. It is against the natural order for the many to govern and the few to be governed. It is unimaginable that the people should remain continually assembled to devote their time to public affairs, and it is clear that they cannot set up commissions for that purpose without the form of administration being changed.[24]

[24.] *Social Contract and Discourses*, p. 217; Launay (ed.), *Oeuvres complètes*, vol. II, p. 544.

So the democratic and sovereign legislator would meet only intermittently, just as Hobbes's sleeping democratic sovereign would. Rousseau made this even clearer in his important discussion at the end of Book III about the maintenance of sovereign authority.

> It is not enough for the assembled people to have once fixed the constitution of the State by giving its sanction to a body of law [*une fois fixé la constitution de l'État, en donnant la sanction à un corps de lois*]; it is not enough for it to have set up a perpetual government, or provided once for all for the election of magistrates. Besides the extraordinary assemblies unforeseen circumstances may demand, there must be fixed periodical assemblies which cannot be abrogated or prorogued, so that on the proper day the people is legitimately called together by law, without need of any formal summoning.
>
> But, apart from these assemblies authorised by their date alone, every assembly of the people not summoned by the magistrates appointed for that purpose, and in accordance with the prescribed forms, should be regarded as unlawful, and all its acts as null and void, because the command to assemble should itself proceed from the law.[25]

This passage suggests that Rousseau recognised that a natural implication of what he had said was that 'legislation' was essentially 'fixing the constitution of the State', but that he was keen to stress that this did not mean that it would then

[25] Chapter 13, Book III, *Social Contract and Discourses*, p. 237; Launay (ed.), *Oeuvres complètes*, vol. II, p. 556.

be a kind of *deus absconditus*. There should be periodical assemblies in which (we may suppose) the people renew their sense of themselves as sovereign, as well as 'extraordinary' assemblies; the parallel we might draw would be with Jefferson's idea that the American Constitution should be revisited at the end of every nineteen years.[26] But there is no suggestion that the democratic legislature should be in session in the way modern legislatures are, and even in the way the eighteenth-century House of Commons was; in Rousseau's eyes those would have counted as 'governments' of a kind, as his remarks on England indeed revealed.[27]

A second area in which Rousseau may have moved beyond Hobbes is one that has, I think, been widely misunderstood. Over the last thirty years or so it has often been said, including by the most perceptive scholars, that Rousseau

---

[26.] See his letters to James Madison and Richard Gem, 6 September 1789 in Albert Ellery Bergh (ed.), *The Writings of Thomas Jefferson*, vol. VII (Washington DC, 1907) (The 'Memorial Edition'), pp. 454–63.

[27.] The limited and foundational character of the assemblies is made clear in chapter 18, Book III: 'The periodical assemblies of which I have already spoken are designed to prevent or postpone this calamity [of usurpation of sovereignty by a government], above all when they need no formal summoning; for in that case, the prince cannot stop them without openly declaring himself a law-breaker and an enemy of the State. The opening of these assemblies, whose sole object is the maintenance of the social treaty, should always take the form of putting two propositions that may not be suppressed, which should be voted on separately. The first is: "Does it please the Sovereign to preserve the present form of government?" The second is: "Does it please the people to leave its administration in the hands of those who are actually in charge of it?"' *Social Contract and Discourses*, p. 246; Launay (ed.), *Oeuvres complètes*, vol. II, p. 563.

rejected the whole Hobbesian idea of the sovereign as *representative*. In the words of Michael Sonenscher, Rousseau was 'openly critical of the idea of representation that was the cornerstone of Hobbes's political theory'.[28] Now, it is of course true that Rousseau denounced the idea that the sovereign general will can be represented:

> Sovereignty, for the same reason as makes it inalienable, cannot be represented; it lies essentially in the general will, and will does not admit of representation: it is either the same, or other; there is no intermediate possibility.[29]

But what he was addressing in this passage was representation by elected deputies, as in England, and, as his remarks shortly afterwards about the modern character of representation make clear, he was engaged here not with Hobbes but with Montesquieu's chapter on the English constitution. Rousseau was not in fact at all critical of the idea of representation as used by Hobbes; there is no criticism in Rousseau of the fundamental Hobbesian thought that *individuals* are represented by the sovereign, that its will is taken to be their will, and that it is this (so to speak) collection of individual representations that makes the sovereign's will general in character. This is, as I have stressed, Rousseau's idea also, and is expressed in words with which Hobbes could not have disagreed: 'Each of us puts his person and all his power in

[28.] Michael Sonenscher (ed.), Sieyès, *Political Writings* (Indianapolis, IN and Cambridge, MA: Hackett Publishing, 2003), p. xlvi.

[29.] Chapter 15, Book III, *Social Contract and Discourses*, p. 249; Launay (ed.), *Oeuvres complètes*, vol. II, p. 558.

common under the supreme direction of the general will', and each person ceases to be 'his own judge'.[30]

What Rousseau profoundly disagreed with was the idea that a *sovereign*, once constituted, could be represented, and in particular that a sovereign people could be represented *in its sovereignty* through deputies; his rejection of this idea was simply part of his general rejection of the standard eighteenth-century view that a people could have an identity as a sovereign and autonomous body, but would be unable to act unless represented by an omnicompetent institution such as a king or Parliament. The denial of representation is thus merely the correlate of the distinction between sovereign and government, for the essence of that distinction is that the government cannot represent the sovereign *as* sovereign. But it can act as the sovereign's agent in specific areas, and Rousseau had no problem about that – 'in the exercise of the legislative power, the people cannot be represented; but in that of the executive power, which is only the force that is applied to give the law effect, it both can and should be represented', he said in Book III, chapter 15 – though he immediately added, 'we thus see that if we looked closely into the matter we should find that very few nations have any laws'.[31] Again, Hobbes could not have disagreed with any of this; this after all was precisely his point in denying that an elective king was a sovereign. The moment at which a

---

[30.] Chapter 6, Book I, *Social Contract and Discourses*, p. 175; Launay (ed.), *Oeuvres complètes*, vol. II, p. 522.

[31.] *Social Contract and Discourses*, p. 241; Launay (ed.), *Oeuvres complètes*, vol. II, p. 559.

sovereign's agent represents a sovereign in the same sense that the sovereign represents the individual citizen – that is, that the will of the representative *fully comprehends* that of the represented person – is for Hobbes, as much as for Rousseau, a moment at which sovereignty has been transferred or usurped, and the vizier has become the king.

But there is one area in which Rousseau unquestionably diverged from Hobbes, and it is the key difference between them. Rousseau, as we all know, did not believe that the sovereign legislature could transfer or alienate its sovereignty to another person or assembly, and Hobbes did – this after all was the basis of his own royalism. But it is fair to say that Rousseau spotted a genuine problem about Hobbes's account. A democratic legislature in Hobbes has the full power to create a new site of sovereignty for its citizens, for its decisions in all potentially controversial matters are authoritative, and among those potentially controversial matters is the location of sovereignty. So much is clear and consistent. The problem arises from the fact that a democratic assembly, for Hobbes, is itself an entity that has a single will and a determinate institutional character, and that Hobbes treats it throughout his work as strictly equivalent to a monarch. But no sovereign agent is entitled to transfer its sovereignty to another: as Hobbes said in chapter 30 of *Leviathan*, 'it is the Office of the Soveraign, to maintain those Rights ["the essentiall Rights of Soveraignty"] entire; and consequently against his duty, First, to transferre to another, or to lay from himselfe any of them'.[32] Moreover, if an assembly dissolves itself, this is

---

[32] *Leviathan*, p. 231, original edn, p. 175.

the equivalent of suicide in a monarch, and no coherent account can be given of why it should choose to do so. Hobbes may have had in mind the thought that a democratic assembly might find its power being undermined by the 'aristocracy of orators'[33] who would hijack its discussions, and that eventually it would have to transfer its powers to a monarch because it could no longer exercise them effectively itself (as in the fall of the Roman Republic); but such a failed sovereign assembly would no longer properly represent its citizens already, before the moment of transfer. Rousseau, who certainly thought that a democratic sovereign assembly would inevitably fail and be corrupted, interpreted this as the 'death of the body politic',[34] and on the face of it this is more consistent with Hobbes's ideas than Hobbes's own claim that a transfer could take place from a democracy to a monarchy. It is true, as I said in the previous chapter, that we might read *Leviathan* as suggesting that there need not be an initial democracy, and thereby avoiding some of these difficulties; but it is not clear that this is a correct reading, and anyway *De Cive* – which was the important text for all Continental

[33.] This is the phrase used (as we saw above p. 101) by Hobbes in the *Elements of Law*: 'a democracy, in effect, is no more than an aristocracy of orators, interrupted sometimes with the temporary monarchy of one orator' (Toennies, ed., ii.2.5, pp. 120–1). See also Rousseau in his *Economie Politique*: 'Athens was in fact not a Democracy, but a very tyrannical Aristocracy, governed by philosophers and orators' (*Social Contract and Discourses*, p. 122; Launay (ed.), *Oeuvres complètes*, vol. ii, p. 279).

[34.] The title of chapter 11, Book iii of the *Social Contract*; see *Social Contract and Discourses*, p. 235; Launay (ed.), *Oeuvres complètes*, vol. ii, p. 555.

readers of Hobbes – is absolutely clear that civil society must begin with democracy. Understood in this way, Rousseau's theory is Hobbes's with an inconsistency removed, rather than a theory that is in fundamental opposition to Hobbes.

But the removal of this inconsistency made an enormous difference, for it completely changed the political implications of Hobbes's ideas and linked them henceforward to the cause of radical democracy. In particular, as I said at the beginning of this book, it allowed for the appearance of a new kind of democracy, appropriate to the modern world, in which citizens could all be true legislators in fundamental matters but leave less fundamental ones to their agents. Rousseau himself (though this has, I think, rather seldom been recognised) plainly understood the modern character of his idea. This comes out particularly clearly from the passage I quoted in the first chapter, from his defence of the *Social Contract* against attacks from Geneva, which was published in 1764 as *Letters from the Mountain*.

> Ancient Peoples are no longer a model for modern ones; they are too alien to them in every respect. You above all, Genevans, keep your place, and do not go for the lofty objects that are presented to you in order to hide the abyss that is being dug in front of you. You are neither Romans, nor Spartans; you are not even Athenians. Leave aside these great names that do not suit you. You are Merchants, Artisans, Bourgeois, always occupied with their private interests, with their work, with their trafficking, with their gain; people for whom even liberty is only a means for acquiring without obstacle and for possessing in safety.

This situation demands maxims particular to you.
Not being idle as ancient Peoples were, you cannot
ceaselessly occupy yourselves with the Government as they
did: but by that very fact that you can less constantly
keep watch over it, it should be instituted in such a way
that it might be easier for you to see its intrigues and
provide for abuses. Every public effort that your interest
demands ought to be made all the easier for you to fulfill
since it is an effort that costs you and that you do not make
willingly. For to wish to unburden yourselves of them
completely is to wish to cease being free.[35]

Rousseauian democracy was not an idyll of an ancient city-
state transported to the present day, but a serious attempt at
working out how a modern commercial state might genuinely
deserve the title of a democracy.[36]

[35.] Launay (ed.), *Oeuvres complètes*, vol. III, p. 483; *Letter to Beaumont,
Letters Written from the Mountain, and Related Writings*, pp. 292–3.
See above p. 3.

[36.] See also his remark in a letter to his friend François Coindet in February
1768 about a constitutional proposal from Paul-Claude Moultou, another
of his Genevan friends, who was trying to steer a path between the
radical democrats and the oligarchs in Geneva. 'M. M[oultou] ne veut
point d'une pure Démocratie à Genève; il a raison. J'ai toujours dit et
pensé de même. Le Gouvernement Démocratique par tout trop orageux,
est Surtout trop remuant dans une Ville de commerce comme Genève,
qui ne Subsiste que par l'industrie, où sont beaucoup de gens riches, et
où tout le monde est occuppé'. (*Correspondance complète* 35, pp. 91–7).
See Whatmore, *Against War and Empire*, p. 94, where, however, the
letter is dated 1767. Whatmore gives a number of instances in which
Rousseau alarmed the radical democrats of Geneva by his insistence that
government should not be democratic.

The full significance of what he had done began to be appreciated as soon as the French started to argue about a new constitution at the beginning of 1789. Though the initial assumption was that (as indeed happened) the constitution would be drawn up and promulgated by the National Assembly without a formal recourse to a popular vote of ratification, a group of members of the National Assembly, almost all of whom were later associated with the Girondins, proposed to introduce a plebiscitary element into the new structure either through a referendum on the constitution as a whole, or, failing that, through a plebiscitary *appel au peuple* triggered by any royal veto of a measure proposed by the newly fashioned legislature. With the important exception of a couple of American cases (to which I will turn in the next chapter), this was the first time that the modern notion of a plebiscite or referendum had been raised, and it is clear that it was intended precisely to give an institutional structure to the idea of a legislative sovereign underlying but separate from the normal governmental structures (which would include the National Assembly).[37] A curious feature of this turn to a plebiscitary sovereign, which as we shall see was defended in explicitly Rousseauian terms, was that Rousseau himself had not considered it. This is

[37.] This is made particularly clear in a speech by Jérôme Pétion de Villeneuve to the Assembly on 10 August 1791, in which he argued that the people of England had alienated their sovereignty to Parliament precisely because they had no extra-Parliamentary means short of insurrection for changing their constitution. *Archives Parlementaires* ... *Première Série (1787 à 1799*, ed. M.J. Mavidal et al. (Paris, 1867–2005), vol. xxix, p. 328.

particularly striking, given that in his later works he had explored various ways of giving the people legislative power in a large state, as well as in the small states which were his preferred option.[38] In *Considerations on the Government of Poland* (drafted in 1772, but not published until his posthumous *Oeuvres* of 1782) he claimed that a system of mandated delegates to an assembly would achieve the objectives he had set out in the *Social Contract*, while in the 1765 *Project for Corsica* (which was not known until it was published in 1861) he seems to have considered the possibility of the sovereign people meeting separately in a number of large assemblies.[39] But something like a modern plebiscitary

[38.] To the well-known constitutional sketches for Poland and Corsica, we can add his brief suggestions for a new settlement of the Genevan constitution in his letter to Coindet, see above n. 15.

[39.] The constitution of Corsica as it already existed in 1765 was praised by contemporaries such as James Boswell as approaching 'to the idea of a Roman comitia' (*An account of Corsica* [London, 1769] p. 147), an assessment endorsed by Dorothy Carrington in her study of the Corsican constitution under Paoli ('The Corsican Constitution of Pasquale Paoli (1755–1769)', *English Historical Review* 88 (1973), pp. 481–503). Each village elected (by manhood suffrage) a representative to be sent to a very large assembly, the Diet, consisting of c. 325 members (Carrington, pp. 495–6). Rousseau appears to have proposed instead that Corsica should be divided into twelve provinces, each of which should send a representative to the government while (apparently) deciding fundamental matters in a general gathering of the province. This seems to be the implication of the fragmentary remarks in the Projet, that the people should assemble 'by sections rather than as a whole', that there should be twelve equally sized provinces as the basis for the government, and that 'the firm establishment of this form of government will produce two great advantages. First, by confining the work of administration to a small number only, it will permit the choice of enlightened men. Second, by

system was a natural extension of Rousseau's ideas, and the implications were duly drawn once the French Revolution began.

The first intimations of these ideas in fact appeared in France before the Revolution. Keith Baker and Roger Barny have drawn attention to the fact that the highly Rousseauian *Catéchisme du citoyen, ou Eléments du droit public français, par demandes et par réponses* by Guillaume-Joseph Saige, which was published and then condemned in 1775, contains a plea for mandated delegates to an Estates General. Without mandation, Saige wrote, '[T]he legislative power would no longer rest with the nation, and it would no longer be the general will that directed the state; instead, sovereign authority would be concentrated in the body of the deputies'.[40]

requiring the concurrence of all members of the state in the exercise of the supreme authority, it will place all on a plane of perfect equality, thus permitting them to spread throughout the whole extent of the island and to populate it uniformly. This is the fundamental principle of our new constitution' (Rousseau, in F. M. Watkins (trans. and ed.), *Political Writings* (London: Thomas Nelson and Sons, 1953), p. 286; Launay (ed.), *Oeuvres complètes*, vol. III, p. 496). Since the population of Corsica in 1780 has been estimated at 140,000 (Stephen Wilson, *Feuding, Conflict and Banditry in Nineteenth-Century Corsica* (Cambridge University Press, 1988), p. 10), Rousseau may have envisaged assemblies of approximately 10,000. So, in line with the importance he gave to the sovereign–government distinction, he was seeking to render the government of Corsica *less* democratic (something Paoli was also seeking in these years – see Carrington art. cit. pp. 49 8ff), but to give a more effective voice to the sovereign.

40. Keith Baker, 'A classical republican in eighteenth-century Bordeaux: Guillaume-Joseph Saige' in his *Inventing the Revolution* (Cambridge University Press, 1990) p. 149. Saige entirely subscribed to the

Interestingly, Saige was writing this seven years before Rousseau's own argument for mandation appeared in print, though his work virtually disappeared after its condemnation and was not generally known until it began to be republished in 1787, by which time the Constitution of Poland had become the authoritative statement on mandation. But like Rousseau himself, Saige did not move on from endorsing mandation to a fully fledged theory of plebiscites. This seems to have happened later, once Frenchmen began to think about what had recently happened in America.[41]

The leading figures in this development were the two later Girondins, Jacques-Pierre Brissot and the Marquis de Condorcet. Brissot's enthusiasm for the radical American state constitutions which I discuss in the next chapter was expressed in a highly and explicitly Rousseauian analysis of

sovereignty/government distinction; see ibid., p. 143 and (for the precise terminology) the 1788 ed. of the *Catéchisme*, p. 11. See also Roger Barny, *Prélude Idéologique à la Révolution Française: Le Rousseauisme avant 1789*, *Annales Littéraires de l'Université de Besançon*, 2nd series 315 (1985), pp. 103ff.

[41.] As we shall see, mandation continued to be discussed as a possibility during 1789, and the erratic Rousseauian, the comte d'Antraigues, published an entire book in its defence, with an epigraph from the *Constitution of Poland*, in the autumn of 1789, though by then plebiscitary ratification of constitutions had moved into the centre of debate. See his *Mémoire sur les mandats impératifs* (Versailles n.d.). Its subject matter is the question of whether delegates to the Estates-General could disregard their mandates; this is an issue that was debated in the summer of 1789 (see Baker, *Inventing the French Revolution*, pp. 248–9), but the *Mémoire* in its final form must date from after 31 August, since it refers on p. 20 to Mounier's report from the constitutional committee on that day (*Archives Parlementaires ... Première Série* VIII, p. 523).

the 1776 Pennsylvania Constitution which he published in 1783; suggestively, he presented the constitution as more plebiscitary in character than in fact it was, and praised this (supposed) feature of it as solving the problem of having democratic government in the modern world;[42] he said of it that '[i]t is easy to see that its framers have drawn many of their articles from the principles of the *Social Contract*'.[43] A full awareness of the genuine plebiscites that had been held in Massachusetts and New Hampshire does not seem to have

---

[42.] He (inaccurately) said that the draft constitution had been printed and distributed six months before it was approved by the general assembly, and that 'its framers sought, in submitting it to the judgement of the citizens, to collect their opinions, to compare them, and to choose those which obtained the greatest support. This is a sure method of making excellent laws, for it is rarely that people deceive themselves about their own welfare, especially when they are already enlightened by instruction. This is a much surer method than those of the ancient republics, for how could a law proposed in a tumultuous assembly be discussed wisely and with order, especially when the greater part of the people allow themselves to be carried away by the eloquence of some corrupt orators? Finally, this is a method that has the advantage of preventing the corruption or the folly of the representatives of the people, because it prescribes for the representatives the path they must follow. This method appears so proper to maintain the principles of the constitution, to prevent them from being attacked, that it is adopted in the code in the form of a rule'. (J. Paul Selsam, 'Brissot de Warville on the Pennsylvania Constitution of 1776', *Pennsylvania Magazine of History and Biography* 72 (1948) p. 33). This is presumably a reference to Article 47 of the Constitution, which prescribed that any constitutional amendments had to be promulgated six months before the election of a special convention to consider them, so that the people 'may have an opportunity of instructing their delegates on the subject'.

[43.] Ibid., p. 30.

dawned in France until a few years later, since the principal collection of state constitutions which French writers could consult was published in 1783 as a translation of the set authorised by the Continental Congress in 1781, and it therefore did not contain the 1784 New Hampshire constitution which was the first to contain a plebiscitary element. Though Massachusetts had held plebiscites on its constitution in 1779 and 1780, the constitution itself did not contain a provision for one until it was amended in 1792 (for these constitutions, see Chapter 4). Accessible accounts of the New Hampshire and Massachusetts plebiscites did not appear in French until 1785–6.[44]

Condorcet also urged the use of a modified plebiscite in his contribution to the American constitutional debate, his

---

[44] The 1784 New Hampshire constitution was translated by Jean-Nicolas Desmeunier in the *Encyclopédie méthodique: Economie Politique et Diplomatique*, chapter 2, vol. ii (Paris 1786); he remarked of it that it is New Hampshire 'qui a établi les dispositions les plus sages pour la révision ou le changement de la constitution' (p. 655). An account of the Massachusetts plebiscite appeared in the record of his conversation on the subject with Samuel Adams in December 1780, which the Marquis de Chastellux included in his *Voyage de Mr. le chevalier de Chastellux en Amérique* (Paris, 1785) pp. 42–53, and which was reprinted three times before 1789; Desmeunier quoted the conversation *in extenso* in vol. iii of the *Encyclopédie méthodique: Economie Politique et Diplomatique* (Paris, 1788), pp. 288–9. For Desmeunier's articles on the American constitutions, of great interest and importance, see Roberto Martucci, 'Les Articles "Americains" de Jean-Nicholas Desmeunier et le Droit Public Moderne' in Claude Blanckaert and Michel Porret (eds.), *L'Encyclopédie Méthodique (1782–1832): Des Lumières au Positivisme* (Geneva: Droz, 2006), pp. 241–64.

Lettres d'un bourgeois de New-Heaven [sic] *à un citoyen de Virginie, sur l'inutilité de partager le pouvoir législatif entre plusieurs corps* which appeared in 1788.[45] What he proposed was an elaborate system in which most legislative acts were referred to the district assemblies that elected the legislators and in which the electors would then vote yes or no on the measure. But this too was not yet a true plebiscite of the Massachusetts kind, as Condorcet wished the final decision to be made on the basis of a weighted majority of *districts*, rather than simply counting heads across the state or nation.

Once the French Revolution began, Brissot moved quickly to propose a similar scheme for France. In his *Plan de Conduite pour les Députés du Peuple aux États-Généraux de 1789* (April 1789) he attacked Sieyès (whose views I shall discuss presently) for having said that the Estates-General could itself write a constitution, and insisted that the *pouvoir constituant* and the *pouvoir constitué* must be kept entirely distinct; it is noteworthy that he had quickly adopted Sieyès's terminology of the two *pouvoirs* and had seen its relevance to what was a broadly Rousseauian theory. Brissot proposed a complex model, expressly drawing on American experience, in which a dedicated constitutional convention would be elected, would send proposals to assemblies elected in each

---

45. They were published in vol. I of Philip Mazzei's *Recherches Historiques et Politiques sur les États-Unis de l'Amérique Septentrionale* (Paris, 1788). Condorcet had been an (honorary) citizen of New Haven since 1785, and Mazzei had been a resident of Virginia since 1773. A translation of the letters can be found in Iain McLean and Fiona Hewitt (eds.), *Condorcet: Foundations of Social Choice and Political Theory* (Aldershot: Edward Elgar, 1994), pp. 292–334.

of thirty-two provinces for discussion and amendment, receive back from the provinces their views, incorporate the views in a final set of proposals and send them to the provinces to be voted on in a simple yes or no vote. If twenty-one of the thirty-two provinces approved it, the constitution would come into force. Three months later Brissot insisted, again against Sieyès, that 'a Nation cannot be constituted by Representatives, even extraordinary ones, without its express approbation of the Constitution', but since he cited his *Plan de Conduite* as a model, he does not yet seem to have thought about a straightforward plebiscitary ratification.[46] The same was true of Condorcet, who published a pamphlet *Sur la necessité de faire ratifier le constitution par les citoyens* in August 1789,[47] in which he urged that all the citizens should vote first on the declaration of the rights of man, and then on whether the proposed constitution contained anything contradictory to the declaration. But since, just like Brissot, he cited as a model his own earlier work, the *Lettres d'un bourgeois*, he too seems not to have envisaged a consolidated national referendum.[48]

[46.] *Le Patriote François* V (1 August 1789), p. 3.

[47.] For the date, see *Archives Parlementaires ... Première Série*, vol. viii, p. 549, n. 1.

[48.] *Oeuvres* (Paris, 1847), vol. ix, pp. 427–8. Condorcet's remarks on the length of time a law accepted by a majority of the population will be valid (which I discuss later on p. 264) might suggest that he envisaged a genuine referendum; but he immediately qualified this discussion with the observation that 'the same is true of constitutions which are produced by a Convention, because then, once again, the plurality (and by extension all) of the citizens agreed to abide by this constitution'.

The first fully plebiscitary scheme appears to have been suggested by some future Girondins in the debates in September 1789 over the royal veto, though it was not yet restricted in their eyes to purely constitutional measures.[49] The idea emerged in the course of these discussions that the king should be given a suspensive veto over acts of the legislature. In the Constitution as it was actually promulgated in 1791, this veto could be overridden if the two following legislatures also endorsed the act; but a number of members of the Assembly proposed during the discussions that the royal veto should trigger a national referendum on the proposed law. Since such a veto (they thought) was likely to be rare, and presumably concerned with matters of fundamental significance, it could be an appropriate object of popular decision-making. The leading exponents of this scheme were Jérôme Pétion de Villeneuve and Jean-Baptiste Salle, both of whom were later to die in the Terror. Responding on 1 September to a work by the liberal monarchist Jean Mounier, which had defended an absolute royal veto on the grounds that popular government was dangerous – the populace 'is essentially

Oeuvres, vol. IX, p. 415, translated in McLean and Hewitt (eds.), Condorcet: Foundations of Social Choice and Political Theory, p. 272.

[49.] The importance of these debates and the proposals for a plebiscite was first stressed by Keith Baker, 'Fixing the French Constitution' in his Inventing the Revolution (Cambridge University Press, 1990), pp. 252–306. Baker, however, saw them as foreshadowing the turn to Jacobinsm. As I argue later in this chapter, I think that Jacobinism represented in fact a different kind of politics, precisely by ignoring the sovereignty-government distinction that was at the heart of the plebiscitary schemes of 1789, and the Girondin constitution of 1793.

credulous; and, in its moments of fury, it uses ostracism against a great man. It wishes the death of Socrates, bewails it the next day, and a few days later dresses the altars for him',[50] Salle wrote,

[t]he people does not know how to govern without passion! But who talks here of governing? Government is not sovereignty; to govern is not to legislate [footnote: 'M. Mounier repeatedly confounds these two things in his last work. This is a familiar sophism of his']; when the people of Athens judged its great men, it was fulfilling the function of magistracy; it had in view a particular object; it governed, it could go wrong, and it often did so. But, when the people of Athens, of those of Sparta, of Rome, etc., exercised sovereignty, that is made law; when they decreed [*stipulaient*] by themselves and for themselves, they did not go wrong, they were wise, and if their political laws were defective, since political science was in its infancy, their civil laws, you well know, Gentlemen, are still today the wonder of the world ... Let us not brand [the French] with the failings of the ancient peoples who wished to judge and govern, let us not, in a word, confuse sovereignty with government.[51]

[50.] Jean Mounier, *Considérations sur les gouvernemens* (Paris, 1789), p. 6.

[51.] *Archives Parlementaires ... Première Série*, vol. VIII, pp. 530–1. A few lines later, Salle remarked, 'The general will cannot err, said the greatest political theorist [*publiciste*] of the age. Why? Because when a nation makes laws, everyone prescribes for everyone [*tous stipulent pour tous*]: the general interest is necessarily the only one to dominate; and it is as absurd to suppose that a people can make a set of bad laws, as that a man should decide for his own good to scratch out his eyes; this does not

Salle's actual scheme was not spelt out in detail, but it seems to have involved 'mandats imperatifs' for delegates, following meetings of the primary assemblies (the basic electoral units) in which the people were not allowed to discuss the law but simply to vote yes or no (p. 531, n. 3). Refusal of deliberation to the sovereign people in this fashion, it should be said, is a feature of all these 'Girondin' proposals, corresponding (as I remarked in Chapter 1) to the hostility in Rousseau to deliberative assemblies.[52]

Five days later Jérôme Pétion produced a clear proposal for a plebiscite in the full modern sense – that is, a simple head count of the population, ignoring the representatives completely. This may have been the first example of such a thing in France, though as I have said, a couple of American states had already used this mechanism to establish their constitutions. Before the Revolution Pétion's ideas were like those of Condorcet and Brissot; in his *Avis au François sur le salut de la Patrie* of 1788, he had attacked the English constitution for permitting a royal veto and had insisted that '[t]he law is the expression of the common will [*volonté*

---

mean that a people cannot make thoroughly bad judgements; but, to repeat myself, to govern or to judge is not to legislate' (p. 531).

[52] Du Pont de Nemours (at this moment close to the radicals) on 4 September also suggested that 'en cas de contradiction, le peuple ou les electeurs pour le peuple, exprimeront leur voeu; si le plus grand nombre regard la loi ou plutôt le projet de loi comme utile, le Roi ne pourra refuser sa sanction' (*Archives Parlementaires ... Première Série*, vol. VIII, p. 573, misprinted as 735); his indifference between 'le peuple' and 'les electeurs pour le peuple' illustrates how slowly the idea of a true plebiscite was emerging.

commune], and it does not belong to a delegate [*mandataire*] to decide on that will, which emanates from those who gave him his powers';[53] he had also denied that a *corps législatif* could 'modify constituting laws [*les loix constitutives*]'. 'If the time and experience make known the need for some reforms of those laws, they can only be undertaken by virtue of express powers sent by the districts, the particular wills of which when unified form the national will [*voeu*]'.[54] But in September he seized on the idea of a plebiscite or *appel* following a royal veto as an appropriate occasion for popular consultation, as the question could be a straight *oui* or *non*. In his *Opinion sur l'appel au peuple* he argued (like Salle) that to give plenary powers to delegates would deprive the nation of its freedom. 'The law ought to be the expression of the general will … if each person can make known his particular will, the combination [*réunion*] of all the wills will truly form the general will'.[55] Government and representation were necessary for practical purposes, but on basic and straightforward matters the sovereign people should make their will known directly.[56]

53. *Oeuvres* (Paris: An I), vol. II, p. 126; *Avis au François sur le salut de la Patrie* (Paris: 1788), p. 89.

54. *Oeuvres*, vol. II, p. 146; *Avis au François*, p. 111.

55. *Oeuvres*, vol. III, pp. 31–2. See also *Archives Parlementaires … Première Série* vol. VIII, pp. 581–4 for his speech.

56. It is interesting that Jeremy Bentham, whose contribution to the French debate is usually treated from an English perspective, broadly shared these ideas. Like Salle and Pétion he believed that the king's veto should trigger an appeal 'from the will of the National Assembly to the nation at large', though unlike them he thought that this appeal should take the form first of a new general election. But if a bill presented by a new Assembly was once again rejected by the king then the major part of the

Accordingly, he argued that if there was a straight choice, the delegates could be mandated by the primary assemblies to vote on the veto, but he now also suggested that

> [w]e could even have the vote of each elector; and however vast this process seems at first glance, it immediately simplifies itself when we see that we can easily draw up a list of everyone in each primary assembly, and that counting these lists will give a general and definite result.[57]

Provincial Assemblies which he proposed, or perhaps even of the subprovincial assemblies, could declare it law. Philip Schofield, Catherine Pease-Watkin and Cyprian Blamires (eds.), *Rights, Representation, and Reform. Nonsense upon Stilts and Other Writings on the French Revolution* (Oxford University Press, 2002), pp. 230, 239. Bentham's links were with the Girondins, through Brissot, who tried to get Bentham elected to the National Convention, and was responsible for making him an honorary French citizen in 1792 (Bentham, *Correspondence*, Alexander Taylor Milne, ed., (London: The Athlone Press, 1981) vol. v, p. 254). See the late J. H. Burns's 'Bentham, Brissot and the challenge of revolution', *History of European Ideas* 35 (2009), pp. 217–26. See Alphonse Aulard, *The French Revolution, A Political History 1789–1804*, Bernard Miall (trans,), (New York: Charles Scribner's Sons, 1910), vol. ii, p. 171, for references to projects sent from England to the Convention on the invitation of the decrees of 19 October 1792 and 16 February 1793.

57. 'Toute la nation, divisée ainsi par grandes sections, s'exprimerait sans paine. On pourrait même avoir le suffrage de chaque votant; et quelqu'immense que paraisse cette opération au premier coup-d'oeil, elle se simplifie à l'instant, lorsqu'on pense que, dans chaque assemblée élémentaire, on dresserait aisément une liste particulière, et que le dépouillement de ces listes donnerait un résultat général et certain', *Oeuvres*, vol. iii, p. 34. For some perceptive remarks on Pétion, see Lucien Jaume, *Le discours Jacobin et la démocratie* (Paris: Fayard, 1989), pp. 287–8.

The tentative fashion in which he put the idea forward suggests strongly that he was aware of its innovative character, and of the fact that he had moved beyond the earlier proposals.[58]

Neither Condorcet nor Brissot supported Salle and Pétion over the royal veto, but by February 1793 both of them, together with most of the other Girondins, had come round to the view that a new constitution must rest on a direct popular vote. As soon as it was formed in September 1792 after the abolition of the monarchy, the Convention had declared that there could be no constitution that was not accepted by the people, though the method of ratification was left vague. Danton, moving the motion, said that it should be accepted 'by the majority of primary assemblies', and others said that the *mode* should be decided later.[59] But when on 15 February 1793 Condorcet presented to the Assembly the report of the committee charged with producing the first republican constitution (the so-called Girondin constitution) (a committee on which Pétion also sat) he now stressed the need for the constitution to be ratified by a majority vote of the French electorate. Nothing else, he said, would 'preserve [the people's]

[58.] Two years later, in the debate over the means of revising the Constitution (29 August 1791), Pétion concluded – rather regretfully, as he took himself in this respect to be dissenting from 'the profound author of the *Social Contract*' – that a new constitution as a whole could not be sent back to the primary assemblies for ratification, as the assemblies would inevitably want to pick it apart and ratify some articles and not others (*Oeuvres*, vol. II, pp. 336ff; see also *Archives Parlementaires ... Première Série*, vol. XXX, pp. 44–54).

[59.] *Archives Parlementaires ... Première Série*, vol. LII, pp. 72–3.

sovereignty in its entirety'.[60] The Girondin constitution allowed for popular votes on two kinds of matters. The first (dealt with under Title VIII) was 'the censure of the people': laws that occasioned disquiet among the people could be recalled to the primary assemblies (the local units in which the citizens gathered to vote) under an elaborate system of petitioning. If 'the majority of votes in the primary assemblies' (Article 22) decided accordingly, a new general election of the 'corps législatif', the unicameral representative legislative assembly, was triggered, rather as in Bentham's proposal two years earlier. The final decision on the law was left up to the assembly, though there could be repeated elections until an assembly was returned whose decisions met with popular approval. The phrase 'the majority of votes in the primary assemblies' rather than, say, 'the majority of primary assemblies' indicates that the Girondins had a genuine plebiscite in mind. They proposed a similar mechanism for constitutional amendments under Title IX, in which the petitioning system could require the legislative assembly to 'straight away consult all the Citizens of the Republic gathered in the primary Assemblies' as to whether a constitutional convention should be called, and 'if the majority of voters say yes [*si la majorité des votants adopte l'affirmative*]' the convention took place (Article 6). Its recommendations were then 'presented to the people' (Article 9), and though Title IX does not specify the form of this presentation, it is clear from the general character of the mechanisms that the Girondins assumed that

---

[60.] *Oeuvres*, vol. XII, p. 345.

it too would require a majority of the voters in the assemblies for a successful ratification.[61]

The distinction between the procedures outlined under Title VIII and those under Title IX was that for ordinary laws, even though there was an element of popular legislation, the ultimate decision lay with the representative legislature, whereas for constitutional laws, the ultimate authority was the people itself. Title VII, on the *corps législatif*, summed up the essential structure, and with it the whole Rousseauian tradition, in Section II, Articles 1 and 2. 'Au Corps législatif seul appartient l'exercice plein et entier de la puissance législative', and 'Les Lois constitutionnelles sont seules exceptées de la disposition de l'article précédent'. This proved to be the major difference between the Girondin project of February 1793 and the constitution rewritten by the Jacobins, which actually was put to the popular vote in July. The Jacobins proclaimed that all laws, however minor, had – in theory – to be enacted by the people, and their constitution allowed for the recall of any piece of legislation to the primary assemblies for their decision, if at least one-tenth of the primary assemblies in at least half of the departments plus one pronounced against the law.[62] Salle accused the Jacobins of having rendered popular

---

[61.] The Girondin constitution can be found in Condorcet, *Oeuvres*, vol. XII, pp. 423ff. Titles VIII and IX are on pp. 469–79.

[62.] Any proposed law was to be sent by the *corps legislatif* to the primary assemblies; Article 59 of the constitution then specified that 'Quarante jours après l'envoi de la loi proposée, si, dans la moitié des départements, plus un, le dixième des assemblées primaires de chacun d'eux, régulièrement formées, n'a pas réclamé [i.e. announced a desire to vote on the law], le projet est accepté et devient loi'. If not, there was a general

control over legislation less effective than in the Girondin proposal, as they left the mechanism by which assemblies would be called together to discuss legislation completely unclear, with the prospect of disorganised mobs taking control of the legislative process. The Jacobins, he thought, had given the citizens of France an impossible choice:

> A mass of 24 million men, dispersed over a territory of twenty-six thousand square leagues, industrious and commercial, strongly attached to their private interests, have to stir themselves *spontaneously*, in order to deal with public affairs ... The People are placed by these articles in a choice each of which is equally dangerous, either to occupy themselves ceaselessly with public affairs, and to completely forget their individual interests ... ; or to entrust the security of their rights entirely to the Legislature.

plebiscite on the law. Aulard in his standard history of the Revolution interpreted this somewhat badly drafted article along the lines I have stated (*The French Revolution: A Political History*, vol. ii, p. 200). But he took this to be similar to the Girondin proposal, which he described as a 'referendum', though on his own account of the Girondin constitution the Legislative Assembly had the final say (ibid., p. 168). Faustin-Adolphe Hélie, also writing from the vantage point of the Third Republic, in 1880, captured more exactly the significance of the move from the Girondin to the Jacobin Constitution in 1793: the provision of a direct vote by the people on the laws confounded 'avec le souveraineté, le pouvoir, qui doit toujours en rester distinct: il diffère essentiellement du système plébiscitaire, dans lequel le peuple, sans délibération, statue seulement sur les bases fondamentales de la Constitution, et règle ainsi le mode de l'exercice de l'autorité, mais ne l'exerce pas lui-même', *Les Constititutions de la France* (Paris, 1880), pp. 387–8.

He contrasted this with the detailed mechanism provided in Condorcet's draft for the scrutiny of legislation, along the lines (he said) of Rousseau's ideas; under the Jacobins 'the apparent homage rendered in these articles to the sovereignty of the people is nothing but a scandalous derision'.[63] From the point of view of these Girondin theorists, the Jacobins had blurred the distinction between sovereignty and government every bit as much as Grotius or Pufendorf had done, though they had done so (allegedly) in the interests of democratic rather than monarchical rule; they had failed to segregate acts of sovereignty, which determined the basic structures of the society, from acts of government – including, most alarmingly, as Salle pointed out, acts of criminal jurisdiction.[64]

Though the Girondins lost the constitutional struggle of 1793, and Brissot, Condorcet, Salle and Pétion all lost their lives, their novel idea, that a constitution should be ratified by a plebiscite, was not to be abandoned. Between 1793 and 1815 seven national referendums were held, with each new constitution being ratified in this way, including the Jacobin constitution of the Year 1, the Directorate constitution of

---

[63.] *Examen critique de la constitution de 1793* (Paris: l'an IIIe), pp. 14–16.

[64.] See, for an earlier example of this Jacobin view, Robespierre's speech to the Assembly on 10 August 1791, in which he insisted that all powers had to be retained by the people. *Archives Parlementaires ... Première Série*, vol. XXIX, p. 326 (the same debate as Pétion's speech, above p. 143 n. 37). Robespierre was already saying something similar in a *Discours* for the Academy of Metz in 1784: in 'les véritables républiques' 'chaque particulier ayant part au gouvernement, étant membre de la souveraineté', (*Oeuvres Complètes ... Première Partie. Robespierre à Arras*), ed. Emile Lesuer (Paris: Ernest Leroux, 1912), vol. I, p. 23.

the Year III, the Constitution of the Year VIII (though as I observe below, this may not have been seen as a true ratification), and the Perpetual Consulship of Napoleon in 1802. After the fall of Bonaparte plebiscites were not used until the rise of Napoleon III; and after 1870 they were not to be used again until the post-war referendums which established the Fourth and Fifth Republics. But in the sixty-seven years since 1945 there have been fourteen national plebiscites in France, and it is clear that the Girondin model is now permanently established there, as it is in most European countries (with the obvious and important exception of Germany).[65]

[65.] Though Germany may not be as exceptional as it first appears. The *Grundgesetz* of West Germany (May 1949) deliberately made no provision for referendums except to change the boundaries of *Länder*, and it was not itself ratified by a popular vote. But technically it was a 'constitution' given to the three western Allied zones by the Western powers on the Allied Control Council, which in theory continued as the sovereign authority over the whole of Germany until it dissolved itself on Reunification in 1990–1. The last article of the *Grundgesetz* specifies that in the event of unification (and therefore the end of Allied rule) the *Grundgesetz* should be replaced by a *Verfassung* (the verbal distinction is significant – a *Verfassung* is a constitution, a *Grundgesetz* is a 'basic law'; the Weimar constitution was a *Verfassung*) chosen as a result of a 'free decision of the German people'. The Western Allies had originally proposed the introduction in 1949 of a new constitution for West Germany based on a referendum, but that was dropped in the final version of the *Grundgesetz*, apparently because of the opposition of German politicians. It is clear that the intention in 1949 was to have a referendum once reunification occurred in order to authorise a new constitutional settlement. This did not happen; the East German *Länder* joined under the terms of the West German *Grundgesetz*, with the result that the German constitution as it now stands is not merely the act of a sleeping sovereign, but of one who has left the room!

However, this ultimate success of the plebiscite in practice should be contrasted with the striking fact that the theorist of the Revolution who has commanded most attention and respect over the last fifteen years or so was a dedicated opponent of this whole way of thinking about politics. This was Emmanuel Sieyès, who is now often regarded (in the words of the title of Pasquale Pasquino's path-breaking book) as the inventor of French constitutionalism.[66] From Pasquino's perspective, this is because Sieyès more than anyone else theorised the role of a constitutional court, which has come to be central to many modern constitutions; but from my perspective in this text Sieyès appears as the most important antagonist to what I have argued is Rousseau's key insight, that by dividing sovereignty and government one could reintroduce something like direct democracy into the modern world.[67] However he did so by co-opting the distinction and

[66.] Pasquale Pasquino, *Sieyès et l'invention de la constitution en France* (Paris: Edition Odile Jacob, 1998).

[67.] For Sieyès's view of Rousseau, see Christine Fauré, 'Sieyès, Rousseau et la théorie du contrat' in Pierre-Yves Quiviger, Vincent Denis and Jean Salem (eds.), *Figures de Sieyès* (Paris: Publications de la Sorbonne, 2008), pp. 213–26. But the gap between them has always been obvious; see for example, the interesting early work by Sir John Clapham, *The Abbé Sieyès: An Essay in the Politics of the French Revolution* (London: P. D. King, 1912), pp. 28–9. And see also the remarks by Pasquino, *Sieyès et l'invention de la constitution en France*, p. 10. Interestingly, Louis-Sébastien Mercier in his *De J.J. Rousseau, considéré comme l'un des premiers auteurs de la Revolution* (Paris, June 1791) criticised Rousseau for not having fully understood the nature of the *pouvoir constituant*: 'Where will this *power* be, if it does not reside essentially in the representatives of the nation? So the first legislature of a people solemnly

turning it to his own purposes, in the process introducing a new terminology for it which has largely supplanted the language of 'sovereign' and 'government'. This was the terminology of *pouvoir constituant* and *pouvoir constitué*.

The terminology appeared for the first time in print in Sieyès's famous *Qu'est-ce que le Tiers Etat* of January 1789, where he remarked that 'in each of its parts a constitution is not the work of a constituted power but a constituent power'.[68] He had already used it in his *Vues sur les moyens d'exécution dont les répresentants de la France pourront disposer en 1789*, which was written in 1788, though it was not printed until April 1789.[69] The occasion of both works was a debate about whether the Estates-General would be able to reconstruct the constitution of France, and whether they were limited in what they could do by the existing rules governing the structure and powers of the Estates. Sieyès argued that the 'constituting power' is the power possessed by any nation to determine its constitution, or the legal rules it is to live by, and by definition this power is not itself limited by any legal rules. As he said in *Qu'est-ce que le Tiers Etat*, 'The nation exists prior to everything; it is the origin of everything. Its will is always

convened is necessarily the *constituant power* produced by the nation' (vol. I, pp. 58–9).

[68]. Sieyès, *Political Writings*, p. 136.

[69]. 'There must not be any confusion between a constituting power and a constituted power' (Sieyès, *Political Writings*, p. 34). It is usually said (e.g. by Sonenscher in ibid., p. xxii) that it was printed in May, but Brissot's *Plan de Conduite*, which has April 1789 on its title page, already refers to it (p. 229).

legal. It is the law itself and 'It would be ridiculous to suppose that the nation itself was bound by the formalities or the constitution to which it had subjected those it had mandated'.[70] At this stage he also accepted that the one rule that did operate at the level of the 'constituting power' was majoritarianism. In *Vues sur les moyens d'exécution*, indeed, he gave an extremely clear statement of the view espoused by both Hobbes and Rousseau, that the essence of a civil association is the individuals' assent to be governed by a majority of the association.

> Every citizen, by his act of adherence to the union, makes a continuous engagement to see himself as bound by the majority view even when his own will forms part of the minority. He submits himself in advance, it should be emphasized, by a free act of his own will, reserving only the right to leave the association and to emigrate if the laws that it makes do not suit him.[71]

So one might have supposed that Sieyès would have thoroughly agreed in 1789 with Pétion and the other future Girondins in their position on the royal veto, and later with the use of plebiscites to ratify the new constitutions. But the heart of his political position during the Revolution was in fact a deep hostility to the plebiscite, and an insistence that everything in a large modern nation must be conducted through *representatives*. This did not mean that he espoused something like the English system, in which a single representative body exercised all legislative powers: the central point, to which

[70.] Sieyès, *Political Writings*, p. 136.   [71.] Sieyès, *Political Writings*, p. 11.

Sieyès returned again and again in his writings and speeches during the Revolution, was that the *pouvoir constituant* should ideally be exercised by a special set of representatives, or (failing that) by a representative body acting in a distinctive fashion.[72] As he said in *Qu'est-ce que le Tiers Etat*,

> I do not mean to say that a nation cannot entrust its ordinary representatives with the type of new commission here in question. The same individuals can undoubtedly gather together to form several different bodies and, by virtue of special proxies, successively exercise powers that by nature should not be conflated with one another. But it is still the case that an extraordinary representation has no similarity to an ordinary legislature. Their powers are quite distinct. The movement of the one always accords with the procedural forms and conditions imposed upon it. The other is not subject to any particular form. It can assemble and deliberate as would the nation itself if, consisting of no more than a small number of individuals, it decided to give its government a constitution.[73]

He had already envisaged this possibility in the *Vues sur les moyens d'exécution*. There he urged that the Assembly (whose future structure, it should be remembered, had not been decided when he wrote) should

---

[72.] In both *Qu'est-ce que le Tiers Etat* (Sonenscher, p. 138) and his *Dire de l'Abbé Sieyes; sur la question du Veto Royal; A la Séance du 7 Septembre 1789* (Paris, 1789), pp. 20–1, he expressly attacked the English constitution for its amalgamation in Parliament of the two powers. See below p. 170 for a discussion of the latter work.

[73.] Sieyès, *Political Writings*, pp. 139–40.

use its initial sittings to give itself the organization and procedural formalities appropriate to the functions that it will be called upon to exercise. This ought not to be taken to mean that at bottom any ordinary legislature can be responsible for giving itself its own constitution. There must not be any confusion between a constituting power and a constituted power. But, since the nation has made no provision for carrying out the great task of constitution-making by way of a special deputation, it has to be supposed that the forthcoming Estates-General will combine the two powers.[74]

The representative body exercising the *pouvoir constituant*, Sieyès believed, should not (except in the exceptional circumstances of 1789) be the same body as the ordinary legislature – that was the great failing of the English constitution.[75] And when the Estates-General turned itself into the Constituent Assembly in July, it was doing exactly what Sieyès wanted.

The works that appeared from Sieyes's pen in the first months of 1789 did not clearly state that *only* a representative body could wield the *pouvoir constituant*. In July he was asked by the Committee on the Constitution, of which he was a member, to prepare a declaration of rights, and on the 21st and 22nd of July he presented it to the committee with a long prefatory statement, which was published at the same time as *Préliminaire de la Constitution. Reconnaissance et exposition raisonée des Droits de l'Homme et du Citoyen*. In the first edition of this as it appeared in July he still merely said that

[74.] Sieyès, *Political Writings*, p. 34.
[75.] Sieyès, *Political Writings*, p. 138, n. 30.

it is not necessary for the members of the society to exercise
the constituting power individually; they can put their trust
in representatives who assemble specifically for that
purpose, without the power to exercise any of the
constituted powers. Furthermore, it belongs to the first
chapter of the projected constitution to make clear the
means of forming and amending all the parts of a
constitution[76]

Brissot reviewed this edition in the August 1st edition of his
journal *Le Patriote François* and criticised this passage in the
terms I quoted earlier.[77] In his *Mémoires* (composed probably
in 1793) he recalled that he had been asked by the Committee
to comment on Sieyès's exposition, despite the fact that he was
not a member of the Assembly and was a mere 'publiciste'.

I was called to give my observations on Sieyès's plan; I put
them forward in front of Sieyès himself; I believed that
I understood his love of truth enough to think that he
would not be offended by my reflections, and that he would
on the contrary be offended if I sacrificed my opinions to
the friendship which bound the two of us; it did not at all
turn out like that.

Among other mistakes, a capital error was to be found in
this scheme for a declaration, an error that could have the

---

[76] *Préliminaire de la Constitution. Reconnaissance et exposition raisonée des
Droits de l'Homme et du Citoyen* (Versailles: Pierres, 1789), p. 13, my
translation. The same passage is on p. 19 of the first Baudouin edition.
See below n. 79 for the bibliographical details of these editions.

[77] 'A Nation cannot be constituted by Representatives, even extraordinary
ones, without its express approbation of the Constitution'. See above,
p. 150.

most dangerous consequences because it threatened the destruction of the constitution itself; this was the author's doctrine of the constituting power. He pretends that this power of constituting a nation definitively and irrevocably ought to be exercised by representatives assembled solely with that purpose. I was of a very different opinion: I thought on the contrary that a nation could not be constituted even by special representatives without having expressly approved the constitution which had been drafted for it and presented to it; but I could not bring Sieyès round to my point of view.[78]

Indeed he could not: Sieyès responded with a new edition of the work in which he made it clear beyond doubt that he believed that the *pouvoir constituant had* to be exercised by representatives. In this new edition, he inserted between these two sentences the following:

> ... constituted powers. In a numerous People this delegation is forced on them by the very nature of things. So the People ought to restrict itself to exercising by itself the one Power of *commiting* [*commettant*], that is, it ought to restrict itself to choosing and delegating the people who will exercise their *real* rights [*droits réels*], starting with the right to constitute the public establishment [*l'établissement public*]. Furthermore, ...[79]

[78.] C. Perroud (ed.), *Mémoires* (Paris, 1902), vol. II, pp. 105–6, my translation.

[79.] *Préliminaire de la Constitution* (enlarged edn), p. 36. There is no proper edition of this important work. The different editions can be distinguished by their length. The first version of the text appears in

He also introduced a swipe at the schemes of Brissot and Condorcet, attacking 'that partial ratification by the *Bailliages*, which many people think necessary. The American system, suitable for *many confederated* States, is foreign to France, which ought to be *one State*'.[80]

When Sieyès spoke of 'the very nature of things', he had in mind not merely the large size of a 'numerous People', but its commercial character, and the centrality in modern life of the division of labour. He had introduced this theme in

editions by Baudouin, the printer to the National Assembly, at Paris (32 pp.) and Pierres, the royal printer, at Versailles (21 pp.). The expanded version is in another edition by Baudouin at Paris containing 51 pp. The Versailles edition contains a prefatory statement by Sieyès recording that he was asked by the Committee to print his speech; the first Baudouin edition does not, but the expanded version does. Brissot reviewed the Versailles edition, and it seems to have been more widely distributed than the others. Roberto Zapperi reprinted one of the shorter editions in his edition of Sieyès's *Écrits politiques* (Paris: Editions des archives contemporaines, 1985) and Eberhard Schmitt and Rolf Reichardt translated one of them in their edition of Sieyès's *Politische Schriften* (Munich and Vienna: R. Oldenbourg Verlag, 1981). The edition used in the collection of Sieyès's works in François Furet and Ran Halévi (eds.), *Orateurs de la Révolution française*, vol. I (Paris: Gallimard, 1989) is also the short version. But the enlarged version was used in the Pergamon Press *French Revolution Research Collection* microfilm, from a copy in the BN, and it also appears as a photographic reproduction (with no apparatus) in Sieyès's *Oeuvres*, Marcel Dorigny (ed.), (Paris: EDHIS, 1989) vol. II, no. 9. Pasquino first drew attention to this difference between the editions: *Sieyès et l'invention de la constitution en France*, p. 47, n. 52.

[80.] *Préliminaire de la Constitution*, p. 19.

the *Vues sur les moyens d'exécution*,[81] and though it plays little part explicitly in *Qu'est-ce que le Tiers Etat*, he enlarged on it in his other important work of late 1789, the *Dire de l'Abbé Sieyes; sur la question du Veto Royal* of 7 September in which he set out his opposition to the proposals for a suspensive veto linked to a plebiscite.[82]

> The modern Peoples of Europe resemble the ancient Peoples very little. We are only concerned with Commerce, Agriculture, Manufactures, &c. The desire for wealth seems to make all the States of Europe nothing but vast Workshops: we dream much more of consumption and production than of happiness [*bonheur*]. In the same way political systems today are based exclusively on labour [*travail*]; man's productive powers are everything; we hardly take account of his moral powers [*facultés morales*] which can however be the source of the truest pleasures. We are thus forced to see in the great part of mankind merely machines for labour. However you cannot refuse the title of Citizen, & the rights of

[81.] 'The more a society progresses in the arts of trade and production, the more apparent it becomes that the work connected to public functions should, like private employments, be carried out less expensively and more efficiently by men who make it their exclusive occupation'. (Sieyès, *Political Writings*, p. 48). Sonenscher observes (p. xxix) that Sieyès later claimed both that he had begun to think about the division of labour before he read Adam Smith, and that Smith had not noticed that the division of labour was a representative system.

[82.] 'We are only concerned here with the suspensive *Veto*. The other, I must say, does not merit a serious refutation'. *Dire de l'Abbé Sieyes; sur la question du Veto Royal; A la Séance du 7 Septembre 1789* (Paris, 1789), p. 20.

citizenship, to this uneducated multitude wholly absorbed in their forced labour. Just as they ought to obey the Law like you, they ought also, like you, come together in making it. This coming together [*concours*] should be equal.[83]

---

83. *Dire . . . sur la question du Veto Royal*, pp. 13–14, my translation. The *Dire* is reprinted in Sieyès, *Ecrits Politiques*, Roberto Zapperi (ed.), (Paris: Editions des archives contemporaines, 1985), pp. 229–44. See also Sieyès's *Observations sur le Rapport du Comité de Constitution, concernant la nouvelle Organisation de la France* a month later:

'Men did not come together in society in order to spend a leisurely life in agreeable pastimes; they had something to do other than organise games and festivals: Nature has put us under the law of labour; she has raised our desires, and then she has said: Do you want pleasure? Work. It was for more reliable, abundant and select consumption, and consequently more and more to secure and develop his labour, that man is supposed to have united with his fellows. Reason, or at least experience, told man: you will succeed better in your activities, to the degree to which you recognise your limits. By bringing to bear all the powers of your mind [*esprit*] on only one part of the set of useful tasks [*travaux*], you will obtain a better product with less pain and expense. From this came the division of labour, the effect and the cause of the increase in wealth and the improvement of human industry. The subject is fully developed in the work of Doctor Smith. This division is in the common interest of all Members of Society. It applies to political tasks [*travaux*] as much as to all kinds of productive labour. The common interest, the improvement of the social State itself, demands that we make of Government a specialised profession; but it is only the voice of superstition & tyranny which urges us to surrender to our Governors, the inalienable right of making law. It is clear that if the Ministers of the Law could do so, they would become its masters; it is clear that the Law ought to be the free creation of those who ought to obey it, the plain and manifest expression of their will.

So, a purely democratic Constitution is not merely impossible in a large society; but even in a State of the narrowest extent, it is much less

Having said that the conditions of modern politics precluded democratic government, Sieyès argued strenuously against the combination of a suspensive veto and a plebiscite or mandated delegates.

> The vast majority of our fellow Citizens have neither enough knowledge, nor enough leisure, to wish to concern themselves directly with the Laws which should govern France; their will [*avis*] is therefore to nominate Representatives; and since it is the will of a large number, the knowledgeable [*éclairés*] should submit like the rest. When a society is formed, we

appropriate to the needs of society, and much less conducive to the end of the political union, than a *representative* Constitution.' (*Observations sur le Rapport*, pp. 34–5, my translation).

Though he wished to include the working class in the electorate, as his remarks in the *Dire . . . sur la question du Veto Royal* make clear, he did not want universal suffrage. In the *Préliminaire de la Constitution* (p. 21) he argued that 'Women, at least in the state as it is at present [*du moins dans l'état actuel*], aliens, and those who contribute nothing to maintain the public establishment, ought to have no active influence on the state [*sur la chose publique*]. *Chose publique* was Sieyès's own term for the *respublica* (Sieyès, *Political Writings*, p. xxi). Sonenscher elsewhere translates it 'public functions' (ibid., pp. xxviii and 48). And in his *Observations sur le Rapport* (p. 20) he said that we should not regard as citizens 'beggars, voluntary vagabonds, or the homeless; and those whom a *servile* dependence keeps attached, not to a trade [*travail quelconque*], but to the arbitrary will of a master'. It should be said that the exclusion of women from the suffrage in the constitutional proposals of 1789 attracted the particular scorn of Bentham, along with most of the other proposals of 'Citizen Sieyès'; see *Rights, Representation and Reform*, pp. 246–50.

know that it is the will of the majority which determines the Law for everyone.

This reasoning, which is good for the smallest Municipalities, becomes irresistible, when we imagine that we are dealing here with Laws which ought to govern twenty-six million men; for I always maintain that France is not, and cannot be, a *Democracy*; nor ought it to become a *federal State*, consisting of a multitude of Republics, united by some political bond. France is and ought to be *one single whole* [*un seul tout*], governed in all its parts by a common code of law [*une Législation*] and Government [*Administration*]. Since it is obvious that five or six million active Citizens, spread out over more than twenty-five thousand square leagues, cannot assemble together; it is certain that they can only hope for a Legislature by *representation*. Therefore the Citizens who nominate Representatives, renounce – and ought to renounce – making the Law directly themselves; so they will have no particular wills to enforce. All influence and all power belong to them in the person of their deputies; but that is all. If they were to insist on their wills, it would no longer be a representative state; it would be a democratic one. (pp. 15–17, my translation)

And in a particularly striking passage, Sieyès revealed that he had noticed the close link between the plebiscitary proposals and a hostility to deliberation. Attacking (apparently) Salle's scheme for mandated delegates, he proclaimed

It is not by examining separate *cahiers*, if there are any, that we can discover the will of their authors [*commettans*]. It is not a question of some democratic head count, but of proposing, listening, consulting, changing one's opinion, in short, forming together a common will.[84]

To allay all doubt in this respect, we should appreciate that even in the strictest democracy this is the only way to form a common will. It is not in the watches of the night, with everyone in their own houses, that the democrats who are most jealous of their liberty form and fix their individual opinion, to be carried from there into the public space – only to return to their houses to start over again in complete solitude, in the event that no will common to the majority could be extracted from these isolated opinions. We would emphatically say that such a means of forming a common will would be absurd. When people gather, it is to deliberate, to know what other people are thinking, to benefit from mutual enlightenment, to compare particular wills, modify them, reconcile them, and eventually achieve a result that is common to a plurality. I now ask: should what would seem absurd in the most rigorous and jealous democracy be the rule for a representative legislature? It is incontestable that the Deputies have come to the National Assembly not to announce the already formed will of their constituents [*Commettans*], but to deliberate and vote freely following their *actual* opinion, illuminated by all the enlightenment which the Assembly can furnish to each of them. (pp. 17–18, my translation)

[84.] 'une volonté commune'. It may be significant that Sieyès uses this term in this passage, rather than *volonté génerale*.

Given his emphasis on representation, it is fair to say that Sieyès's theory of the *pouvoirs constituant* and *constitué*, unlike Rousseau's theory of sovereignty and government, was really a theory of separation of powers or functions at what Rousseau would have regarded as the level of government – where, as we saw, Rousseau was not opposed to separate powers or mixed regimes.[85] The unusual twist that Sieyès gave to the idea of the separation of powers was that one of them was the power to draft constitutions, but this did not in his eyes make it fundamental, nor lead him to think that it could be exercised directly by the people. He remained silent on the Girondin and Jacobin proposals in 1793, despite having sat on the committee that produced the Girondin draft, and he famously 'survived' the Terror; but when in the Year III (1795) he returned to public life during the debates over the new constitution of the Directory he reaffirmed and clarified his ideas. In a manuscript essay written at this time he argued that the initial act by which individuals formed themselves into a civil society was (as in Hobbes and Rousseau) *unanimous* – anything else would derogate from their natural liberty. But this act was not an agreement to be bound by a majority. Instead, it was an agreement to respect a constitutional order that put a brake (*frein*) on majorities, and

---

[85.] This is a point made clear by Paul Bastid in his *Sieyès et Sa Penseé* (Paris: Hachette, 1939), p. 579, following Carré de Malberg in his *Contribution à la Théorie général de l'Etat* (Paris: Sirey, 1922), vol. II, pp. 487–9, 530–4. See also Carré de Malberg's *Considérations théoriques sur la question de la combinaison de referendum avec le parlementarisme* (*Annuaire de l'Institut International de Droit Public* 10) (1931), pp. 271–2.

since this *brake* can only be located in the separation of
powers and the organisation of each of them, but
especially in the organisation of legislation, I say that
the separation of powers and their organisation, that is
the constitution (for it is nothing else) is a
fundamental law anterior to all law passed by a simple
majority. Obedience to the constitution is part of the
primordial commitment [*engagement*] of each
individual in the association ... *If the constitution did not
exist before the action of the majority* ... or if the
majority could break the constitutional laws, then
aristocracy would show itself in place of liberty. It is a
mistake to talk of the sovereignty of the people as if it
had no bounds.[86]

He also now explicitly attacked the idea of popular sovereignty.
As we have seen throughout this book, sovereignty was
the leitmotiv of the tradition we have been studying, but, as
Pasquino has observed, the term *sovereignty* appears in Sieyès's
texts only 'in a negative and critical form'. Pasquino has indeed
seen this as part of Sieyès's dissociation from Rousseau.[87] In his
Opinion of 2 Thermidor Sieyès proclaimed that

This word [sovereignty] only looms so large in our
imagination because the spirit of the French, full of royal
superstitions, felt under an obligation to endow it with
all the heritage of pomp and absolute power which made
the usurped sovereignties shine ... [P]eople seem to say,
with a kind of patriotic pride, that if the sovereignty

86. *Sieyès et l'invention de la constitution en France* p. 178.   87. Ibid., p. 10.

of great kings is so powerful and so terrible, the sovereignty of a great people ought to surpass it.[88]

And in terms of constitutional design, Sieyès now pushed for a powerful *jury constitutionnnaire*, which would act like a modern constitutional court, annulling acts of the legislature it judged unconstitutional. After an extensive debate, the proposal was unanimously thrown out by the Convention, with many speakers claiming that it would lead to 'usurpation' or 'tyranny'.[89] The constitution of the Year III as passed by the Convention in Thermidor contained none of Sieyès's suggestions, and retained from the constitutions of 1793 the method of ratification by plebiscite.

But Sieyès did not abandon his scheme of a constitutional court, and when after the 18th Brumaire in the Year VIII (1799) he joined Bonaparte in devising yet another constitution the scheme reappeared under the name (in Sieyès's draft) of the *collège des conservateurs* or (in the

---

88. *Les Discours de Sieyès dans les débats constitutionnels de l'an*, vol. III, Paul Bastid (ed.), (Paris: Librairie Hachette, 1939), p. 17.

89. 'It is said that among some People of the Indies the popular belief is that the world is supported by an elephant, and the elephant by a tortoise; but when they are asked what the tortoise rests on, they have nothing to say [*adieu l'érudition*]. This picture is perfectly applicable to the subject we are dealing with. The safeguard [*garantie*] of the Republic lies in the separation of powers and a good organisation; the safeguard of the powers is in the *jury constitutionnaire*; but when one asks what is the safeguard of the jury itself, and of the powers, against usurpation, there is no answer'. (Antoine Claire Thibaudeau in the *Gazette Nationale, ou Le Moniteur Universe l'an* III, p. 1330. The discussion about Sieyès's proposals is on pp. 1326–36).

final version as promulgated) the *sénat conservateur*. In his version of the Constitution of the Year VIII Sieyès even wanted to give it the power to enact a kind of ostracism; this was too much for the other members of the drafting commission, who complained (in the words of Antoine Boulay de la Meurthe, in other respects a staunch supporter of Sieyès) that to do so would be 'to erect a supreme judge, an absolute sovereign over all the officers of state and all the citizens?'[90] They also decided against another of Sieyès's ideas, that there should be a 'Great Elector' who would do nothing but represent the nation as a single person, the beginning of the modern idea of a constitutional president or constitutional monarch. Bonaparte in particular feared that such a figure would turn out to have real and not merely notional power, and that Sieyès wished to acquire the office himself. But in other respects Sieyès saw quite a lot of what he favoured written into the new constitution. In particular, it broke with the constitutions of both 1792 and 1795 in that it included *no explicit provisions for its own amendment*, and (on one view) did not even require ratification to be declared law. Though the very last article declared '[t]he present Constitution will be offered at once for the acceptance of the French people', it in fact came into force before the plebiscite was held, and the consular proclamation presenting the constitution for

[90.] Sieyès's notes are in Christine Fauré, Jacques Guilhaumou and Jacques Valier (eds.), *Des Manuscrits de Sieyès 1773–1799* (Paris: Honoré Champion, 1999), pp. 519ff. The negotiations over the constitution are recorded in Boulay de la Meurthe's *Théorie constitutionelle de Sieyès. Constitution de l'an VIII* (Paris, 1836); see p. 67 for his own objections to the powers of the *sénat conservateur*.

ratification famously proclaimed 'Citoyens, la Révolution est fixée aux principes qui l'ont commencée: elle est finie'.[91] It also declared that the new constitution was based 'on the true principles of representative Government, on the sacred rights of property, equality, and liberty'; in other words, no comprehensive revision of the constitution could be appropriate. The imperial constitution of the Year XII was also not put to the people as a whole, though Article 142, on the hereditary nature of the new office, was put to a plebiscite. The danger of a constitution which could not be democratically amended had already been observed by Bentham in his attacks on 'Citizen Sieyès' and the other supporters of the Constitution of 1791,[92] but even the Constitution of 1791 had allowed for amendment, albeit at the end of an extremely laborious process with no direct appeal to the people.

[91.] Faustin-Adolphe Hélie noted with his customary perspicuity that the Constitution of the Year VIII did not specify the nature of constituent power nor the means of amendment (*Les Constititutions de la France* (Paris, 1880), p. 602), though this has seldom been discussed by later commentators.

[92.] 'We the unlawful representatives of the people will govern the people for ages and in spite of ages: we will govern them for ages after we are no more. The only lawful representatives, the first and all succeeding lawful representatives of the nation, the deputies appointed by the people for the time being, shall not govern them as we do, shall not exercise any jurisdiction over them except such as it has been our pleasure to allow', *The Necessity of an Omnipotent Legislature* (1791) in *Rights, Representation and Reform*, p. 272. For his explicit attacks on 'Citizen Sieyès' see his *Observations on the Declaration of Rights* from 1789(?), ibid., pp. 389ff. Bentham believed that Sieyès had blocked the consideration of his scheme for a new judicial establishment in France, *Correspondence*, vol. VII, p. 280.

With the Constitution of the Year VIII the full implications of Sieyès's views became apparent. Unlike the Constitutions of 1791 and the Years I and III, the Constitution of the Year VIII avoided any mention of sovereignty. There was to be no single site of fundamental legislation, not even by a representative body entrusted with the task; instead, politics and law were to be spread out among multiple representatives, and the distribution of roles among them was not to be called into question. Without in any way returning to the pre-Revolutionary structures, and in particular without any renunciation of the principle of *election*, Sieyès had succeeded in closing down both the Girondin and the Jacobin routes to modern democracy. His success can be illustrated by the extent to which even in our own time he has been regarded as the principal theorist of the modern state,[93] and as the only systematic alternative to Jacobinism. But as I have said, the actual *practice* of modern states has increasingly come to resemble not the ideas of Sieyès, nor those of the Jacobins, but those of the Girondins. Despite the slaughter visited upon them, in the end they came to have more influence upon modern politics than any of their rivals; though, as we shall see in Chapter 4, they were helped by the fact that in the next generation in the United States constitutional schemes very like theirs became widespread and acceptable.

[93.] See not only the work of Pasquino, but the use made of Sieyès by the most important current British constitutional theorist Martin Loughlin, in *The Idea of Public Law* (Oxford University Press, 2003), pp. 61–71 and *Foundations of Public Law* (Oxford University Press, 2010), pp. 221–8.

4

America

In the aftermath of their revolution the American revolutionaries found themselves (almost, one might say, by accident)
creating a constitutional structure which could most easily be
theorised in the language I have been tracing throughout this
book, though it was not until the first generation of post-
revolutionary jurists that the language began actually to be
employed. When the revolution began, the understanding of
the participants was that the rebellious provinces of British
North America had severally declared their independence
and constituted themselves as independent states[1] – indeed,
it is precisely from 1776 that the term *state* began to be applied
generally to each province. Though Massachusetts had styled
itself, as it still does, a *commonwealth* in the early days of the
settlement, by the eighteenth century the term seems to have
been used much less and had been replaced by the legally

[1.] For provincial declarations, see Pauline Maier, *American Scripture:
Making the Declaration of Independence* (New York: Knopf, 1997). The
united declaration was taken initially to be a coordinated act by the
separate provinces. And as Antifederalists later observed, the first Article
of the Treaty of Paris reads 'His Brittanic Majesty acknowledges the said
United States, viz., New Hampshire, Massachusetts Bay, Rhode Island and
Providence Plantations, Connecticut, New York, New Jersey,
Pennsylvania, Delaware, Maryland, Virginia, North Carolina, South
Carolina and Georgia, to be free sovereign and Independent States'.

correct name of *province*.² After 1776 Massachusetts, Virginia and Pennsylvania chose to call themselves commonwealths rather than provinces, while the other provinces opted for the name of 'state'. The binding of these states into a union initially took the form (under the Articles of Confederation) of a straightforward treaty in which it was expressly decreed that 'Each state retains its sovereignty, freedom, and independence, and every Power, Jurisdiction, and right, which is not by this confederation expressly delegated to the United States, in Congress assembled' (Article 11), and in which the 'Confederacy' was described as 'a firm league of friendship' (Article 111). The treaty was sent back to the states for ratification, and no procedure was specified for the process of ratification within each state, though the accompanying letter from the Congress asked that 'the legislatures' should be consulted. But in most cases the ratifying act was passed according to the usual local procedures by the state senate, or its equivalent, as well as the legislature, and was signed by the governor.³ So no fundamentally new constitutional forms

---

²· Alas, the Latin description of Harvard College as 'in Republica Massachusettensium', which appears on the college diplomas, seems to be a post-Revolutionary expression. The regular Latin title of Harvard before the Revolution was *Collegium Harvardinum in Cantabrigia Nov-Anglorum*, and the Latin style for the province was *Colonia Massachusettensis* in the seventeenth century and *Provincia* in the eighteenth century.

³· For two examples, see the full documentation of the process in *The votes and proceedings of the Assembly of the state of New-York, at their first session, begun and holden in the Assembly chamber, at Kingston* (Kingston, NY, 1777) and *Resolves of the General Assembly of the state of Massachusetts-Bay, begun and held at Boston, in the county of*

had been created, and the United States of America might well have continued to be precisely analogous to the United Provinces of the Netherlands in their constitutional structure.

The theoretical innovations of this early period of the revolution instead took place at the state level. Their declarations of independence naturally entailed the refashioning of their political structures in a way that was not true at first at the Continental level, and in the process some of the states were led to give a new institutional character to the popular politics to which (like all English-speaking radicals of the period) they paid at least lip service. The most striking instance of this was (perhaps unsurprisingly) in Massachusetts, and it is the case which has been most closely studied by modern historians.[4] In the majority of the other states the new constitutions were produced by a process very similar to that by which the new constitutions of the revolutionary era in England in the previous century had been created – that is, either by an act of the existing governmental institutions or by an act of some version of the former institutions, modified by the exigencies of revolution and war (such as the 'Provincial Congress' of New York, which replaced the old Assembly in 1775 and promulgated a new constitution in

Suffolk, on Wednesday the twenty-eighth day of May, (being the last Wednesday in said month) anno domini, 1777 (Boston, 1777). In Massachusetts the ratifying Act was signed by the President of the Council, there being no Governor between 1776 and 1780.

[4.] See the great work by Oscar and Mary Handlin, *The Popular Sources of Political Authority* (Harvard University Press, 1966), and Ronald M. Peters, *The Massachusetts Constitution of 1780: A Social Compact* (University of Massachusetts Press, 1978).

1777). Like the seventeenth-century English constitutional experiments, these procedures mostly continued to presuppose the existence of a sovereign legislature which could decree the fundamental terms of political life in its territory – a presupposition that has continued in England down to the present day, though it is now looking rather shaky. And like their English precedents, these new constitutions implied nothing about any separation between 'sovereign' and 'government' or the existence of a distinctive procedure for creating written constitutions; the 'government' *was* the 'sovereign', insofar as its acts constituted the fundamental rules of the society.

In England, these irregular or revolutionary bodies had on two occasions been termed 'conventions' – that is, the Conventions or Convention Parliaments of 1660 and 1689.[5] This was partly to signify that they had not been summoned in the ordinary way, but partly to signify that they had a fundamental task to perform; thus John Locke wrote to a friend in January 1689 that

> I have seen the Princes letter to the convention, which carys weight and wisdom in it. But men very much wonder here

[5.] The Parliament that deposed Richard II in 1399 is sometimes called a Convention Parliament, but the description does not seem to go further back than *The Report into the Dignity of a Peer* in 1820 (*Report from the Lords Committees . . . for all matters touching the Dignity of a Peer of the Realm* (London 1820–23), p. 350. The use of the term to describe Parliamentary assemblies is frequent in that work). The word *convention* was standardly used in sixteenth-century Scotland to describe a non-Parliamentary gathering of the Estates, and it is likely that it came into seventeenth-century English usage from Scotland.

to heare of Committees of Priviledges of Greivances etc
as if this were a formall Parliament and were not
something of an other nature and had not businesse to doe
of greater moment and consequence, sufficiently pointed
out to them by the Princes letter. People are astonishd
here to see them medle with any small matters and
When the setlement of the nation upon the sure grounds of
peace and security is put into their hands, which can noe
way soe well be don as by restoreing our ancient
government, the best possibly that ever was if taken and
put togeather all of a peice in its originall constitution.
If this has not been invaded men have don very ill to
complain. and if it has, men must certainly be soe wise by
feeling as to know where the frame has been put out of
order or is amisse and for that now they have an oportunity
offerd to finde remedys and set up a constitution that
may be lasting for the security of civill rights and the
liberty and property of all the subjects of the nation.
These are thoughts worthy such a convention as this, which
if (as men suspect here) they thinke of them selves as a
parlament and put them selves into the slow methods of
proceeding usuall there in, and thinke of mending some
faults peice meale or any thing lesse then the great frame of
the government, they will let slip an oportunity which
cannot even from things within last long.[6]

The contrast Locke drew between 'convention' and 'parliament' made the point that the meeting was intended,
as he said, to address fundamental issues; but both the

[6.] Esmond De Beer (ed.), *Correspondence* (Oxford University Press, 1979),
vol. III, pp. 545–6.

seventeenth-century conventions turned into regular parliaments once the issues of the succession were dealt with, and there was little sense that the convention had a wholly different function from that of a parliament.

One exception to this was a famous pamphlet by Sir Henry Vane the younger in 1656. In that year he published *A Healing Question* as part of the extensive debate then taking place over what form of government should replace the rule of the Major Generals under the Protectorate. Vane argued as follows:

> The most natural way ... would seem to be by a General Council, or Convention of faithful, honest, and discerning men, chosen for that purpose by the free consent of the whole Body of adherents to this Cause in the several parts of the Nations, and observing the time and place of meeting appointed to them (with other circumstances concerning their Election) by order from the present Ruling Power, but considered as General of the Army [i.e. Cromwell, the Protector].
>
> Which Convention is not properly to exercise the Legislative Power, but only to debate freely, and agree upon the particulars, that by way of fundmental [sic] Constitutions shall be laid and inviolably observed, as the conditions upon which the whole body so represented, doth consent to cast it selfe into a Civil and Politique Incorporation, and under the visible forme and administration of Government therein declared, and to be by each individual member of the Body subscribed in testimony of his or their particular consent given thereunto. Which conditions so agreed (and amongst them an Act of Oblivion for one) will be without danger of

> being broken or departed from; considering of what it is
> they are the conditions, and the nature of the Convention
> wherin they are made; which is of the people represented in
> their highest state of Soveraignty, as they have the sword in
> their hands unsubjected unto the rules of Civil
> Government, but what themselves orderly assembled for
> that purpose, doe think fit to make.[7]

Strikingly, his proposal included both a dedicated constitutional convention, and (apparently) a kind of plebiscite, though with the vote restricted to 'the adherents to this Cause', as it was in a number of these constitutional proposals of the interregnum. Vane had been very closely associated with the radicals of New England, having lived there in the late 1630s and having acted as Governor for a year; it is quite possible that what we see in *A Healing Question* is an echo of the ideas of the New England separatists which I mentioned in Chapter 2.

In the event his ideas were not picked up; and the principal response to them could have come straight out of Bentham in the 1790s.

> These fundamentals are to be agreed upon by the peoples
> Representatives, and to oblige the supream Legislative
> power (which is to be the peoples Representatives also)
> so, that the peoples Representatives once met, are to
> oblige the Representatives for ever after: which is a thing
> not only absurd in itself in the nature of it, but of the
> highest improbability in the practice of it; for who can
> dream that Representatives of the people, when chosen

[7.] Sir Henry Vane, *A Healing Question* (London, 1656), sig. C2v.

and met, will ever hold themselves obliged by any
constitution of former Representations, farther then they
shall according to time and circumstance agree with
their liking? since they all stand upon one foot of power,
as entrusted by the people; and the latter may as well,
and by as good right alter constitutions and laws agreed
by the former, as the former could make such: so that if
our Author will trust the peoples Representatives at first
to make fundamentals, by as good reason he may
trust them ever without any at all, since that the power
and choice of observing or not observing those
fundamentals will always rest in themselves, and this
unavoidably so.[8]

[8.] *A letter from a person in the countrey to his friend in the city: giving his
judgement upon a book entituled A healing question* (n.p., 1656) sig. C2.
This is a curious work, written in defence of the Army; it contains an
account of the state of nature as a state of war (B3v), and a defence of the
Instrument of Government as having been agreed to in a kind of
plebiscite. '[T]his forme of Government we now are under ... was sent
down into every Shire and County of the Nations, that none (except
enemies and people not worth 200.*l.*) might pretend ignorance, or be
denied his opinion and vote; and upon such proofe and tryal, the people
not only embraced it, but even tied every individual of their
Representative not to alter it. But our Author may say, that indenture by
which they did so, was sent down to them to sign; and I say, but it was
signed by them; the Government did but offer the condition, but 'twas the
people did accept it'. (C1). This refers to Article xii of the Instrument of
Government, which required an 'indenture' between the returning officer
'on the one part, and the electors on the other part; wherein shall be
contained, that the person elected shall not have power to alter the
government as it is hereby settled in one single person and a Parliament'
(S. R. Gardiner (ed.), *The Constitutional Documents of the Puritan
Revolution 1625–1660* (Oxford University Press, 1906), p. 410).

The Americans in the 1770s returned to this seventeenth-century language, and most of the newly independent provincial assemblies that drafted new constitutions called themselves conventions; the three that did not were New Hampshire, South Carolina and Massachusetts.[9] And these conventions mostly behaved like those of 1660 and 1689 in that they both passed fundamental legislation and constituted themselves the new states' legislatures; in a number of cases these were the bodies that ratified the Articles of Confederation. But there were two striking exceptions to this, which presaged in their different ways the new constitutional arrangements of the United States. The first was Delaware, where the House of Assembly in 1775 called for a 'convention' to be elected specifically to draft a new constitution;

An example of one of these indentures survives from Manchester (briefly represented in Parliament under the Interregnum), signed by twenty-nine electors (Manchester Archives M71/4/3/1). But (leaving aside the extremely attenuated character of the electorate, radically reduced from its 1640 level) this was not a true plebiscite, as there could be no vote against the new constitution! It resembled more the administrations of various oaths to the population during the 1640s and 1650s, such as the Engagement of 1650 'to be true and faithful to the Commonwealth of England, as it is now established, without a King or House of Lords'.

9. New Hampshire, New York, New Jersey and South Carolina summoned 'provincial congresses', but the New York and New Jersey congresses rechristened themselves 'conventions'; Massachusetts reconstituted its prerevolutionary General Court. Information about these early conventions is from John Alexander Jameson, *The Constitutional Convention: Its History, Powers, and Modes of Proceeding* (New York: Charles Scribner and Co., 1867), pp. 118–44; the text of the various constitutions can be found in Francis Newton Thorpe (ed.), *The Federal and State Constitutions* (Washington DC, 1909), vols. I–VII.

the preamble to the Constitution accordingly described it as 'agreed to and resolved upon by the Representatives in full Convention of the Delaware State ... , the said Representatives being chosen by the Freemen of the said State for that express Purpose'. The convention's draft was not ratified but simply came into force by virtue of the convention's final vote in September 1776; the convention then dissolved itself, and the new state legislature took office. This has remained the system in Delaware ever since; uniquely among American states it has no procedure for the popular ratification of amendments produced by a constitutional convention.[10] The Delaware model was picked up by the drafters of the Pennsylvania constitution; although the convention that produced it operated also as a legislature, the constitution passed in September 1776 introduced for the first time a formal provision for its own amendment by a dedicated convention called expressly for that purpose by an elected 'council of censors', which the constitution also introduced as a body to monitor 'whether the constitution has been preserved inviolate in every part; and whether the legislative and executive branches of government have performed their duty as guardians of the people, or assumed to themselves, or exercised other or greater powers than they are intitled to by the constitution' (Sect. 47). It was this feature – the provision of a separate route for constitutional amendment – which seems to have fascinated

---

[10] The 1792 Delaware constitution allowed constitutional amendments by a vote of the legislature, if proposed before a general election, but it also allowed voters to call for a constitutional convention at any general election.

the contemporary French readers of the constitution (along with the fact that the legislature was to be unicameral), as it was genuinely innovatory in this respect, though it was followed the next year by Vermont and (without the council of censors) by Georgia.[11]

The other exception was Massachusetts, which took in one important respect the opposite route from Delaware and Pennsylvania, and which eventually created a structure remarkably similar to that which its former governor had suggested in 1656. The General Court decided in 1777 to draft a new constitution without calling a convention. At the conclusion of its deliberations, in May 1778, it then declared that it was submitting the constitution to the people and would require a two-thirds majority of the freemen for ratification. A statewide referendum was organised, which promptly rejected the proposals by a majority of 9,972 nays against 2,083 yeas (with 129 out of the 298 towns not submitting returns).[12] The General Court responded with a new proposal that there should now be a dedicated constitutional convention to draft a second version of the constitution, but that this version should also be ratified by a referendum. The vote of

---

[11.] The Maryland constitution was the other document from 1776 which prescribed means for its own amendment, though in its case this was simply the requirement that amendments had to pass by a two-thirds majority in the legislature – a system of what were later called 'entrenched clauses', which other Parliamentary jurisdictions (notably South Africa under the 1909 South Africa Act) have occasionally used.

[12.] Peters, *The Massachusetts Constitution of 1780*, p. 19 (the total number of towns from the Handlins, *The Popular Sources of Political Authority*, Appendix, pp. 933 ff.)

1778 was the first general referendum or plebiscite ever mounted in any state anywhere in the world – fifteen years before the Girondin *projet* and the Jacobin constitution. But extraordinarily, there was no extensive discussion about its significance either in the General Court or the Massachusetts press. It seems that the General Court was simply agreeing with arguments that had been put forward by Massachusetts radicals during statewide discussions over what the new constitution should be.

As the residents of Pittsfield, in the remote west of the state, put it in the most extensive version of these arguments,

> we have always been persuaded that the people are the fountain of power.
>
> That since the Dissolution of the power of Great Britain over these Colonies they have fallen into a state of Nature.
>
> That the first step to be taken as a people in such a state for the Enjoyment or Restoration of Civil Government amongst them, is the formation of a fundamental Constitution as the Basis and ground work of Legislation.
>
> That the Approbation of the Majority of the people of this fundamental Constitution is absolutely necessary to give Life and being to it. We often hear of the fundamental Constitution of Great Britain, which all political writers (except ministerial ones) set above the King, Lords, and Commons, which they cannot change, nothing short of the great national Majority of the people being sufficient for this.
>
> That a Representative Body may form, but cannot impose said fundamental Constitution upon a people . . .

> If this fundamental Constitution is above the whole
> Legislature, the Legislature cannot certainly make it, it
> must be the Approbation of the Majority which gives
> Life and being to it . . .[13]

The authors of the Pittsfield Petition accepted that as things stood there was no actual constitutional structure of this kind in Massachusetts; this was why the Pittsfield authors claimed that they were now living in a state of nature and could proceed to rebuild their society. But it was not necessary to go this far to argue for a majority vote on a constitution; another resident of Berkshire County, William Whiting, reproved the Pittsfield writers on the grounds that they still belonged to the political community of Massachusetts Bay, and were not in a state of nature, but

> when men emerge from a state of nature, and unite in
> society, in order to forming a political government; the
> first step necessary is, for each individual to give up his
> alienable natural rights and privileges, to be ordered,
> directed, and disposed of, as the major part of the
> community shall think fit; so far as shall be necessary for
> the good of the whole, of which the majority must be the
> judges. And this must necessarily take place previous to
> the community's forming any particular constitution,
> mode, or form of government whatever: For, to be in a state
> of society, so far as to be under obligation to obey the
> rules and orders prescribed by the major part of the society,
> is one thing; and for that society to be under any
> particular constitution or form of government, is another.

[13.] Handlins, *The Popular Sources of Political Authority*, pp. 90–1.

> The latter is necessarily subsequent to the former, and
> must depend intirely on the pleasure of the supreme judge;
> that is, the major part of the community, who have an
> undoubted right to enter upon, or postpone that matter,
> when, and so long as they see fit.[14]

So Whiting thought that without destroying an existing civil
society the majority of its members could at any time declare
some new set of principles by which the society should govern
itself, particularly when (as at the time of writing)

> [t]here cannot indeed with propriety, be said to be now,
> any constitution of government existing in this state, which
> is designed to be permanent, and to remain for
> generations to come; but we are now in a proper condition
> to form one, whenever the major party of the community
> shall think proper to enter upon so import an undertaking:
> And then, every individual must submit to such a
> constitution as the majority shall agree to; though, the
> larger that majority, the happier will it be.[15]

So general was this sense in Massachusetts of the obviousness
of plebiscites that even John Adams remembered urging them
on his fellow delegates in the Continental Congress in 1775.
He recalled that some members

> began to ask me civil questions. How can the People
> institute Governments? My answer was by Conventions

[14] William Whiting, *An Address to the Inhabitants of the County of
Berkshire: Respecting Their Present Opposition to Civil Government*
(Hartford, CT, 1778), p. 11.
[15] Ibid., p. 17.

of Representatives, fairly, freely, and proportionably
chosen. – When the Convention has fabricated a
Government, or a Constitution rather, how do We know
the People will submit to it? If there is any doubt of that,
the Convention may send out their Project of a
Constitution, to the People in their several Towns,
Counties, or districts, and the People may make the
Acceptance of it their own Act ... I believe that in every
considerable portion of the People, there will be found
some Men, who will understand the Subject as well as
their representatives, and these will assist in enlightening
the rest.[16]

Adams hoped (as he went on to say) that the people would
choose a government based on a tripartite legislature, and
not the unicameral legislature which the Massachusetts radicals sought, but nevertheless he saw the point of seeking
explicit ratification by the citizens of any constitutional
proposal.

Massachusetts was not the only state in which radicals
urged a plebiscite for a new constitution, though it was the
first actually to accede to the demand. Among the papers of
Philip Mazzei, the friend of Jefferson and Condorcet, is a draft
appeal to the Virginia Constitutional Convention of 1776 to
send the constitutional plan out for a vote of the electors
(though the author of the appeal wanted it to be validated
by a majority of the counties, not the entire population as in
Massachusetts). The plea was disregarded and may not even

[16.] L.H. Butterfield (ed.), *Diary and Autobiography of John Adames*
(Harvard University Press, 1961), pp. 355–6.

have been read.[17] In the event only New Hampshire initially followed Massachusetts's example; there too the first proposed constitution was thrown out in a referendum in 1778, though unlike Massachusetts the second was also rejected (in 1781), and it was the third which was finally accepted in 1783. New Hampshire, however, unlike Massachusetts, wrote into its new constitution a clause both prescribing a convention for amendments, and expressly decreeing that 'no alteration shall be made in this constitution before the same shall be laid before the towns and unincorporated places, and approved by two-thirds of the qualified voters present, and voting upon the question', so it may count as the first state formally to enact this provision.[18] Massachusetts did not follow suit until 1820, when the first nine amendments to the 1780 constitution were passed, though those amendments were themselves put to popular vote.[19] Although as we have seen, the 1776 Pennsylvanian constitution was of great interest to foreign observers in the 1780s, Pennsylvania did not at that stage choose a plebiscite. The legislature attempted to bypass the 1776 constitution in 1778 by organising a direct appeal to the people on the question of whether there should be a new constitutional convention. But in the event it did not take place, and the constitution that replaced the 1776 document

---

[17] Philip Mazzei, *Selected Writings and Correspondence*, ed. Margherita Marchione (Prato: Edizioni di Palazzo, 1983) p. 96. Mazzei, or whoever composed this manuscript, went even further, down the Jacobin route: he demanded that not only the constitution but the regular laws issued by the legislature should be ratified in the same way (p. 94).

[18.] *The Federal and State Constitutions*, vol. IV, p. 2470.

[19.] Ibid., vol. III, pp. 1913, 1922.

in 1790 not only abolished the unicameral legislature and the council of censors, it made no provision for its own amendment. Not until 1838 did Pennsylvania hold a plebiscite on its constitution, which now prescribed plebiscites for future amendments. But by then Pennsylvania was looking in this respect rather tardy: between 1778 and the beginning of the Civil War almost all American states moved to a plebiscitary basis for their constitutions, with a particular rush occurring (unsurprisingly) in the heyday of Jacksonian democracy. At the start of 1861 only five states out of a Union of thirty-four did not use the plebiscite.[20]

20. Constitutional plebiscites were held for the first time as follows: Massachusetts 1778, New Hampshire 1779, Mississippi 1817, Connecticut 1818, Maine 1819, New York 1821, Rhode Island 1824 (the constitution was thrown out by 3,206 to 1,668 and Rhode Island did not receive a written constitution until 1842, when one was passed by another plebiscite; see p. 234 for a further discussion of this), Alabama 1828, Virginia 1830, Tennessee 1834, North Carolina 1835, Michigan 1835, Pennsylvania 1838, New Jersey 1844, Iowa 1844, Louisiana 1845, Texas 1845 (the independent Republican constitution of 1836 was also ratified by plebiscite), Missouri 1845, Wisconsin 1846, Illinois 1848, California 1849, Kentucky 1850, Maryland 1851, Indiana 1851, Ohio 1851, Kansas 1855, Oregon 1857, Minnesota 1857, Georgia 1861 (very unusually, Georgia introduced the plebiscite to ratify its secessionist constitution). Neither Arkansas, Delaware, Florida, South Carolina nor Vermont had used plebiscites before 1861; Arkansas introduced them in 1864, South Carolina and Florida were given them in their Reconstruction constitutions of 1868, Vermont introduced them in 1870, and Delaware has never used plebiscites for ratification. In not all of these cases did the constitution ratified by a plebiscite itself prescribe this method of amendment: Massachusetts, New Hampshire, Kentucky, Louisiana, Indiana, Mississippi, Arkansas and Maryland did not (Massachusetts

What explains this move to direct popular control over the Constitution? As I said, there was surprisingly little discussion of the issue in Massachusetts; what there was tended to refer back not to the constitutional proposals of the Interregnum, but to the arguments about Parliamentary corruption in eighteenth-century England. It has long been recognised that mistrust of Parliament lay at the heart of the Americans' actions, and had even led some of them (as Eric Nelson has recently stressed) to turn to a kind of 'patriot royalism' in which the King could be seen as a guarantor of freedom for the American provinces from

prescribed it in 1820, New Hampshire in 1784, Kentucky in 1890, Louisiana in 1845, Indiana in 1851, Mississippi in 1832, Arkansas in 1868 and Maryland in 1864). The Iowa constitution of 1844 prescribed one, but it was thrown out by the people; the 1846 constitution did not prescribe one but was ratified by a popular vote, and the 1857 constitution reinstated it. Virginia is an interesting case: not until 1870 did its constitution prescribe *any* method of amendment, but new constitutions and constitutional amendments from 1830 to 1870 were always ratified by popular vote. Nor, on the other hand, were constitutions prescribing plebiscites always themselves ratified by one: Alabama prescribed the plebiscite in its constitution of 1819, but did not hold a plebiscite until the first amendment in 1828 (see T. M. Owen, *History of Alabama and Dictionary of Alabama Biography* (Chicago, 1921), vol. I, p. 364) and the 1836 constitution of the independent republic of Texas was not itself ratified by a plebiscite. For accurate information (surprisingly hard to come by) see *The Federal and State Constitutions*, together with the information on various state government websites. There is a good discussion by Christian G. Fritz of the Jacksonian period's move to conventions and popular ratification in his *American Sovereigns: The People and America's Constitutional Tradition Before the Civil War* (Cambridge University Press, 2008), pp. 235–45.

Parliamentary rule.[21] This was not an unknown element in English radicalism,[22] but more significant for my purposes was the turn to an idea of popular control over the activities of Parliament which would go well beyond the mere act of election. As both Isaac Kramnick and, more recently, Mark Goldie have emphasised, Locke began to be read by these radicals as a theorist of this kind of popular control.[23] They did so by taking his remarks about the 'community' retaining residual rights, and about the salience of majoritarianism, and pushed them in a direction Locke himself may not have wished to go; though one should always remember that Locke himself was wary of Parliament, and – strikingly – argued that the executive should control the franchise and not, as the other Whigs wanted, the legislature itself. From the early eighteenth century these radicals emphasised the tradition in England of mandates for Members of Parliament from their constituents, and sought to refashion the Commons as a house of mandated delegates.[24] On the

---

[21.] See his *The Royalist Revolution: Monarchy and the American Founding* (Harvard University Press, 2014).

[22.] See, for example, James Burgh's *Remarks historical and political collected from books and observations. Humbly presented to the King's most excellent majesty*, British Library King's MS 433. See below for the continuation of Burgh's patriot royalism into the 1770s.

[23.] Isaac Kramnick, 'Republican revisionism revisited', *American Historical Review* 87 (1982), pp. 629–64; Mark Goldie, 'Situating Swift's politics in 1701' in Claude Rawson (ed.), *Politics and Literature in the Age of Swift: English and Irish Perspectives* (Cambridge University Press, 2010), pp. 31–51.

[24.] An early example, cited by Goldie: 'for Members, who are sent up by the People of *England*, who are their true Electors, to pretend to be

eve of American independence this programme was given a particularly thorough statement, and linked to Locke, in James Burgh's *Political Disquisitions* (1775), which was reprinted in Philadelphia that year with a list of 'Encouragers' headed by 'His Excellency George Washington, Esq; Generalissimo of all the Forces in America, and a Member of the Honorable, the American Continental Congress', and including many of the other delegates.[25] The Pittsfield authors in their plea for a plebiscite said that they were 'countenanced in believing' these 'Truths' by 'the most respectable political Writers of the last and present Century, especially by Mr. Burgh in his Political Disquisitions for the publication of which one half of the Continental Congress were subscribers'.[26]

Absolute, and to act without Controul, and yet at the same time to call themselves the Representatives of the People in those Counties, Cities, and Corporations, for which they serve, is such a Blunder of Words, as is not reconcileable to common Understanding'. *The Electors right asserted* (London, 1701), pp. 1–2. The author of the pamphlet then lists many examples of such mandates. For more, see Derek Hirst, *The Representative of the People? Voters and Voting in England under the Early Stuarts* (Cambridge University Press, 1975), pp. 161–7, 182–5. Lord Somers in his *Jura Populi Anglicani* of the same year cited many cases of other states which used or had used mandation.

[25.] *Political Disquisitions* (Philadelphia, 1775), vol. III, pp. [1] ff. See Isaac Kramnick, 'Republicanism revisited: the case of James Burgh', *Proceedings of the American Antiquarian Society* 102 (1992), pp 81–98 and Carla H. Hay, *James Burgh, Spokesman for Reform in Hanoverian England* (Washington DC: University Press of America, 1979).

[26.] Handlins, *The Popular Sources of Political Authority*, p. 91.

Burgh repeated the need for a mandate, devoting the whole of Book ɪv, chapter 3 to the subject, and he insisted on the power of the majority:

> If revolution-principles are justifiable, that is, if the *people* may take the *power* out of the hands of a *king*, or government, when they abuse it, it follows, that the king and government are in all cases *responsible* to the *people*, and that a majority of the people can at any time change the government.[27]

In a striking section, he calculated that in the contemporary House of Commons a majority of the members could be elected or a bill passed by the votes of only 5,723 people![28] But like all these English radicals, Burgh's concern was with a mandate and an equitable representation; he explicitly ruled out any move to a non-representative system on the standard argument that it could not be fitted to a populous country.[29] Indeed, even in *Political Disquisitions* he turned to the crown as a possible solution to the imbalances of Parliament, explicitly endorsing Locke's argument for executive control of the

---

[27.] *Political Disquisitions*, vol. ɪ, p. 200.

[28.] That is, the majority in each of the smaller boroughs which together sent a majority of MPs to Westminster totalled 5,723. See *Political Disquisitions*, Book ɪɪ, chapter 4.

[29.] 'It may be said, "Why might not (in *Britain* for instance) the inhabitants of single counties meet together to deliberate on those subjects, which are now debated in parliament, and afterwards communicate the result of their consultation to a grand national assembly?" The answer is, "This would still be government by representation; because the national assembly must be the elected representatives of the people."' *Political Disquisitions*, vol. I, pp. 5–6.

franchise.[30] But at the end of the work he attacked the idea that 'the people are annihilated, or absorbed into the parliament; that the voice of the people is no where to be heard but in parliament; that members of parliament are not responsible to their constituents, &c.', and called for a 'grand national association for restoring the constitution', with

> a copy of the ASSOCIATION for every parish, and a parochial committee to procure subsciptions from all persons whose names are in any tax-book, and who are willing to join the Association. And there must be a grand committee for every county in the three kingdoms, and in the colonies of *America*.[31]

The functions of the Association were to be

> 1. The securing of public credit.[32] 2. Obtaining the undoubted sense of the people, on the state of public affairs. 3. Presenting petitions, signed by a clear majority of the people of property, for the necessary acts of parliament. 4. To raise, and have in readiness, the strength of the nation, in order to influence government, and prevent mischief. (p. 434)

[30.] Ibid., vol. I, pp. 74–5.   [31.] Ibid., vol. III, pp. 432 and 429.

[32.] Like many eighteenth-century writers, Burgh believed that the existing system of public credit acted as a permanent barrier to constitutional change, since any suggestion of instability would destroy the value of the funds. See *Political Disquisitions*, vol. III, pp. 328–30, and Istvan Hont, 'The rhapsody of public debt: David Hume and voluntary state bankruptcy', *Jealousy of Trade: International Competition and the Nation-State in Historical Perspective* (Harvard University Press, 2005), pp. 325–53.

And Burgh even toyed with the idea that the King might put himself at the head of this Association (pp. 432–3).

So on the eve of American independence we have in place some elements of the new constitutional developments, and in particular we have a sense in England of the possibility of action by the sovereign people as an organised body against their representatives. But we are still a long way from the idea that there should be an institutionalised method of fundamental legislation by the people: Burgh's Association was essentially, as he admitted, a mechanism for petitioning the legislature, rather than for taking over part of its power. It is true that, as we have seen in the French context, the distinction between mandation and a plebiscite can be quite fine, and the English radicals' stress on the need for mandation was edging towards a plebiscitary system; but it is nevertheless significant that the move to a plebiscite, and to the authorisation of a constitution by a legislative body which was not the normal legislature, was not made among the English writers until the radicals of Massachusetts made it. In their support they cited Locke and Burgh, despite the fact that neither had quite made the case the Massachusetts radicals wished to make; but it is interesting and may be important that some also quoted Rousseau in support of their majoritarianism.[33]

[33.] See *Result of the convention of delegates holden at Ipswich in the county of Essex, who were deputed to take into consideration the constitution and form of government, proposed by the Convention of the state of Massachusetts-Bay* (Newbury-port, MA, 1778), pp. 10, 14–15. It is worth observing that Rousseau himself, discussing the American revolution with an English visitor in 1776, fully supported the Americans, and was even prepared to countenance the continued existence of slavery among

Responding to the American developments in the late 1770s and early 1780s some English opponents of the revolution also found that the best way of thinking about what the Americans were doing was to use Rousseau's categories; thus George Chalmers in his *Political Annals of the present United Colonies* (1780) described the early colonists of both Massachusetts and Pennsylvania as having anticipated 'the true spirit of Rousseau' in their hostility to representation, and praised them for their 'humiliation' in eventually recognising the necessity of it.

> J.J. Rousseau insists, with his accustomed spirit; that, as the sovereignty cannot be represented, no sooner are representatives introduced than the state is already enslaved; that, though the English imagine themselves free, yet, when their elections are over, they become instantly slaves: Nor does he consider it as any objection to the assembling of the freemen that their numbers amount to 400,000 or more. – Social Comp. b. 4. – The wisdom of Massachusetts thought otherwise [by the later seventeenth century].[34]

And Josiah Tucker with his characteristic perspicuity noted in his attack on the modern Lockeans that the English radical

them, on the presumption that it would prove short-lived. Thomas Bentley, *Journal of a Visit to Paris 1776*, ed. Peter France (Brighton: University of Sussex Library, 1977), p. 60.

[34] George Chalmers, *Political Annals of the Present United Colonies* (London, 1780), p. 169. See also p. 8 on the Plymouth Plantation, and p. 645 for the 'humiliation' (i.e. modesty) of the Pennsylvanians in choosing representation. The eighteenth-century translation of the *Social Contract* entitled it *A treatise on the social compact* (London, 1764).

writers had not quite provided a theory for the course of action which (he believed) the Americans had taken.

> Honest, undissembling Rousseau clearly saw, where the Lockian Hypothesis must necessarily end. And as he was a Man who never boggled at Consequences, however extravagant or absurd, he declared with his usual Frankness, that the People could not transfer their indefeasible Right of voting for themselves to any others . . . The Doctors Priestley and Price do not indeed absolutely join Rousseau in condemning the Use of national Representatives; but it is plain, that they admit them with a very ill Grace, and, with great Reluctance.[35]

So far we have been considering the constitutional innovations of the new American states. But, of course, though they were interesting and remain important, the state constitutions have been overshadowed by the federal constitution, and I now want to turn to that. The delegates at Philadelphia in the summer of 1787 had to settle the procedures for ratification and amendment of the new constitution; though one or two people spoke out against specifying any method of amendment,[36] it was quickly agreed both that the constitution had to be ratified by a body or bodies other than the

---

[35.] *A treatise concerning civil government, in three parts. Part 1. The notions of Mr Locke and his followers, concerning the origin, extent, and end of civil government, examined and confuted* . . . (London, 1781), pp. 39–40. In his *A letter to Edmund Burke, Esq* ('Glocester', 1775), p. 13, Tucker had already cited Rousseau's remarks in *A Letter from the Mountain* as expressing the colonists' ideas.

[36.] Charles Pinckney of South Carolina spoke against the idea of a clause specifying the means of amendment, June 5, in Max Farrand (ed.),

Convention itself, and that it would have to dictate the means of its own amendment. On ratification, though Gouverneur Morris called for a single national ratifying convention,[37] he was alone in thinking this, and the real argument was over the question of whether (like the Articles of Confederation) it should be ratified by the state legislatures. The 'Virginia Plan', which was the basis for the debates at the convention, proposed that the constitution should 'after the approbation of Congress to be submitted to an assembly or assemblies of Representatives, recommended by the several Legislatures to be expressly chosen by the people, to consider & decide thereon' (I, p.22). (The final version, Article VII of the Constitution, reads 'The Ratification of the Conventions of nine States, shall be sufficient for the Establishment of this Constitution between the States so ratifying the Same'). This initial proposal was repeatedly attacked by delegates who wanted only the legislatures to ratify; in response James Madison said that 'He considered the difference between a system founded on the Legislatures only, and one founded on the people, to be the true difference between a *league* or *treaty*, and a *Constitution*', and 'the new national constitution ought to have the highest source of authority, at least paramount to the powers of the respective constitutions of the states'.[38]

The Records of the Federal Convention of 1787 (New Haven: Yale University Press, 1911), vol. I. p. 121.

[37.] July 23, *The Records of the Federal Convention of 1787*, vol. II, pp. 92–3.

[38.] July 23 and June 5, *The Records of the Federal Convention of 1787*, vol. II, p. 93 and vol. I, p. 126. The latter quotation is not from Madison's own notes, and may be inaccurate – 'at least paramount' is an odd way of putting it.

James Wilson concurred: '[T]he people by a convention are the only power that can ratify the proposed system of the new government'.[39] Even antifederalists in the Convention could agree; George Mason, for example, said that 'The Legislatures have no power to ratify [the Constitution]. They are the mere creatures of the State Constitutions, and cannot be greater than their creators ... Whither then must we resort? To the people with whom all power remains that has not been given up in the Constitutions derived from them'.[40] And they finally agreed Article VII gave no explicit role to the legislatures at all, though a separate resolution of the convention accompanied the submission of the Constitution to Congress, expressing 'the Opinion of this Convention, that it should afterwards be submitted to a Convention of Delegates, chosen in each State by the People thereof, under the Recommendation of its Legislature, for their Assent and Ratification'.

It should be noted (since this issue became hugely important in the later interpretation of the Constitution) that at least in Mason's eyes an appeal to the people over the heads of the legislatures was compatible with the separate identity of those people in their respective states; it was possible to believe in the necessity of a democratic process within each state as the guarantee of the federal Constitution's legitimacy, without believing that the appeal to the people had created a new and unitary nation. (This was also to be the position in the next generation of Mason's fellow Virginian St George Tucker.)[41]

[39.] June 5, ibid., vol. I, p. 127.   [40.] July 23, ibid., vol. II, p. 88.

[41.] The US is 'a confederate republic, composed of several independent, and sovereign democratic states, united for their common defence, and

Similarly, conservative federalists such as Roger Sherman or Oliver Ellsworth were strongly in favour of restricting ratification to the legislatures without (apparently) thinking that this committed them to a clearly antifederalist position.[42] No delegate proposed plebiscites as the method of ratification: the debate was entirely between legislatures and conventions, or what one might term the 'Maryland' versus the 'Delaware' methods of ratification.[43] But even the opponents of conventions supposed that they represented a kind of democratic control over the process; that, after all, was precisely the objection that delegates such as Elbridge Gerry (from Massachusetts!) raised: 'He seemed afraid of referring the new system to [the people of the Eastern states]. The people

security against foreign nations, and for the purposes of harmony, and mutual intercourse between each other; each state retaining an entire liberty of exercising, as it thinks proper, all those parts of its sovereignty, which are not mentioned in the constitution'. See his *Blackstone's Commentaries: With Notes of Reference to the Constitution and Laws of the Federal Government of the United States and of the Commonwealth of Virginia* (Philadelphia, 1803) vol. 1, note D.I.8, appendix p. 171; I discuss his general views below, p. 217. Another Virginian defender of states' rights, John Taylor 'of Caroline', expressed indifference between legislatures and conventions, since each (he thought) represented the people of a state: 'a concurrence or rejection of either, was considered as a sovereign act of a state people by their representatives'. *New Views of the Constitution of the United States* (Washington DC, 1823), p. 8.

[42.] Sherman, June 5, *The Records of the Federal Convention of 1787*, vol. 1, p. 122; Ellsworth, June 20, *The Records of the Federal Convention of 1787*, vol. 1, p. 335.

[43.] And the fact that Maryland's constitution prescribed that only the legislature could amend it was raised by their opponents as a stumbling block for the advocates of conventions.

in that quarter have <at this time> the wildest ideas of Government in the world. They were for abolishing the Senate in Massts. and giving all the other powers of Govt. to the other branch of the Legislature'.[44] And indeed it was the case that in the event many delegates to the ratifying conventions were mandated by their electors, while in Massachusetts there was an attempt to present the convention with a plebiscitary vote on the Constitution, and Rhode Island's convention actually organised such a plebiscite (it voted 2,708 against ratification and 237 for it).[45] So though the argument over conventions *versus* legislatures, from the point of view of (say) the Girondins, was not really an argument over the possibility of democracy in the modern world, conventions could most easily be assimilated to the plebiscitary model, and seen as a direct expression of the electors' wills with regard to specific legislative proposals, while legislatures remained within the tradition of English Parliamentary government.

When it came to the discussion over what became Article v, covering future amendments, the advocates of ratification by legislatures were able gain more of a victory. The initial discussion concentrated on the question of whether the 'National Legislature' should have a veto on any amendments, and it was generally agreed that it should not. The first specific proposal was simply that 'On the application of the

---

[44.] June 5, *The Records of the Federal Convention of 1787*, vol. I, p. 123.

[45.] See Pauline Maier, *Ratification: The People Debate the Constitution 1787–1788* (New York: Simon and Schuster, 2010) for cases of mandation or plebiscites: pp. 106 (Pennsylvania), 135 (Connecticut), 141–53 (Massachusetts), 218–19 (New Hampshire), 223 (Rhode Island), 235 (Virginia), 406 (North Carolina).

Legislatures of two thirds of the States in the Union, for an amendment of this Constitution, the Legislature of the United States shall call a Convention for that purpose' (Farrand II, pp. 148, 159). But when on 10 September the delegates finally turned their attention properly to this article there was a successful move first to allow the National Legislature an equal right with the states to propose amendments, and then to allow state legislatures potentially to be the ratifying body. The proposal that incorporated these features was put forward by Madison himself and was accepted:

> The Legislature of the U.S. whenever two thirds of both Houses shall deem necessary, or on the application of two thirds of the Legislatures of the several States, shall propose amendments to this Constitution, which shall be valid to all intents and purposes as part thereof, when the same shall have been ratified by three fourths at least of the Legislatures of the several States, or by Conventions in three fourths thereof, as one or the other mode of ratification may be proposed by the Legislature of the U.S.[46]

But five days later there was a revolt and Madison gave way, agreeing that there should be a mechanism for calling a national constitutional convention. The 'circulating murmurs of the small States' also succeeded in inserting the clause that 'no State, without its Consent, shall be deprived of its equal Suffrage in the Senate', an odd anomaly, which is the only

---

[46.] *The Records of the Federal Convention of 1787*, vol. II, p. 559. At the same time an amendment was accepted preventing any amendment to the articles involving slavery for twenty years.

element of the Constitution that in theory cannot be changed (unless one takes the view that an amendment to Article v simply removing that provision, without at that stage depriving any state of its 'equal suffrage', would be valid, in which case a subsequent amendment could proceed to change the voting arrangements in the Senate). The final Article reads

> The Congress, whenever two thirds of both Houses shall deem it necessary, shall propose Amendments to this Constitution, or, on the Application of the Legislatures of two thirds of the several States, shall call a Convention for proposing Amendments, which, in either Case, shall be valid to all Intents and Purposes, as Part of this Constitution, when ratified by the Legislatures of three fourths of the several States, or by Conventions in three fourths thereof, as the one or the other Mode of Ratification may be proposed by the Congress; Provided that no Amendment which may be made prior to the Year One thousand eight hundred and eight shall in any Manner affect the first and fourth Clauses in the Ninth Section of the first Article; and that no State, without its Consent, shall be deprived of its equal Suffrage in the Senate.

So the legislators, in Congress and in the states, had been handed a substantial victory, compared with the defeat they had suffered over the ratification of the Constitution, because future amendments could become valid without ever passing through either a national or a state convention. The delegates, rushing through the Article in the dying days of the Convention, had found themselves in the strange position of prescribing a method for changing the Constitution, which they were not willing to use for ratifying it. And indeed, since 1789 there has been no national constitutional convention, and only one amendment ratified by state conventions – of all things, the twenty-first amendment abolishing Prohibition! Nevertheless, the revolt of the delegates against Madison's proposal on September 15 had at least succeeded in placing in the Constitution a possible means of bypassing Congress, and forcing into existence the kind of general gathering of representatives from the states in a national convention, which the meeting at Philadelphia had been. George Mason had written against his copy of Madison's proposal, 'By this article Congress only have the power of proposing amendments at any future time to this constitution and should it prove ever so oppressive, the whole people of America can't make, or even propose alterations to it; a doctrine utterly subversive of the fundamental principles of the rights and liberties of the people'; but he voted for the Article as finally drafted, apparently believing that it met his objection.[47] The fact remained, however, that if one were to suppose (as the majority of delegates earlier had done) that the essence of popular sovereignty was a mechanism whereby one had to appeal in some way to the people in order to pass fundamental laws, then in the new American nation the people would have spoken as sovereign only to deny themselves sovereignty in the future – Hobbes not Rousseau!

Anxiety about what they had done was expressed by some of the former delegates during the debate in the House of Representatives in August 1789 over the first ten amendments to the Constitution, the Bill of Rights. Defending his

---

[47.] *The Records of the Federal Convention of 1787*, vol. II, pp. 629–30.

motion that they should be listed as a separate supplement
to the Constitution rather than interspersed into the existing
text (which of course is what was eventually agreed), Roger
Sherman of Connecticut argued that the Bill of Rights should
be thought of as a second constitution, but

> I would desire gentlemen to consider the authorities
> upon which the two constitutions are to stand. The original
> was established by the people at large, by conventions
> chosen by them for the express purpose. The preamble to
> the constitution declares the act: but will it be a truth in
> ratifying the next constitution, which is to be done
> perhaps by the State Legislatures, and not conventions
> chosen for the purpose? Will gentlemen say it is 'We the
> people' in this case? Certainly they cannot; for, by the
> present constitution, we, nor all the Legislatures in the
> Union together, do not possess the power of repealing it.
> All that is granted us by the 5th article is, that whenever
> we shall think it necessary, we may propose amendments
> to the constitution; not that we may propose to repeal the
> old, and substitute a new one.[48]

[48.] Joseph Gales (ed.), *The Debates and Proceedings in the Congress of the
United States* (Washington DC, 1834), vol. I, col. 742. See also his remarks
coll. 734–5. Samuel Livermore of New Hampshire said the same: 'neither
this Legislature, nor all the Legislatures in America, were authorized to
repeal a constitution; and that must be an inevitable consequence of an
attempt to amend it in a way proposed by the committee [i.e. amending
the original text]'. And James Jackson of Georgia drew an interesting
parallel with acts of Parliament carrying constitutional significance,
which simply succeeded one another: 'the [English] constitution is
composed of many distinct acts; but an Englishman would be ashamed

This might appear a strange position to take up; the fact that Sherman did so is testimony to his worries about Article v (despite the fact that, as we saw above, at Philadelphia he had argued against ratifying the Constitution through conventions). Elbridge Gerry responded to it with the obvious argument, but in doing so revealed his own continued suspicion of anything like direct democracy.

> The conventions of the States, respectively, have agreed for the people, that the State Legislatures shall be authorized to decide upon the amendments in the manner of a convention ... Does he [Sherman] mean to put amendments on this ground, that after they have been ratified by the State Legislatures, they are not to have the same authority as the original instrument? If this is his meaning, let him avow it; and if it is well founded, we may save ourselves the trouble of proceeding in the business. But, for my part, I have no doubt but a ratification of the amendments, in any form, would be as valid as any part of the constitution. The Legislatures are elected by the people. I know no difference between them and conventions, unless it be that the former will generally be composed of men of higher character than may be expected in conventions; and in this case, the ratification by the Legislatures would have the preference.[49]

Sherman's proposal eventually carried the day in the full House, having lost earlier in the Committee of the Whole

to own that, on this account, he could not ascertain his own privileges or the authority of the Government', ibid., coll. 741–2.

[49.] Ibid., col. 744.

House, though we do not have details of what was said in the final debate (the quotations above come from the debate in the Committee).[50] But it is worth considering the implications of Sherman's argument, particularly as they seem to have underlain the decision to treat amendments as supplemental, an apparently technical decision which may have, in this light, considerable theoretical importance. Sherman offers us a third way of thinking about popular sovereignty and the Constitution, an alternative both to the standard view (in effect, Gerry's) that the only way to change the Constitution is through the provisions of Article v, and the radical view put forward recently in a series of stimulating works by Akhil Reed Amar, that Article v is non-exclusive and that a national convention and plebiscite could legally amend the Constitution, as they would be in keeping with the fundamentally popular character of the document.[51] Though I have a great deal of sympathy with Amar's views, it should be said that no one in the eighteenth century (I believe) said anything precisely like this, since the general remarks from the founders which he cites about popular sovereignty were not clearly focused on the specific question of constitutional

[50.] Ibid., p. 795 (August 19); the motion had first been lost on August 13 (p. 744).

[51.] See his 'Philadelphia revisited: amending the Constitution outside Article v', *The University of Chicago Law Review* 55 (1988), pp. 1043–104; Sanford Levinson (ed.), 'Popular sovereignty and Constitutional amendment' in *Responding to Imperfection. The Theory and Practice of Constitutional Amendment* (Princeton University Press, 1995) pp. 89–116; *America's Constitution. A Biography* (New York: Random House, 2005), pp. 298–9.

amendment.[52] And if we do not read Article v as non-exclusive, it remains a stumbling block for Amar's goal of building in popular sovereignty as a *legal* principle, and renders his view closer to that of Bruce Ackerman, according to whom major changes to the Constitution have been brought about in ways that the Constitution itself did not specify, but in accordance with its fundamentally democratic character.[53] Ackerman instances most spectacularly the Fourteenth Amendment, but also the creation of the modern federal government in the twentieth century without constitutional amendment. What Sherman's remarks can alert us to is the thought that whereas Article v is exclusive, the Constitution *as a whole* could not be changed except by the process that created it. What 'as a whole' means, is then going to be a question of judgement, and clearly its character can be quite radically changed, as it has been, by relatively small amendments (witness the Thirteenth, which merely changed a very minor clause in Article IV);[54] but it

---

[52.] It is, however, worth observing that Jameson in his *The Constitutional Convention* was willing to entertain the idea that Article v is non-exclusive (pp. 530–1). This seems to have been an issue discussed (for obvious reasons) during the passage of the Fourteenth Amendment. I discuss Jameson's general views (in other respects the antithesis of Amar's) later, p. 241.

[53.] Bruce Ackerman, *We The People* (Harvard University Press, 1991, 1998).

[54.] Lysander Spooner, indeed, argued with some reason that even this clause ('No Person held to Service or Labour in one State, under the Laws thereof, escaping into another, shall, in Consequence of any Law or Regulation therein, be discharged from such Service or Labour, but shall be delivered up on Claim of the Party to whom such Service or Labour may be due') did not strictly imply slavery. See his *The Unconstitutionality of Slavery* (Boston, 1860), pp. 67ff.

would not be unreasonable to baulk at the use of Article v to write a wholly new constitution for the United States, and a successful case might well be made in some court (particularly given the evidence from the congressional debates of August 1789) that the only procedure which could be followed in this instance would be that specified in Article vii, duly adjusted for fifty states. This gives less than Amar wants as it does not allow for a national plebiscite, but that might simply be the consequence of living in a federation.

Some thought of this kind allows one to make sense of the fact that (apart from Gerry) the founders and their succeeding generation do not seem to have thought that they had undermined the genuinely popular character of the American Constitution by passing Article v. A particularly good example of this is provided by the most perceptive of the early commentators on the Constitution, the Virginian St George Tucker. He put what he took to be the general political theory underlying all American constitutional arrangements entirely clearly.

> The American revolution seems to have given birth to this
> new political phenomenon: in every state a written
> constitution was framed, and adopted by the people, both
> in their individual and sovereign capacity, and character.
> By this means, the just distinction between the sovereignty,
> and the government, was rendered familiar to every
> intelligent mind; the former was found to reside in the
> people, and to be unalienable from them; the latter in
> their servants and agents: by this means, also, government
> was reduced to its elements; its object was defined, it's [sic]
> principles ascertained; its powers limited, and fixed;
> its structure organized; and the functions of every part of

the machine so clearly designated, as to prevent any interference, so long as the limits of each were observed. The same reasons operated in behalf of similar restrictions in the federal constitution, whether considered as the act of the body politic of the several states, or, of the people of the states, respectively, or, of the people of the United States, collectively. Accordingly we find the structure of the government, its several powers and jurisdictions, and the concessions of the several states, generally, pretty accurately defined, and limited.[55]

He was in general very scrupulous about the sovereignty-government distinction, remarking that the two things were often wrongly confused;[56] it is clear from his terminology, such as his description of government potentially 'usurping' sovereignty, that he was drawing upon Rousseau, whom indeed he cited as the authority for some of his basic principles.[57]

He was accordingly entirely clear that the sovereign had to have a specific institutional character and act as a legislator. Since the Constitution was

completed by conventions, especially called and appointed for that purpose, in each state; the acceptance of the

[55.] St. George Tucker, *Blackstone's Commentaries*, vol. 1, note D I.5, appendix, pp. 153–4.

[56.] 'The sovereignty, though always potentially existing in the people of every independent nation, or state, is in most of them, usurped by, and confounded with, the government'. Ibid., note B, appendix, p. 10.

[57.] 'The right of governing can, therefore, be acquired only by consent, originally; and this consent must be that of at least a majority of the people ... See Rousseau's Social Compact'. Ibid., note B, appendix, p. 8. He also cited Locke and Burgh.

constitution, was not only an act of the body politic of each state, but of the people thereof respectively, in their sovereign character and capacity: the body politic was competent to bind itself so far as the constitution of the state permitted, but not having power to bind the people, in cases beyond their constitutional authority, the assent of the people was indispensably necessary to the validity of the compact, by which the rights of the people might be diminished, or submitted to a new jurisdiction, or in any manner affected. From hence, not only the body politic of the several states, but every citizen thereof, may be considered as parties to the compact, and to have bound themselves reciprocally to each other, for the due observance of it and, also, to have bound themselves to the federal government, whose authority has been thereby created, and established.[58]

But rather strikingly, Tucker assumed that this institutional structure applied equally to amendments to the Constitution, despite the fact that Article v in fact stipulated that the *governments*, the legislatures, could amend it. He said that the states had agreed that

amendments to the constitution, when proposed by congress, shall not be valid unless ratified by the legislatures of three fourths of the several states; and that congress shall, on the application of two thirds of the legislatures of the several states, call a convention for proposing amendments, which when ratified by the conventions in three fourths of the states shall be valid to all intents and

[58.] Ibid., note D I.7, appendix, p. 169.

> purposes, as a part of the constitution; that the
> ratification of the conventions of nine states, should be
> sufficient for the establishment of the constitution, between
> the states so ratifying.

That is, he blandly presumed that amendments would not be valid unless *conventions* ratified them, and that there was no difference between the ratification of amendments and the ratification of the Constitution.[59]

As I said earlier, Tucker took the view that the United States remained a confederation; his commitment to popular sovereignty was primarily a commitment to popular sovereignty at the level of the states. As a consequence, he found no problems in putting forward a strong defence of majoritarianism as a political principle, including even a reduction of supermajoritarianism to a form of straight majoritarianism.[60]

---

[59]. Ibid., note D.I.2, appendix, p. 144. This was no mere slip, since he said the same some pages later: the constitution 'cannot be controlled, or altered without the express consent of the body politic of three fourths of the states in the union, or, of the people, of an equal number of the states. To prevent the necessity of an immediate appeal to the latter, a method is pointed out, by which amendments may be proposed and ratified by the concurrent act of two thirds of both houses of congress, and three fourths of the state legislatures: but if congress should neglect to propose amendments in this way, when they may be deemed necessary, the concurrent sense of two thirds of the state legislatures may enforce congress to call a convention, the amendments proposed by which, when ratified by the conventions of three fourths of the states, become valid, as a part of the constitution'. Ibid., note D.I.8, appendix, p. 171.

[60]. It is interesting that Condorcet in his 1788 comments on the American constitutional proposals argued for a substantial supermajority of states in the ratification process as a means of increasing the probability that

The right of the majority to bind the minority, results from a due regard to the peace of society; and the little chance of unanimity in large societies or assemblies, which, if obtainable, would certainly be very desirable; but inasmuch as that is not to be expected, whilst the passions, interests and powers of reason remain upon their present footing among mankind, in all matters relating to the society in general, some mode must be adopted to supply the want of unanimity. The most reasonable and convenient seems to be, that the will of the majority should supply this defect; for if the will of the majority is not permitted to prevail in questions where the whole society is interested, that of the minority necessarily must. The society therefore, in such a case, would be under the influence of a minority of its members, which, generally speaking, can on no principle be justified.

It is true there are cases, even under our own constitution, where the vote of a bare majority is not permitted to take effect; but this is only in points which have, or may be presumed to have, received the sanction of a former majority, as where an alteration in the constitution is proposed.[61]

On the whole, the states had decided constitutional matters initially by plain majorities, and in particular the Constitution had been ratified by straight majorities within the conventions.

there would be a majority of the population in favour of the Constitution. *Oeuvres*, vol. VIII, p. 104.

[61.] Ibid., note D I.6, appendix, pp. 168–9.

Strikingly, Tucker quoted *in extenso* in support of his reading of the Constitution Federalist No. 39 by James Madison. Madison had argued there that

> the constitution is to be founded on the assent and ratification of the people of America, given by deputies elected for the special purpose; but on the other, that this assent and ratification is to be given by the people, not as individuals composing one entire nation, but as composing the distinct and independent states to which they respectively belong. It is to be the assent and ratification of the several states, derived from the supreme authority in each state . . . [ellipsis in the original] the authority of the people themselves. The act, therefore, establishing the constitution, will not be a *national*, but a *federal* act.
>
> That it will be a federal, and not a national act, as these terms are understood by the objectors, the act of the people, as forming so many independent states, not as forming one aggregate nation, is obvious from this single consideration, that it is to result neither from the decision of a *majority* of the people of the union, nor from that of a *majority* of the states. It must result from the *unanimous assent* of the several states that are parties to it, differing no otherwise from their ordinary assent than in its being expressed, not by the legislative authority, but by that of the people themselves. Were the people regarded in this transaction as forming one nation, the will of the majority of the whole people of the United States would bind the minority; in the same manner as the majority in each state must bind the minority; and the will of the majority must be determined either by a comparison of the individual votes, or by considering the will of the majority of the

states, as evidence of the will of a majority of the people of
the United States. Neither of these rules has been adopted.
Each state, in ratifying the constitution, is considered as a
sovereign body, independent of all others, and only to be
bound by its own voluntary act. In this relation, then, the
new constitution will, if established, be a *federal*, and not a
national constitution.[62]

If we read this passage (so to speak) through Tucker's eyes, we
see that Madison too was using the distinction between sovereign and government, and that he was claiming that a sovereign people (in each state) could share its *government*, but not
its *sovereignty*, with other peoples. He was also using, as a test
for the location of sovereignty, the majority will – it was
precisely because the Constitution did not have to be ratified
by a majority of American citizens that one could say that
there was not a national sovereign. The idea that sovereign
states could share governments, though uncommon in the
tradition I have been discussing, was not inconsistent with it,
as long as the sovereigns retained some kind of institutional
shape and power of fundamental legislation – which ratifying
conventions plausibly possessed. Madison has often been seen
as inconsistent in his views, with examples of both federalist
and anti-federalist sentiments easily extracted from his
writings and speeches;[63] but if we too distinguish between

[62] George W. Carey and James McClellan (ed.), *The Federalist*
(Indianapolis: The Liberty Fund, 2001), pp. 196–7.
[63] For a discussion, see Gordon Wood, 'Is there a "James Madison
problem"?' in David Womersley (ed.), *Liberty and American Experience
in the Eighteenth Century* (Indianapolis: Liberty Fund, 2006), pp. 425–48.

sovereignty and government we can see that he was no more inconsistent than Rousseau had been when he opposed democratic government while upholding democratic sovereignty. It was perfectly possible to defend almost any form of national government, and any degree of its power over, for example, states' legislatures, while still holding that the people of each state remained separate and sovereign entities, though their sovereignty would be expressed only through ratifying conventions. All the disputes over how to interpret the Constitution, and the balance it drew between state and federal legislatures, were then merely disputes over the form of *government*.[64] On this account, Tucker was correct to see Madison as an ally (something Madison may have recognised when as president he appointed him judge of the federal court for the district of Virginia).

But this view, that a national government was consistent with sovereign states, became increasingly unpopular, no doubt because of the struggles over such things as the Virginia Resolutions (which Madison had supported). Instead, federalists came to insist that the Constitution had been ratified over the heads of the state legislatures by the American people *as a whole*, despite the obvious cogency of the remarks

---

[64.] See the interesting remarks by Madison in a letter of 29 December 1798, to Jefferson: 'Have you ever considered thoroughly the distinction between the power of the *State*, & that of *the Legislature*, on questions relating to the federal pact. On the supposition that the former is clearly the ultimate Judge of infractions, it does not follow that the latter is the legitimate organ, especially as a Convention was the organ by which the Compact was made'. Julian P. Boyd et al. (ed.), *The Papers of Thomas Jefferson* (Princeton University Press, 1950), vol. xxx, p. 606.

in Federalist No. 39 against this idea. Thus John Marshall, in perhaps the most famous statement of this principle, asserted in his judgement in the case of *McCulloch* v. *the State of Maryland* (on whether Congress had the power to found a bank) in 1819 that

> The Convention which framed the constitution was indeed elected by the State legislatures. But the instrument, when it came from their hands, was a mere proposal, without obligation, or pretensions to them. It was reported to the then existing Congress of the United States, with a request that it might 'be submitted to a Convention of Delegates, chosen in each State by the people thereof . . .' This mode of proceeding was adopted, and by the Convention, by Congress, and by the State Legislatures, the instrument was submitted to the people. They acted upon it in the only manner in which they can act safely, effectively, and wisely, on such a subject, by assembling in Convention. It is true, they assembled in their several States – and where else should they have assembled? No political dreamer was ever wild enough to think of breaking down the lines which separate the States, and of compounding the American people into one common mass.[65] Of consequence, when they act, they act in their States. But the measures they

[65] This was not in fact true: George Read, one of the Delaware delegates to the Constitutional Convention, urged that 'The State Govts must be swept away' (*The Records of the Federal Convention of 1787*, vol. i, p. 143) and 'There can be <no> cure for this evil but in doing away States altogether and uniting them all into <one> great Society' (vol. i, p. 202). See also vol. i, pp. 206, 463, 471. He apparently found no support for this in the Convention. See Maier, *Ratification*, p. 142 for a similar plea from a township in Maine.

adopt do not, on that account, cease to be the measures of the people themselves, or become the measures of the State governments.[66]

This picture, in which the conventions operated like English constituencies or French districts, was endorsed by the founder of the Harvard Law School Nathan Dane in his *Abridgement of American Law* (1829). As he said,

> The *ratification* alone gave it [the constitution] validity, and this was all done by *individual* voters, voting in 13 places by majorities, minorities individually opposing, absent persons and voters submitting, as far as any of them were legally able to submit. Voting, to ratify in different states, could be no more in principle than voting to ratify in different departments in France, or here, in different counties and towns ... I repeat, the ratification alone was of any importance, and that was by *individual* citizens, voting in their natural sovereignty.[67]

---

[66] US Reports 17 (4 Wheaton) (1819), p. 403. It should also be noted that Marshall's most famous judgement, his defence of judicial review in *Marbury* v. *Madison*, relied precisely on the claim that the sovereign legislative power of the people was expressed in the Constitution and was always intended to control acts of the government. US Reports 5 (1 Cranch) (1803), pp. 176–7. See also Hamilton in Federalist No. 78: 'where the will of the legislature, declared in its statutes, stands in opposition to that of the people, declared in the constitution, the judges ought to be governed by the latter, rather than the former' (*The Federalist*, p. 404).

[67] *General Abridgement and Digest of American Law*, vol. ix (1829), appendix, pp. 37–8.

This was on the face of it quite inconsistent with a strong majoritarian commitment, as Madison had observed. But Dane was wholly unwilling to abandon the principle that a majority must make political decisions and was led by this to produce the remarkably fallacious argument that the requirement that a supermajority of states had to approve an amendment or ratify the Constitution meant that a majority of the *population* of the Union had to approve it.

> [I]n ratifying the Federal Constitution, the major votes of *individuals* in nine states were required to ratify it, counting by *states*. Counting *individual* votes had been the same, as a majority of them was required in each, and every one of the nine states; the ratifying majorities put together, were, necessarily, more in numbers, than the opposing minorities put together.[68]

But the very fact that he felt it necessary to make this claim shows how much jurists of his generation and location were still wedded to the will of the majority as a basis for all political association, and were desperate to find some way of combining this with their support for a fully federal union.

The views of Marshall and Dane were summed up in the most authoritative account of the Constitution before the Civil War, that was produced by their protégé Joseph Story. As he said,

> The truth is, that the majority of every organized society has always claimed, and exercised the right to govern the whole of that society, in the manner pointed out by the

[68.] Ibid., appendix, p. 38.

fundamental laws, which from time to time have existed in
such society . . . The minority are bound, whether they
have assented or not; for the plain reason, that opposite
wills in the same society, on the same subjects, cannot
prevail at the same time; and, as society is instituted for the
general safety and happiness, in a conflict of opinion the
majority must have a right to accomplish that object by the
means, which they deem adequate for the end. The
majority may, indeed, decide, how far they will respect the
rights or claims of the minority . . . But this is a matter on
which it decides for itself, according to its own notions
of justice or convenience. In a general sense the will of the
majority of the people is absolute and sovereign, limited
only by its means and power to make its will effectual.[69]

But Story also repeatedly insisted that the ratification of the
Constitution had produced a single people, devoting several
pages to a point-by-point refutation of Tucker's argument,
and endorsing Daniel Webster's famous speech to the Senate
in 1830, in which he had said that 'Doubtless the people of

[69.] *Commentaries on the Constitution of the United States*, vol. 1 (Boston,
1833), p. 299. See also the striking remarks by Henry Baldwin in the
Supreme Court in 1831. 'We can . . . expound the constitution without a
reference to the definitions of a state or nation by any foreign writer,
hypothetical reasoning, or the dissertations of the Federalist. This would
be to substitute individual authority in place of the declared will of the
sovereign power of the union, in a written fundamental law. Whether it
is the emanation from the people or the states, is a moot question, having
no bearing on the supremacy of that supreme law which from a proper
source has rightfully been imposed upon us by sovereign power. . .'
The Cherokee Nation v. *The State of Georgia* (30 US (5 Peters) 131)
pp. 40–1.

the several states, taken collectively, constitute the people of the United States. But it is in their collective capacity, it is as all the people of the United States, that they establish the Constitution'.[70]

This commitment to majoritarianism ran very deep in the early American republic, something Amar (again) has correctly observed.[71] It was expressed repeatedly by the delegates at Philadelphia; thus Madison said that 'According to the Republican theory ... , Right & power being both vested in the majority, are held to be synonimous', James Wilson said that 'The majority of people wherever found ought in all questions to govern the minority' and that 'It was surely better to let the [minority] be bound hand and foot than the [majority], and Gouverneur Morris said that 'within the State itself a majority must rule, whatever may be the mischief done among themselves'.[72] Madison on occasion voiced

---

[70] Ibid., p. 332. Story's refutation of Tucker takes up the whole of Book III, chapter 2, pp. 279–343. For Webster's speech, in the form cited by Story, see Jonathan Elliot (ed.), *The Debates in the Several State Conventions on the Adoption of the Federal Constitution [etc]*, 2nd ed. (Washington DC, 1836) vol. IV, p. 518.

[71] See in particular his 'Popular sovereignty and constitutional amendment'.

[72] *The Records of the Federal Convention of 1787*, vol. I, p. 318; vol. I, p. 605; vol. II, p. 451; and vol. II, p. 439. Wilson insisted on the same principle in his well-known law lectures of 1790: 'the voice of the majority must be deemed the will of the whole', Kermit L. Hall and Mark David Hall (ed.), *Collected Works* (Indianapolis: Liberty Fund 2007), vol. I, p. 639; a constitution can be changed, and 'A majority of the society is sufficient for this purpose; and if there be nothing in the change, which can be considered as contrary to the act of original association, or to the intention of those who united under it; all are bound to conform to the

anxiety that 'In all cases where a majority are united by a common interest or passion, the rights of the minority are in danger', but the only solution he saw was

> to enlarge the sphere, & thereby divide the community into so great a number of interests & parties, that in the 1st place a majority will not be likely at the same moment to have a common interest separate from that of the whole or of the minority; and in the 2d place, that in case they shd. have such an interest, they may not be apt to unite in the pursuit of it.[73]

In other words, there could be no general constraint on the principle of majoritarianism, and its supposedly dangerous effects could be countered only by making a state sufficiently large that there would as a matter of fact be no single preponderant interest. Even the most famous statement of an apparently anti-majoritarian position from this generation of Americans – Jefferson's appeal in his First Inaugural that all 'will bear in mind this sacred principle, that though the will of the majority is in all cases to prevail, that will, to be rightful, must be reasonable: that the minority possess their equal rights, which equal laws must protect, and to violate would be oppression' – was (to say the least) qualified: it does after all

resolution of the majority. If the act of original association be infringed, or the intention of those who united under it be violated; the minority are still obliged to suffer the majority to do as they think proper; but are not obliged to submit to the new government. They have a right to retire, to sell their lands, and to carry off their effects. (Ibid., p. 712).

[73.] *The Records of the Federal Convention of 1787*, vol. I, pp. 135–6. See also vol. II, pp. 273–4.

contain the flat assertion that 'the will of the majority is in all cases to prevail'.[74] And elsewhere Jefferson repeatedly endorsed majoritarianism (one example: 'Every man, and every body of men on earth, possess the right of self-government: they receive it with their being from the hand of nature. Individuals exercise it by their single will: collections of men, by that of their majority; for the law of the *majority* is the natural law of every society of men').[75] This stress on majoritarianism, it should be said, sat awkwardly with the actual shape of the Constitution as it had emerged from the compromises of Philadelphia, and the twists and turns of American jurists in the first generation or so of the new republic testify to their difficulties in reconciling their fundamental principles with what had been agreed by the delegates. As so often, it was the state constitutions rather than the federal one that most closely corresponded to the political convictions of the Americans.

It should also be said that from the late 1830s this commitment to majoritarianism began to fade, on the part of both nationalists and defenders of states' rights; and part of

[74.] *The Papers of Thomas Jefferson*, vol. xxx, p. 149.

[75.] Ibid., vol. xvii, p. 195 ('Opinion on the constitutionality of the Residence Bill', 15 July 1790). John Adams was a notable exception to this general commitment to majoritarianism – 'the people, when they have been unchecked, have been as unjust, tyrannical, brutal, barbarous, and cruel, as any king or senate possessed of uncontroulable power: the majority has eternally, and without one exception, usurped over the rights of the minority'. (*A Defence of the Constitutions of Government of the United States of America* [London, 1788], vol. iii, p. 218).

the explanation for this may be a recognition that it could not after all be squared with the federal constitutional facts. But it was also the case that Jacksonian democratic movements in the 1830s and 1840s, with their rhetoric of popular majority power, turned out to have disturbing implications, and not only at the level of the ratification of state constitutions,[76] and in pushing back against them many jurists now found themselves repudiating the majoritarian position. An excellent though little-known example is provided by the German nationalist refugee Francis Lieber (most famous for his later drafting of the 'Lieber Code', which set out the legal rules for the Union forces in the Civil War). In his *Manual of Political Ethics* (1839) Lieber expressly attacked the principle of majority rule that had been so important to the earlier Americans.

> One of the great errors into which philosophical politicians have frequently fallen, in consequence of seeking for a government absolutely and abstractedly good, is the idea that the people, being themselves the object of all government as well as the real source of power, the best government will be there, where the people have absolute power ... [T]his proposition rests as so many others, on a deception, owing to the personification of an idea, which means an aggregate, not an abstract. Who are the people?

[76.] See Kyle G. Volk, 'The perils of 'pure democracy': minority rights, liquor politics, and popular sovereignty in antebellum America', *Journal of the Early Republic* 29 (2009), pp 641–79, for an interesting discussion of how temperance movements in the late 1830s and early 1840s tried to use direct local democracy to secure their ends, and how they were met with the cries of 'minority rights' and 'representation'.

Is it one individual or a number of individuals, called, for convenience sake, by one name ...? Are the people an aggregate of a number of individuals with one mind, one will, one impulse, or do the people consist of a majority and a minority? Giving unbounded power to the people means, then, nothing less than giving unbounded power to a majority; for, as a matter of course, the majority must possess it, if the people have it at all. We are repeatedly told, that the people can do what they like; but have they the right to deprive the minority of their property ..., to enslave them, to kill them, as ... the French [did] during the first revolution.[77]

And when it came to the question of sovereignty, Lieber argued – along the lines of what had become standard in Germany in the early nineteenth century – that sovereignty was 'inherent' in the 'nation', or the 'society', and that acts of sovereignty were not merely – or even at all – the acts of a duly constituted sovereign legislator. Instead, like everyone in his tradition, he stressed public opinion and cultural forces as the expression of the national will. 'I understand by public opinion the sense and sentiment of the community, necessarily irresistible, showing its sovereign power everywhere. It is this public opinion which gives sense to the letter, and life to the law: without it the written law is a mere husk'.[78] Beneath Lieber's bombastic prose we can see exactly the theory which Hobbes and Rousseau had so disliked, that a society is the site of sovereignty without being an author of law, and that appeals to 'public opinion' as representative of its views can

[77] *Manual of Political Ethics* (London, 1839), p. 349.   [78] Ibid., pp. 238–9.

carry as much or more weight as clear and express statements of political intention. Lieber's hostility to majoritarianism and his stress on society rather than the state as the site of sovereignty are particularly interesting, given his close relationship to Tocqueville;[79] both in *Political Ethics* and in *Democracy in America* we see European fear of the radical democracy of the French Revolution transplanted to what one might have expected would be the unpropitious soil of America.

The most dramatic illustration of how the political culture of the United States had changed by the 1840s was the response to 'Dorr's Rebellion' in Rhode Island.[80] As I mentioned earlier (above p. 197, n. 20), in 1824 Rhode Island had held a plebiscite on a new constitution and had voted it down. The state continued (uniquely) to be governed by its colonial charter, with inter alia a restricted franchise. Because the General Assembly persistently refused to produce a new constitution, in 1841 a group of citizens led by Thomas Dorr called an unauthorised convention to draft a new one, which was then put to a plebiscite of all white males and overwhelmingly approved.[81] The state government insisted that the new

---

[79.] He assisted Tocqueville and Beaumont in gathering information during their visit, and translated and annotated their work. He remained quite close to Tocqueville.

[80.] For a good discussion of the political ideas involved in the Rebellion, see Christian G. Fritz, *American Sovereigns: The People and America's Constitutional Tradition Before the Civil War* (Cambridge University Press, 2008), pp. 246–76.

[81.] Dorr had apparently originally wanted to include African Americans, but was forced by his supporters to drop the proposal in a characteristic episode of Jacksonian democracy.

constitution was illegal, and in 1842 there were parallel elections for state offices, one under the charter and one under the new constitution. Dorr himself was elected governor by the new electorate. But the governor elected under the charter declared martial law, and the insurgency was forcibly suppressed (though the defenders of the charter later that year themselves called a plebiscite on the old franchise for a new constitution with a much wider suffrage, though it was more limited than on Dorr's constitution). An episode in which one of Dorr's supporters had been arrested eventually made its way in 1849 to the US Supreme Court, since the supporter (appropriately named Martin Luther) claimed that his arrest had been illegal, as the legitimate government of the state was that put in place by the Dorr plebiscite.[82] The case for Luther was argued by the Massachusetts Democrat Benjamin Hallett, and the case against by Daniel Webster, and it became an object of great public interest, with the speeches being printed and widely circulated.

To read Hallett's speech to the court is to be transported back to the world of the 1780s, complete with the express use of the sovereignty–government distinction. In defence of popular majoritarianism he cited extensively Algernon Sidney, Locke, and above all Burgh, as well as the

---

[82.] In particular, he claimed that Article IV of the US Constitution, committing each state to a 'republican form of government', implied that the state constitution had to rest on a popular vote. The judgement of the court was that this article is non-justiciable, a ruling which still stands. *Luther* v. *Borden*, US Reports 48 (7 Howard) (1849), pp. 1–88.

Founders (especially James Wilson), and indeed Story. And he put the essential point absolutely clearly.

> The proposition on the other side is, you must have a statute law to call your Convention and count your votes, and say who shall vote and how, or you cannot take a step to make or alter the frame of government.
>
> It is not so, unless this boasted sovereignty is but a mockery, a delusion, and a snare. Will this Court say to the people of each State in this Union, that true it is they are the source of all political power, but if they [are] to presume to exercise their sovereignty in establishing or changing constitutions of government, without consent of the Legislature, they shall be followed with pains and penalties, enforced by the lawless despotism of Martial Law, and backed by the whole military power of the United States, called out by the President to suppress insurrection and domestic violence! Whenever this tribunal shall proclaim this to be the law, it will have decreed that, in contemplation of law, the people here, as in Great Britain, do not exist.
>
> The serious objection to this position is, that it resolves sovereignty into the government, and takes it from the people. This is plain, because he who *alone* can take the first step is the sovereign.[83]

He went on to argue that sovereignty could not be restricted to a particular set of legally defined voters, even if the definition

---

[83.] *The Right of the People to Establish Forms of Government. Mr Hallett's Argument in the Rhode Island Causes, before the Supreme Court of the United States* (Boston, 1848), pp. 40–1.

was included in a constitution: the majority of the *population* must always have the right to change the Constitution. If the people excluded from the franchise 'are a majority, as in France, in England, and in Rhode Island, then there can be a State wherein the sovereignty is rightfully held by a minority, and the majority of the people are *not* sovereign!' 'This is the theory of the old world, which American liberties have exploded'.[84] Hallett indeed repeatedly contrasted America with Europe in this respect, distinguishing between what he termed 'the American principle of POPULAR government and the European principle of LEGITIMATE government'.[85] He also stressed that in recent years movements such as Dorr's had succeeded in refashioning the constitutions of other states.[86]

But Dorr's Rebellion was the last time such a thing was attempted, and Daniel Webster's speech to the Court expressed the view that was becoming dominant (and which could have come out of the mouth of Sieyès in the 1790s). Having conceded that 'the aggregate community is sovereign,

---

[84.] Ibid., p. 41. On pp. 51–2 he tried to deal with the fact that women and children, in free states, and women, children and slaves in the others, were never included in the franchise, saying that this had been done 'on the common consent of mankind in all governments', but *if a doubt were raised here, it is no argument in favor of limiting the sovereignty to a less number* than all the adult males'. As always, American democrats of this period found it hard to extend their principles to either women or slaves.

[85.] Ibid., p. 47.

[86.] For the truth of this claim see Christian G. Fritz's discussion, above p. 198, n. 20.

but that is not *the* sovereignty which acts in the daily exercise of sovereign power',

> the next principle is, that as the exercise of legislative power and the other powers of government immediately by the People themselves is impracticable, they must be exercised by REPRESENTATIVES of the People: and what distinguishes American Governments as much as anything else from any governments of ancient or of modern times, is the marvellous felicity of their representative system ... The power is with the people; but they cannot exercise it in masses or *per capita*; they can only exercise it by their representatives.[87]

Webster had primarily in mind representative legislatures rather than special conventions, but he conceded that representation could also be exercised through conventions:

> It is true that at the Revolution, when all government was immediately dissolved, the people got together, and what did they do? Did they exercise sovereign power? They began an inceptive organization, the object of which was to bring together representatives of the people, who should form a government. This was the mode of proceeding in those States where their legislatures were dissolved. It was much like that had in England upon the abdication of James the Second.[88]

It was the plebiscite that attracted his special scorn. 'Is it not obvious enough, that men cannot get together and count

---

[87.] *The Rhode Island Question. Mr Webster's Argument in the Supreme Court of the United States, in the Case of Martin Luther v. Luther M. Borden and others* (Washington DC, 1848), pp. 6–7.

[88.] Ibid., p. 8.

themselves, and say they are so many hundreds and so many thousands, and judge of their own qualifications, and call themselves the people, and set up a government?'[89]

This turn against plebiscites, in what had been the region of their birth (and Webster was a native of New Hampshire and senator for Massachusetts), was matched – with much graver consequences – in the South. By the 1850s, the South had been lectured for a generation by John C. Calhoun on the dangers of majoritarianism – though in his case the solution was not simply representation or reserved rights, but 'concurrent majorities', that is, the representation of interest groups rather than individuals (something that intrigued John Stuart Mill, in his own turn from the radical democracy of Bentham and his father, as a possible means 'of limiting the tyranny of the majority').[90] And by 1861 the southern states were able to act accordingly. It is a fact of great interest and importance that of the eleven secessionist states in 1861, seven were legally committed to plebiscites for any constitutional change, but of those seven only Texas and Virginia put their secession to the vote. Virginia split over the result into the present states of Virginia and West Virginia, and Texas shied away from putting the consequential constitutional amendments to the people, including its accession to the Confederacy – which was bitterly opposed

[89] Ibid., p. 9.

[90] In his *Considerations on Representative Government* Mill famously described Calhoun as 'a man who has displayed powers as a speculative political thinker superior to any who has appeared in American politics since the authors of the Federalist'. Mill in *Collected Works*, John M. Robson (ed.), (University of Toronto Press, 1977), vol. XIX, p. 558.

by some who were willing to accept secession from the Union (notably Sam Houston the governor himself, who reluctantly accepted the legality of the secession ordinance, but not of the subsequent constitutional amendments). So in all the plebiscitary states there was what amounted to a coup d'état by the supporters of the Confederacy, and a repudiation of their earlier democratic history. (Though it should also be acknowledged that Georgia decided at just this moment to introduce a plebiscite in order to ratify its secession.) A number of the secessionist conventions in these states addressed the issue but voted popular ratification down; in Alabama one of the speakers revealingly expressed himself as follows, in words which (ironically) mirrored Webster's speech on Dorr's Rebellion:

> I would say a few words upon the proposition to submit the Ordinance of Dissolution to a popular vote. This proposition is based upon the idea that there is a difference between the people and the delegate. It seems to me that this is an error. There is a difference between the representatives of the people in the law-making body and the people themselves, because there are powers reserved to the people by the Convention of Alabama, and which the General Assembly cannot exercise. But in this body [i.e. the Secessionist Convention] is all power–no powers are reserved from it. The people are here in the persons of their deputies. Life, Liberty and Property are in our hands. Look to the Ordinance adopting the Constitution of Alabama. It states 'we the people of Alabama', &c., &c. All our acts are supreme, without ratification, because they are the acts of the people acting in their sovereign capacity.

As a policy, submission of this Ordinance to a popular vote is wrong ... The policy is at war with our system of government. Ours is not a pure Democracy–that is a government by the people–though it is a government of the people. Ours is a representative government, and whatever is done by the representative in accordance with the Constitution is law; and whatever is done by the deputy in organizing government is the people's will.[91]

And we should remember that this fear of the popular vote on the part of the secessionists was fear of a *white* electorate.

The most extensive response to the means which the Southern secessionists had chosen to force their views on their populations came just after the Civil War had ended, in the form of the Chicago jurist John Jameson's book *The Constitutional Convention* (1867), which proved influential well into the twentieth century.[92] The book was a sustained attack on the idea that constitutional conventions had some kind of sovereignty, including (as one would have expected) a

---

[91.] William Lowndes Yancey in *The History and the Debates of the Convention of the People of Alabama*, William R. Smith (ed.), (Montgomery, AL, 1861), pp. 114–15. He went on to claim that 'The Constitution of the State of Alabama was never submitted for popular ratification', a misleading remark since, as I observed above in p. 198, n. 20 the 1819 Alabama constitution, while not itself ratified by a plebiscite, prescribed them for constitutional amendments, which were duly passed by the procedure until 1861.

[92.] A particularly good and (given Jameson's views on the franchise) surprising example: John Dewey in his early essay on sovereignty cites Jameson as an authority and follows his account of the US Constitution. 'Austin's theory of sovereignty', *Political Science Quarterly* 9 (1894), pp. 31–52.

denunciation of Hallett's argument in the Dorr case as a 'most ingenious defence of anarchical principles' and an endorsement of Webster's 'masterly statement of the principles of the American system of government'.[93] And Jameson made absolutely clear in his attack on Hallett that the way to think about the issue was in terms of *corporate identity*, using a language that could have been found in, for example, Pufendorf.

> [I]f the entire population of a State could, as it often expressed, 'meet upon some vast plain,' so long as that population was organized under a Constitution, like those with which we are familiar, though it would be physically able to carry into execution such ordinances as should get themselves passed at its tumultuous parliament, it clearly would have no *constitutional* or *legal* right to pass an ordinance at all. Such an assemblage would not constitute, in a political sense, The People. The people of a State is the *political body – the corporate unit –* in which are vested ... the ultimate powers of sovereignty; not its inhabitants or population, considered as individuals.[94]

Accordingly, Jameson did not criticise the Southern Conventions for their refusal to put secession to the electorate (though he did attack the idea that for constitutional change 'there was needed but a vote of a few conspirators, sitting as a Constitutional Convention, pretending to utter the voice of the people, and refusing to submit their ordinances to the test of a popular vote').[95] Instead, he explicitly followed Lieber in

---

[93.] Jameson, *The Constitutional Convention*, p. 227. [94.] Ibid., p. 232.
[95.] Ibid., p. 3.

seeing multiple sites of representation within the American state, of which the electorate was merely one.

> Within the sphere allotted to the electors in the scheme of government, they constitute a strictly representative body. But it is only one of a number of such bodies. The three ordinary departments of a government – the legislative, executive, and judicial – are also representatives of the same constituent, the sovereign ... Because, judging from the visible operations of government, the electors seem to be the basis of the entire system, they are usually denominated [by] *the people*. From this circumstance has arisen a common misapprehension, to the effect, that the electors are the source and possessors of all sovereign rights – the real sovereign. When it is considered, however, that this body is a variable one, the number and qualifications of those who compose it depending on the determinations from time to time of that power lying still further back, by whom the Constitution itself is enacted, the position of electoral sovereignty is seen to be untenable. The electors merely represent the sovereign, and are under all the conditions of responsibility and of limitation of power which attach to the departments at the next remove from the source of sovereignty, generally denominated the government.[96]

[96.] Ibid., pp. 314–15. For his continued belief in this position (with further praise of Lieber), see his essay 'National sovereignty', *Political Science Quarterly* 5 (1890), pp. 193–213. See *The Constitutional Convention*, pp. 317–18, for his attack on universal suffrage as impractical – 'The "right of suffrage" comes thus to be practically only a right of one man to represent many other men'. So a convention (he thought) can disenfranchise existing electors.

And he also sounded like Lieber (or, indeed, Pufendorf) in his criticisms of majoritarianism:

> Nature knows nothing of any majority but that of force. Anterior, then, to any positive institutions, and this side an appeal to force, nothing less than the whole can rightfully bind the whole. It is only when a political society, with positive laws and compacts, has been established, that the whole can be bound by the action of a number less than the whole; and the number to which shall be accorded the power to act for the whole, and the conditions under which it may so act, are matters of positive regulation, in which alone they find their warrant.[97]

We should bear in mind that Jameson's book was published during the run-up to the Fifteenth Amendment, which conferred the vote upon African Americans, and against that background his repeated opposition to universal suffrage, and majoritarianism gains added significance. What we might call the 'representative' (or even, the 'German') theory of sovereignty, in the context of the 1860s, could act as a brake on the extension of the franchise, something Jameson himself illustrated when as a judge he ruled against an attempt to include women in the franchise in Hyde Park, Chicago, in a judgement which repeated almost word for word his arguments in Constitutional Conventions.[98] And it is hard not to

---

[97] Ibid., p. 526.

[98] *Chicago Legal News*, vol. IV, no. 14 (13 January 1872). 'For our present purposes, the most important fact . . . is that our government is a *representative* one . . . [T]he right *to be represented* is not the right *to be a representative*'.

think that the rolling back of Reconstruction and the introduction of Jim Crow may have been made intellectually easier
by this turn away from majoritarian democracy even among
supporters of the Union in mid-century America.

The kind of approach that Jameson followed was to be
found in many late-nineteenth-century accounts of the American
Constitution.[99] In the first decade or so of the twentieth century it
was challenged by writers of the Progressive Era, as popular
ballot initiatives came to be enshrined in many states' laws
(and as interest in referendums also spread across Europe).[100]

[99.] For the idea that the American political system is profoundly *anti*-
majoritarian, see, for example, Thomas Cooney's *The General Principles
of Constitutional Law in the United States of America* (Boston: Little,
Brown and Company, 1880), pp. 40–1. 'All the safeguards which under
kingly government were ever interposed against the tyrannical power of
rulers are incorporated in the bills of rights in the American
constitutions as absolute limitations laid on the power of the majority
for the protection of the liberty, property, privileges, and immunities
of the minority, and of every individual citizen; and the judiciary is
given a power to enforce these limitations, irrespective of the will or
control of the legislature, such as it has never possessed in any other
country. So far then from the government being based on unlimited
confidence in majorities, a profound distrust of the discretion, equity,
and justice of their rule is made evident in many precautions and
checks, and the majority is in fact trusted with power only so far as is
absolutely essential to the working of republican institutions'.

[100.] A good example from America is the introduction by Charles Beard and
Birl E. Schultz to their *Documents on the State-Wide Initiative,
Referendum and Recall* (New York: The Macmillan Company, 1912).
(Beard was the famous Progressive historian.) See also Charles Sumner
Lobingier, *The People's Law or Popular Participation in Law-making
from Ancient Folk-Moot to Modern Referendum: A Study in the
Evolution of Democracy and Direct Legislation* (New York:

But, as is well known, this revival of direct democracy petered out in the United States after the Progressive period ended and the European interest in referendums faded after the First World War (with the notable and unfortunate exception of the Weimar Republic, whose adoption of the referendum and ballot initiative in these years needs more explanation than it usually receives),[101] and the Left between the wars was not

The Macmillan Company, 1909), with its resounding epigraph from Rousseau: 'Every law which the people in person have not ratified is invalid; it is not a law', and Walter Fairleigh Dodd, *The Revision and Amendment of State Constitutions* (Baltimore: The Johns Hopkins Press, 1910) in which Jameson is specifically rebutted (pp. 73–9, and p. vi: 'Judge Jameson's work constructed a theory regarding constitutional conventions, which conformed more or less closely to the facts, but in which the facts were subordinated to the theory'). There seems to be no full modern discussion of this aspect of Progressive politics' (though see Thomas Goebel, *Government by the People: Direct Democracy in America, 1890–1940*), (University of North Carolina Press, 2002). For England there is a useful brief survey in J. Meadowcroft and M. W. Taylor, 'Liberalism and the referendum in British political thought 1890–1914', *Twentieth-Century British History* 1 (1990), pp. 35–57. An interesting link between the English and American debates in these years is provided by the American Samuel Robertson Honey's *The Referendum Among the English: A Manual of 'Submissions to the People' in the American States* (London: Macmillan and Co. Ltd, 1912), which had an Introduction advocating the use of constitutional referendums in England by John St. Loe Strachey.

101. The fullest study of the adoption of the referendum in Weimar is Reinhard Schiffers, *Elemente direkter Demokratie im Weimarer Regierungssystem* (Dusseldorf: Droste Verlag, 1971). Schiffers takes the story of the referendum in Germany to begin with Moritz Rittinghausen, who was a kind of Utopian Socialist in the 1840s (for an English translation of his principal work, published unsurprisingly in the US in 1897, see Martin [sic] Rittinghausen, *Direct Legislation by the*

particularly interested in reversing this trend.[102] By the 1950s and 1960s the 'representative' account of politics in general and the American Constitution in particular seemed always to have been true; so that even Bernard Bailyn could say of the Revolution that 'the course of intellectual, as well as of political and military, events had brought into question the entire concept of a unitary, concentrated, and absolute governmental sovereignty', thereby confusing exactly the two things – sovereignty and government – which the Revolutionaries had wished to keep distinct.[103] The same could be said of Edmund Morgan, despite his recognition of a difference between the two terms, since his *Inventing the People* (1988) had as its central theme what he repeatedly termed the 'fiction' of popular sovereignty, represented (on his account) by a shifting set of institutions, from the English Parliament to the American

People, trans. Alexander Harvey) (New York: The Humboldt Library, 1897). But Rittinghausen was really a kind of Jacobin, keen on putting every policy issue to the popular vote; Marx and Engels (who knew him) treated him with some disdain, and Karl Kautsky attacked his ideas – an interesting further example (in at least Kautsky's case) of the Left's hostility to plebiscitary democracy. The origins of the referendum in Weimar still need explaining, and in particular it would be helpful to have some sense of the degree to which recent American practice made its way into the Constitution. Max Weber certainly drew on the example of America in his argument for a plebiscitary presidency for Germany, and his protégé Richard Thoma in his analysis of the plebiscitary elements of the Weimar constitution used the term *recall*, in English, suggesting that he had in mind American Progressive practice. (Arthur J. Jacobson and Bernhard Schlink (ed.), *Weimar: A Jurisprudence of Crisis* (University of California Press, 2000), p. 161).

[102.] For the English Left, see Meadowcroft and Taylor, pp. 56–7.

[103.] *The Ideological Origins of the American Revolution* (Harvard University Press, 1967), p. 228.

constitutional conventions to a national government.[104] In recent years this has once again begun to change; in particular Bruce Ackerman and Akhil Amar have stressed the role of democratic politics in the American Constitution, though seen from my perspective Ackerman has continued to incorporate some of the 'representative' view, since he has argued that moments such as the New Deal represent a refashioning of the Constitution, despite the fact that it did not involve the kind of deliberate action at a foundational level which the eighteenth-century democrats envisaged.[105] My own view is closer to Amar's, though (unlike him) I want to place the American democratic experience in a broader European context, and I also see it as more contested and fragile – the history of the United States, like that of Europe, consists of counter-revolution as much as revolution.

[104] Edmund S. Morgan, *Inventing the People: The Rise of Popular Sovereignty in England and America* (New York: W.W. Norton and Company, 1988). See pp. 80–1 for his discussion of constituent power. In general, his governing assumptions were broadly those of Sieyès.

[105] Bruce Ackerman, *We The People* (Harvard University Press, 1991, 1998). For this aspect of the New Deal see particularly vol. ii, pp. 342–50; and see vol. ii, pp. 100–16 for Ackerman's discussion of the awkward legal status of the Thirteenth and Fourteenth Amendments (important examples of refashioning which seem to ignore the provisions of the original Constitution).

Conclusion

I now want to make some general points about the story I have been telling in this book. As I have stressed from the start, the appearance of a clear conceptual distinction between *sovereignty* and *government* was a necessary precondition for the emergence of a distinctively modern idea of democracy, in which the mass of the citizens could genuinely participate in politics as long as their participation was limited to a set of fundamental acts of legislation. Paradoxically, as we saw in Chapter 1, the distinction arose in the context of ancien régime France, and Jean Bodin's attempt to theorise the unusual constitutional arrangements of his society; but even in Bodin's work, and certainly immediately after it, the implications of his idea for a theory of democracy were quickly grasped. Before Bodin, democracy implied *government* by citizens, in a legislature of some kind, and though it was widely supposed that in some sense 'the people' lay behind all political structures, they did not do so as legislators. After him, the citizens could be thought of (if one wished) as Bodinian sovereigns, formally authorising a set of fundamental laws, though not necessarily of *authoring* it – does Parliament as a whole *write* the law? Under any system the legislator or legislature is unlikely to be the person or body that actually drafts the wording of a piece of legislation.

From antiquity down to the eighteenth century all societies had characteristically possessed sites of legislative

249

authority that dealt indifferently with matters of general constitutional significance and matters of limited or local importance. The United Kingdom is a fine example of such an
arrangement: it still possesses a site of this kind, for there is
no institutional or structural difference between acts of Parliament, which undeniably have a fundamental or constitutional
character, such as the Act of Settlement, the Act of Union, the
Parliament Act or the European Communities Act, and –
say – an act prescribing the organisation of the London police
force.[1] In this respect (as one might expect on other grounds)
the United Kingdom remains premodern in its political structures, if modernity is marked (as I think it is) by precisely
the kind of theorising with which I am concerned. It can be
contrasted with societies in which there is an institutional
division between constitutional and other kinds of legislation,
and in which as a consequence it is possible to talk about the

[1.] This may be changing, in two ways. First, some jurists have begun to
speculate that beneath the surface constitutional acts may be seen in a
different light from ordinary ones. For example, Lord Justice Laws
suggested in *Thoburn* v. *Sunderland City Council* (2003, QB 151) – the
famous so-called Metric Martyrs Case dealing with the implications of the
European Communities Act – that these constitutional acts are immune
to implied repeal; that is, whereas acts of Parliament have normally been
taken to repeal implicitly previous statutes or clauses of statutes with
which they are in conflict, Laws argued that this doctrine might not apply
to constitutional statutes, which could only be explicitly repealed or
amended. This view has so far remained speculation and has not become
a standard part of British jurisprudence. Second, it is increasingly the case
that constitutionally significant acts have been passed (or are thought to
need passage) against the background of a 'consultative' referendum,
something which is moving the United Kingdom towards the default
constitutional structure of a modern state.

society as possessing a written constitution, in the sense of a segregated set of laws generated in some distinctive fashion, as in the United States. As has often been observed (most recently by John Gardner in a stimulating essay),[2] Britain *does* have a written constitution, as much as any country does: the foundational Acts I just mentioned are, after all, written down, and the fact that there is a great deal *unwritten* which is part of constitutional practice would not distinguish Britain from the United States or any other country with a written constitution. What Britain does not have is a separate legislator for specifically constitutional measures, and in this respect, as I said, it is the same as all political associations used to be until the eighteenth century.

It is a familiar piece of history that written constitutions did not appear until (arguably) the 1770s when (as we saw in Chapter 4) the newly independent states of North America began to draft them, followed by the current US Constitution, the French constitutions of the 1790s, and all the modern constitutional documents thereafter. And we tend to think that what was new was the idea of writing a constitution down. But once we approach the question from the direction with which I have been concerned, we can see that what was really new was the idea not of writing fundamental laws – for legislators had always done that – but of handing the authority to write the laws to an institution that might put in only fleeting appearances and be largely forgotten during

---

[2] Leslie Green and Brian Leiter (eds), 'Can there be a written constitution?' in *Oxford Studies in Philosophy of Law*, vol. 1 (Oxford University Press, 2011), pp. 162–94.

the actual political activity of a community. I expect, for example, that there will be no new amendment to the US Constitution in my lifetime (unless Larry Lessig can miraculously succeed in his campaign to use the amending procedure to overturn the Citizens United judgement). Put in this way – that the sovereign legislator has an institutional shape but is usually dormant – we can see the oddity of the idea, and why it proved so hard to imagine prior to the eighteenth century and prior to a proper understanding of the distinction whose history I have been tracing.

It was also an idea that has always occasioned a great deal of explicit opposition. As we saw in Chapter 2, the opponents of Bodin and (later) Hobbes, in their enmity towards the possibility of democratic sovereignty in a modern state,[3] reverted to something strikingly close in practice to the medieval theories of representation. (Though Hobbes, too, uses the language of representation, as I also showed in Chapter 2 he did so in a way that significantly differed from both his medieval predecessors and his contemporaries, and which linked him much more closely to Rousseau than to Pufendorf.) What these opponents, beginning with Grotius and Pufendorf, asserted was that (in the imagery of Grotius's *De Iure Belli ac Pacis*) the 'common subject of sovereignty' was a political community (what Grotius termed a *coetus*), just as the 'common subject' of sight was the body, while the 'proper subject' of sovereignty was the government, just as

---

[3.] They were much less troubled by a theory of democracy as possible through a small governing assembly of the whole people, since few modern Europeans lived under such a system.

the 'proper subject' of sight was the eye. The eye sees on behalf of the body, but the body does not itself see – so that the legislative activity in which the 'proper' subject engaged was quite different from the activity of the 'common' subject. The common subject was not the sovereign legislator of the Bodinian or (the Hobbesian/Rousseauian) theory, but was much closer to the vaguely specified people or *respublica* of Vitoria. Fifty years later, and spurred on by the need to refute Hobbes, Pufendorf took this idea and gave it a more technically precise formulation with his theory of the double contract: individuals in a state of nature formed a society by contracting with one another, and that society then determined its form of government. But before government was established, Pufendorf made clear, the society had a kind of provisional status, since by definition it could not rule itself or its members; he expressed this by describing it as based on an agreement by the citizens to *discuss* the conditions for their common existence, rather than to *decide* them. And when the society made the decision about its government, that need not have been – and in fact ought not to have been – a decision to be ruled democratically. Hobbes had rejected the Grotian version of this idea, insisting that the formation of a society by individuals *was* the formation of a fundamental site of legislation, and moreover (he argued in *De Cive* of 1642) necessarily a democratic one, and it was this in particular that seems to have alarmed Pufendorf. Both Grotius and Pufendorf were fully aware of the fact that their view was an alternative to the idea of a distinction between sovereign and government, and both expressly attacked the distinction, Pufendorf describing it with disdain as something merely 'with Subtilty enough [to] be disputed in the Schools'. So when Rousseau in the mid-eighteenth century turned against both Pufendorf and Grotius as the representatives of the ideology that underpinned the ancien régime, he naturally returned both to the Hobbesian picture, though purged (as he thought) of its dangerous inconsistencies, and to the distinction, which he used repeatedly in his works and upheld as the new key needed to understand democracy.

But the two views remained in contest with one another throughout the Revolutionary period. In the newly independent states of America the settlers quickly realised that they could give an appropriate institutional expression to the idea of democracy at the level of sovereignty but not government by the institution of a referendum on the articles of a written constitution. The first such plebiscite in the world was duly held in Massachusetts in 1778 to ratify the state constitution, to be followed within the next two generations by almost all the states of the Union (though of course the federal Constitution was not to be ratified in this manner). The Girondins in France went down the same route, as I showed in Chapter 3, though apparently in some ignorance of what Massachusetts had done twelve years earlier (as distinct from the federal Constitutional Convention, which the Girondins studied closely). But just as the ideas of Bodin or Hobbes had been challenged from the point of view of older political theories in the seventeenth century, so too were the ideas of Rousseau, the Americans and the Girondins.

And once again the principal alternatives resembled pre-Bodinian ideas. Monarchism of the old kind was now dead, but its principal executioner, Jacobinism, was also in effect pre-Bodinian. It claimed to be in the vanguard of modern democracy, but it wished to have democratic government as well as democratic sovereignty, as if France could be ruled by an ancient citizen assembly or a medieval commune. As the Jacobins' opponents tirelessly observed, this led inevitably in practice for obvious reasons to the rule of the Parisian mob and the marginalisation of the rest of France. But after the Terror and the slaughter of so many of the Girondin leaders, the principal challenge to the Jacobins was voiced by the Abbé Sieyès, and though some recent scholars have linked Sieyès to the Rousseauian tradition, I argued in Chapter 3 that he was in fact a critic of it. In its place, like Pufendorf, he wanted to see a distinction between the site of legislation and the 'nation', and he asserted strenuously that representation must be the key feature of any modern state, including, ideally, even the authorisation of a constitution by representatives. Unlike Pufendorf, however, he believed in multiple sites of representation, and he became increasingly unwilling to use the language of sovereignty – 'this word [sovereignty] only looms so large in our imagination because the spirit of the French, full of royal superstitions, felt under an obligation to endow it with all the heritage of pomp and absolute power which made the usurped sovereignties shine'.[4]

The liberal anti-Jacobin constitutionalism of Sieyès became in many ways the default theory of the nineteenth century, even in America (as I argued in Chapter 4). And it

---

[4] See above p. 176. Paul Bastid (ed.), *Les Discours de Sieyès dans les débats constitutionnels de l'an III* (Paris: Librairie Hachette, 1939), p. 17.

has remained the most congenial approach to constitutional theory for many contemporaries. A particularly good example is the principal English constitutional theorist of our time, Martin Loughlin, who has argued (with express references to Grotius, Pufendorf and Sieyès)[5] that we should think of sovereignty not as a power located in a specific site, but rather as an expression of the fact that there are no political constraints on what an independent community can do. Like Sieyès, he claims that 'the people' is an entity that cannot act in its own right but can act only through representation, and that there can be multiple sites of representation. One such site, on this modern view, is public opinion;[6] this is a thought that became particularly important in the immediate post-Revolutionary period,[7] and which (as we saw in Chapter 4) made its way to the United States through the German legal

---

[5.] And to Hobbes, interpreted as a believer in the representation of a state (rather than purely of individuals) by the sovereign. See earlier p. 107 for a discussion of this question.

[6.] *Foundations of Public Law*, pp. 232–3

[7.] A striking example of this is provided by Fichte. In his 1796 *Foundations of Natural Right* he provided a well-known account of a formal constitutional device, the 'ephorate', which could call the people together to remake their constitution and to control their government. (See Frederick Neuhouser (ed.), *Foundations of Natural Right* (Cambridge University Press, 2000), pp. 151–61.) In its broad outlines this clearly owed a great deal to Rousseau. But by 1812, when Fichte returned to the subject in his *System der Rechtslehre*, he repudiated his earlier idea as too subversive of orderly government, and instead asserted that the role of an ephorate in 'civilized' peoples was played not by a formal institution but by public opinion and (*in extremis*) by the possibility of revolution. J. G. Fichte (ed.), *Nachgelassene Werke* (Bonn, 1834), vol. II, pp. 632–4. For a translation of this passage, see *The Science of Rights*, A. E. Kroeger

theorist Francis Lieber, who came to have enormous influence in his adopted country. This is a particularly striking contrast to the ideas of Bodin, Hobbes or Rousseau (though Rousseau did allow a role for opinion in the formation and maintenance of a state), for the essence of their view was that the politics of a society had to be controllable from a single and specific site, so that it was clear what mechanism could be utilised in order to change the circumstances of the citizens' collective existence. The vagueness and multifariousness of representation implied by the modern view, from their perspective, would hand power over to a set of institutions that claimed authority without ever having been clearly given it – this, after all, is exactly why Hobbes was so strenuously opposed to the notion of the common law, which he took to have allowed lawyers to exercise power over their fellow citizens in the name of a set of principles they had themselves invented.

There are, I think, three major reasons for the modern disinclination to accept the radical seventeenth- or eighteenth-century view that a sovereign people can act like a monarchical sovereign through the process of majority voting (apart from a fear about what such a process can give rise to – but there is no known political process that cannot threaten us, and the track record of democratic majoritarianism is actually better than many people suppose).[8] The first

---

(trans.), (Philadelphia: J. P. Lippincott & Co., 1869), pp. 284–5. I owe this observation about Fichte to Isaac Nakhimovsky.

[8.] See, for example, what I said in Chapter 4 about the fear of the American secessionists in 1861 to put their plans to a majority vote of their populations, even despite the limited nature of the electorate in their states. And we should also remember that despite the post-war fear of

is the belief that majoritarianism has no special claim as a principle of political action, and that it does not necessarily correspond to the 'will' of a people.[9] It is merely one among many procedures all of which can issue in results that might be taken to represent the intentions of the community, and it cannot be invoked as the means of choosing among those procedures. The second is a concern that the relationship between states is in danger if we cannot stipulate that they possess an identity over time capable (for example) of being the bearer of the obligation to repay debts, and this identity cannot be expressed in terms of the constantly shifting results of democratic voting. On this account, it cannot be the case that a 'people' is simply the set of nameable individuals whose views on a subject concur and form the majority, or even that it is simply the set of nameable individuals who either form the majority or who accept the majority view as determinative (i.e. including the minority who agree to be bound by the

---

plebiscites in Germany, the Weimar Republic prior to the Hitlerian regime held only two of them, both initiated by groups of citizens rather than the government, and both were lost (one dealt with the position of the princes in the new republic, and the other proposed the withholding of reparations). The legal foundation of Hitler's dictatorship was the Enabling Act of 23 March 1933, which was a Parliamentary statute. Hitler, it should be acknowledged, did put three measures to a popular vote once his dictatorship was in place: cession from the League of Nations, the unification of the offices of Chancellor and President, and *Anschluss*. All were (naturally) passed. But it is not clear that this is enough on which to base a general mistrust of referendums, as distinct from parliamentary acts.

9. This is a view quite commonly attributed to Rousseau, though with very little textual support, as we saw in Chapter 3.

result of the vote). The members of that set change (in a large modern state) every minute or so as people die off and are replaced, so the 'people' will have no stable existence. It has therefore to be a kind of imaginary construct, best understood as an entity represented by some set of institutions with a continuous existence. The third reason is more technical, but carries a great deal of weight with modern jurists; it is that the authority of a law cannot be understood as issuing from the will of a sovereign legislator, since most of the laws that govern us were promulgated by assemblies whose members are long since dead. Modern jurists almost without exception reject the old view that old laws are tacitly renewed by an existing sovereign when it fails to repeal them, and as a consequence they usually take the authority of preexisting law to rest on a set of conventions about what we as a society recognise as authoritative, which once again allow a multiplicity of sites of authority.

None of these objections, I believe, carries as much weight as is often supposed; there are relatively straightforward responses to them which obviate the need to enter upon the unsatisfactory territory of a imagined people. I addressed the first objection in effect in my book *Free Riding* (Harvard University Press 2008); briefly, what I argued there was that from the point of view of an *agent* it makes sense to seek to be part of a majority for a particular course of action he desires, as there is a high probability that (if there is indeed a majority for it) he will be part of what I termed there an 'efficacious set' – that is, a set sufficient (but not *necessary*) to bring about the result. If I care about being someone who contributes causally to an outcome, I have a reason to vote (if I think enough other people are going to do likewise) and to be part of the successful group, though it is true that were I to abstain, the same result would probably be achieved – but without *my* agency. This is an example of what is known as 'redundant causation' – I can cause something to happen even if, were I not to perform the relevant action, another person would take my place – which, though entirely familiar as a phenomenon, has proved remarkably resistant to philosophical analysis. Partly because it is so difficult to understand redundant causation in terms of the standard counterfactual analysis of causality, most modern theorists have simply ignored it and have supposed that the only instrumental reason I might have for voting is that I think I will be the pivotal voter. Because it is highly unlikely that any particular voter will be pivotal, they have then tended to rule out instrumental considerations entirely from voting and have concentrated instead on ideas such as the 'expressive' character of the vote. Once we do this, it is indeed true that majoritarianism loses its distinctiveness, and there may well be more appropriate ways of arriving at political decisions; but if we continue to think in terms of agency then majoritarianism remains an obvious way of structuring politics. Something like this, I believe, was taken for granted by the early writers on majoritarianism.

Jeremy Waldron has sought to defend majoritarianism by stressing its connection to the principle of *equality*,[10] and that is clearly correct: majoritarianism does treat each voter as strictly equivalent to every other, with no distinctions

---

[10.] In his *Law and Disagreement* (Oxford University Press, 1999), especially pp. 101–18.

between them of (e.g.) intelligence or judgement. But Waldron's view in the form he has stated it is vulnerable, as he has acknowledged, to the response that something like a fair lottery for participation in political decision-making would also fulfil the condition of equality among the citizens – every citizen would have an equal chance to play his part as a legislator. This has indeed been argued in recent years by some leading theorists of democracy, notably Bernard Manin, and Waldron's own response is not particularly compelling.[11] However, if one adds to Waldron's argument the need for citizens to *think of themselves as agents*, bringing about (as far as possible) by their own actions the conditions of their common life, then the lottery ceases to be a plausible alternative, as only a very small subset of the group will actually contribute to the outcome. The distinctive feature of majoritarianism is that it is the only principle that offers both equality and agency.[12] Viewing it in this light also allows one to tackle the surprisingly under-theorised question of supermajorities, as a supermajority requirement will bring more people into the position of being causally responsible for the outcome than will a plain majority requirement, but this will need to be balanced against the fact that supermajority requirements may be so hard to meet that the group can take *no* effective action (which generally rules out

[11.] His principal argument is that 'majority-decision differs from the cointossing method in giving positive decisional weight to the fact that a given individual member of the group holds a certain view'. (p. 113).

[12.] It may be significant that Waldron accepts that a vote cast in a large group 'may be said to carry no weight at all' (p. 114), though he is troubled by the implications of this for majoritarianism.

the most extreme version of a supermajority requirement, namely unanimity). (We saw in Chapter 4 that the distinction between majority and supermajority seems in fact to have been of curiously little interest to the eighteenth-century writers.)

Some people have also been troubled by the fact that the population whose votes are counted is not – so to speak – a natural set: even after the democratic revolutions of the nineteenth century, culminating in the extension of the vote to women, it excludes many inhabitants of the state's territory such as children or foreigners. If those inhabitants' views are going to play any part in the political process, it can only be by representation. I agree that this is a problem, but it is an aspect of a very general problem for theories of democracy, namely the territoriality of a modern state. Hobbes, Rousseau and the other writers of this kind finessed the problem by presuming that the formation of a state is the association of individuals, who might then permit other individuals to join them, and in this way come to possess a defined territory – but there are many difficulties to this account, some pointed out by Locke when he stressed that land must already have been owned by the individuals when they entered civil society if their state was to acquire territorial rights. A modern version of these theories is to be found in Robert Nozick's *Anarchy, State, and Utopia*, and we can see from his discussion the problems involved. But it is hard on any view of democratic politics to explain the significance of boundaries and the rights that the state possesses over anyone who steps across them; the merit of the kind of view I am outlining is that at least it makes it the default position that everyone within the boundaries should take part in the vote in order to render its outcome authoritative for everyone, and exclusion of any kind has to be carefully justified. (I would say, for instance, that the modern distinction between 'residency' and 'citizenship', upon which Locke laid so much stress, is hard to justify on a non-representational account of the state, and its role has usually been (as it undoubtedly was in Locke) to privilege one group in the society over another).[13]

On the second issue, the need to ascribe identity to a people in order to permit such things as foreign debt, it is not clear to me that one cannot get quite a lot of what one might want purely by supposing that every member of the voting group takes the outcome to reflect his individual will, however he may have voted (the conventional Hobbesian or Rousseauian view). If a community, for example, takes on a foreign debt through a majority vote in 2012, then the debt has in effect been agreed to by every member of the community that year, and it would not be unreasonable to suppose that those individuals are bound by the undertaking, just as they would be if they incurred a debt solely as individuals. There will not be a possible majority composed of people who had not as individuals been bound by the undertaking until half the voting population of 2012 is dead – which one can roughly calculate as around

[13.] As is now generally understood, I think, the well-known distinction in Locke between 'express' and 'tacit' consent, with only the former implying citizenship, was primarily intended to justify the exclusion from public life of Catholics, who would not take the oath of allegiance in the form in which it had been phrased since its introduction in 1606, which required them to abjure the authority of the Pope.

42 years.[14] Indeed, precisely this argument was put forward by Condorcet in his *Sur la nécessité de faire ratifier la constitution par les citoyens* of August 1789.

> Any law accepted by the plurality [*pluralité*] of the inhabitants of a nation can be taken as having unanimous support: given the need to accept or to reject the law and to follow the plurality opinion [*l'opinion du plus grand nombre*], anyone who rejects a proposed law will already have decided to abide by it if it is supported by the plurality. This kind of unanimous approval will continue for as long as those who were alive at the time continue to form a plurality, since they were all able to consent to live by this law for this length of time. But such approval becomes meaningless as soon as these individuals cease to form a plurality of the nation.
>
> Thus, the length of time for which any constitutional law [*loi constitutionnelle*] can remain in force is the time it takes for half of the citizens alive when the law was passed to be replaced by new ones. This is easily calculated, and takes about 20 years if the age of majority is fixed at 21, and 18 years if the age of majority is 25 [given a much lower life expectancy in eighteenth-century France than in the twenty-first century U.K.].
>
> The same is true of constitutions which are produced by a Convention, because then, once again, the plurality (and by extension all) of the citizens agree to abide by this constitution.

[14.] For example, the UK has an electorate of 45 million and a death rate in the adult population of about 540,000 p.a., so half the current electorate will be dead after approximately 42.5 years.

I consider it very important to set a maximum period for which a law can remain irrevocable. People no longer dare claim that there can legitimately be perpetual laws.[15]

The idea that a society should be free to revisit all its agreements, and potentially repudiate them, after they have been in force (in our case) for forty-two years or so is not (at least as far as I am concerned) at all disturbing, and it is not obvious why one would want a more robust notion of national identity

---

[15.] Condorcet, *Oeuvres*, vol. ix (Paris, 1847), p. 415, translated in *Condorcet: Foundations of Social Choice and Political Theory*, Iain McLean and Fiona Hewitt (trans. and ed.), (Aldershot: Edward Elgar, 1994), p. 272. He added that one should also not have laws that can be 'instantly revoked', though he recognised the problems of this: why should a citizen who had not participated in their formation, because he was born too late, be obliged to obey them? Thomas Jefferson said exactly the same as Condorcet in his well-known letters from Paris to James Madison and Richard Gem, 6 September 1789 (*The Papers of Thomas Jefferson*, vol. xv, pp. 379–99), concluding that nineteen years was the appropriate time. He had presumably just read Condorcet's pamphlet. Twenty-seven years later he was still saying the same thing; see his letter to Samuel Kercheval in 1816: 'It is now forty years since the constitution of Virginia was formed. [The European tables of mortality] inform us, that, within that period, two-thirds of the adults then living are dead. Have then the remaining third, even if they had the wish, the right to hold in obedience to their will, and to laws heretofore made by them, the other two-thirds, who, with themselves, compose the present mass of adults? If they have not, who has? The dead? But the dead have no rights ... This corporeal globe, and everything upon it, belongs to its present corporeal inhabitants, during their generation. They alone have a right to direct what is the concern of themselves alone, and to declare the law of that direction; and this direction can only be made by their majority.' Albert Ellery Bergh (ed.), *The Writings of Thomas Jefferson* (The Memorial Edition), (Washington DC, 1907), vol. xv, pp. 42–3.

in order to meet these kinds of pragmatic objectives. As I have suggested, the modern stress on collective identity frequently looks like a means to counter mass politics, with all their disturbing social possibilities, rather than a genuine response to a major theoretical difficulty. This is, after all, precisely the contrast between Condorcet and Sieyès.

To turn to the last of my three objections: all the theorists of sovereignty with whom I have been dealing in these chapters agreed on one thing, which seemed to them obvious. *All law has force by virtue of the will of the current sovereign*. Bodin voiced this thought when he said in his chapter on sovereignty that

> it is well known that the laws, ordinances, letters patents, privileges and concessions of princes, have force only during their lifetimes unless they are ratified by the express consent, or at least the sufferance, of a prince who is cognizant of them.[16]

(I am not sure this was exactly 'well known' before Bodin, but certainly medieval princes quite regularly formally ratified the acts of their predecessors – Magna Carta, for instance, was confirmed thirty-seven times). Hobbes, unsurprisingly, put the general point in entirely clear terms: 'the Legislator is he, not by whose authority the Lawes were first made, but by whose authority they now continue to be Lawes'.[17]

[16.] Translation from Franklin, *Bodin On Sovereignty*, p. 12. *Republique* 1576, p. 132; 1579, pp. 91–2; *Republica* 1586, p. 85; McRae, p. 91.

[17.] *Leviathan*, pp. 185–6, original ed., p. 139.

Or, some pages later, commenting on *The Decrees of the whole people of Rome*:

> These were Lawes, at first, by the vertue of the Soveraign Power residing in the people; and such of them as by the Emperours were not abrogated, remained Lawes by the Authority Imperiall. For all Lawes that bind, are understood to be Lawes by his authority that has power to repeale them. Somewhile like to these Lawes, are the Acts of Parliament in *England*.[18]

And Rousseau:

> The State subsists by means not of the laws, but of the legislative power. Yesterday's law is not binding to-day; but silence is taken for tacit consent, and the Sovereign is held to confirm incessantly the laws it does not abrogate as it might. All that it has once declared itself to will it wills always, unless it revokes its declaration.
>
> Why then is so much respect paid to old laws? For this very reason. We must believe that nothing but the excellence of old acts of will can have preserved them so long: if the Sovereign had not recognised them as throughout salutary, it would have revoked them a thousand times.[19]

But, very strikingly, exactly the same thing was said by the early American jurists of the Constitution, such as Tucker.

[18.] Ibid., p. 196, original ed., p. 147.
[19.] Book III, chapter 11; Launay (ed.), *Oeuvres complètes*, vol. II, p. 555; *The Social Contract and Discourses*, p. 235.

That mankind have a right to bind themselves by their own voluntary acts, can scarcely be questioned: but how far have they a right to enter into engagements to bind their posterity likewise? Are the acts of the dead binding upon their living posterity, to all generations; or has posterity the same natural rights which their ancestors have enjoyed before them? And if they have, what right have any generation of men to establish any particular form of government for succeeding generations?

The answer is not difficult: 'Government,' said the congress of the American States, in behalf of their constituents, 'derives its just authority from the consent of the governed.' This fundamental principle then may serve as a guide to direct our judgment with respect to the question. To which we may add, in the words of the author of Common Sense, a law is not binding upon posterity, merely, because it was made by their ancestors; but, because posterity have not repealed it. It is the acquiescence of posterity under the law, which continues its obligation upon them, and not any right which their ancestors had to bind them.[20]

[20.] Tucker, *Blackstone's Commentaries*, vol. I, note D I.8, appendix pp. 172–3. Paine's views are set out in the *Rights of Man*, with its fierce attack on Burke for allegedly claiming that the 1688 settlement bound all of posterity. 'It requires but a very small glance of thought to perceive that although laws made in one generation often continue in force through succeeding generations, yet they continue to derive their force from the consent of the living. A law not repealed continues in force, not because it cannot be repealed, but because it is not repealed; and the non-repealing passes for consent' (Eric Foner (ed.), *Rights of Man* (Penguin Books, 1984), p. 44).

And both Bentham and Austin, as is well known, said the same.[21]

But five pages in H. L. A. Hart's *The Concept of Law* seem to have been enough (in the eyes of most modern writers) to have demolished this theory, and this is something on which people seem to be agreed irrespective of whether they agree with Hart's general account of legislation or not.[22] So I would like briefly to deal with Hart's argument. There are in fact two separate claims in *The Concept of Law*, though they are not always clearly distinguished.[23] One is the claim that what Hart considers the 'Austinian' theory of sovereignty is not a necessary account of law *as such*: we can have a 'concept of law' in which the defining characteristic of a valid law is not that it has been promulgated by a person or institution whom we recognise as having a general authority over us, but instead has simply been picked out in accordance with what he called a 'rule of recognition' generally accepted in the society (like a Humean convention). The rule may be simple and specify a king's words as law, or it may be complex, as it is (he thinks) in a modern society, and specify (in a Sieyès-like fashion)

[21.] For Bentham, see, for an example, his remarks on 'susception' in J. H. Burns (ed.), *Of Laws in General* (London: The Athlone Press, 1970), p. 21; for Austin, see H. L. A. Hart (ed.), *The Province of Jurisprudence Determined* (London: Weidenfeld and Nicholson, 1954), chapter 6, p. 347 (and see also Chapter 1, pp. 30–2, on customary law).

[22.] Again, Amar is an honourable exception. See his 'Philadelphia revisited: amending the Constitution outside Article v', p. 1074.

[23.] See *The Concept of Law* (Oxford University Press, 1961), pp. 60–4 (for general principle), pp. 44–8 (for customary law).

several independent sites of legislation.[24] This is clearly true, though whether it would have been of much interest to the people with whom I have been concerned may be doubted. The rustling of the leaves in the oak at Dodona could in this sense be a valid source of law (with the priestess as the Supreme Court interpreting the sound), but of course the theorists of modern democratic sovereignty would not have taken this seriously as an objection to their position. They were intent on showing that one could – contrary to received opinion – have a practical and consistent system of democratic sovereignty, rather than that *all* legal systems had as a matter of logic to take this form, and they also thought that such a system would fit onto the ideas of human freedom and intentional collective decision-making far better than any other. To that extent they were not 'positivists', at least as Hart uses the term, because they believed that only rules generated through these democratic and open processes were fully valid, just as the old school of natural law held that only laws which corresponded to the principles of natural reason were fully valid.[25] This was true

---

[24.] It should be said that Sieyès does not make an appearance in *The Concept of Law*. Hart acknowledges that these independent sites may be orderable – thus, statute in the UK trumps common law – but as he rightly says, it does not follow (on this account) that they are derivative from one another.

[25.] See Hart's discussion of this issue, pp. 205–6, making clear his own 'positivism'. The term is an awkward one, since it usually acquires its meaning through a contrast with a conventional account of moral principles which must underlie law. In the case of these theorists, human will is the sole origin of law, but it has to be will in a specific setting or following a specific procedure.

even of Hobbes, as otherwise we cannot make sense of his fierce opposition to the common lawyers.

The other claim in *The Concept of Law* is more relevant to my concerns, as it is (or appears to be) the claim that the idea of a sovereign as the sole source of law cannot make sense of the actual practices of modern societies, and a fortiori the idea of a *democratic* sovereign cannot do so. It is in this context that Hart makes his argument against the idea of tacit legislation by the current sovereign. Again, this might not strictly trouble the earlier theorists, who might just say (as they usually came close to saying in general) 'so much the worse for modern societies'; but as we have just seen they (not unreasonably) took the view that the persistence of law needs explaining in their terms – it is indeed hard (though not impossible) to imagine a legal order which does not rely on the continuation of old laws. Here Hart brings two arguments together, saying that they are in fact the same: one is the claim that obedience to a sovereign cannot explain the persistence of law, and the other is the claim that it cannot explain the use by courts and other bodies of customary rules which have not been formally promulgated by the sovereign.[26] It is true that the adoption of customs has also often been defended in terms of tacit legislation by a sovereign, as by Hobbes in *Leviathan*: 'When long Use obtaineth the authority of a Law, it is not the Length of Time that maketh the Authority, but the Will of the Soveraign signified by his silence, (for Silence is sometimes an argument of Consent)'.[27] But there are some important differences between this and the persistence under a new sovereign

---

[26.] *The Concept of Law*, p. 63.   [27.] *Leviathan*, p. 184, original ed., p. 138.

of laws enacted by an old one, and sovereignty theorists have usually been much more concerned with the latter than with the former.

What Hart says about custom is as follows.

> What absurdity is there in the contention that, when particular cases arise, courts apply custom, as they apply statute, as something which is already law and because it is law? It is, of course, *possible* that a legal system should provide that no customary rule should have the status of law until the courts, in their uncontrolled discretion, declared that it should. But this would be just *one* possibility, which cannot exclude the possibility of systems in which the courts have no such discretion. How can it establish the general contention that a customary rule *cannot* have the status of law till applied in court?[28]

And in the same way old statutes simply are law already, and need no tacit repromulgation by the current sovereign to render them authoritative. Hart's last point in the quotation brings out clearly what I was saying earlier, that he is interested in a wholly general account of what 'law' means. The question that should concern us in this context, however, is not whether a customary rule *cannot* have the status of law, but whether the theory of tacit legislation cannot accommodate the incorporation into law of custom. It is certainly true (*pace* Hobbes) that the idea of tacit legislation by a sovereign does have a certain difficulty in dealing with the adoption of custom into a legal system; this is not so much because of the

---

[28] Ibid., p. 46.

deficiencies of the general principle, but rather because there is an implausibility in the picture that the sovereign randomly permits the courts to use this set of customary rules, and not any other rules that simply come into their heads. Customs do have some sort of force in the law (or at least in legal systems of the kind which admit them) because they are thought already to have some kind of normative status. But what that status is, is far from clear, even if we are not sovereignty theorists: they are obviously not law in the same sense as ordinary statutes before the sovereign or his agents put their stamp of approval on them, whatever Hart might say. I cannot, for example, be punished for not having complied with the custom before it was authorised. This is not true of old statutes which are not repealed: an offence against them is punishable now even if it was committed before the present sovereign came into office. English lawyers of Hobbes's generation were sufficiently puzzled by the status of the customary rules of the common law that they eventually concluded (under the influence of John Selden, whom Hobbes greatly admired) that common law was to a great extent simply lost statute.[29] So it is not clear that we can rely on an

---

[29.] Selden made this point in his *History of Tythes*, observing that Parliamentary statutes still properly counted as part of the common law; in his *Titles of Honour* he gave a number of examples of common law principles that could be traced to lost statutes. See David Wilkins (ed.), *Opera Omnia* (London, 1726) vol. III, coll. 742, p. 1330. Hale spelt it out clearly: 'those Statutes or Acts of Parliament that were made before the Beginning of the Reign of King Richard I and have not since been repealed or altered, either by contrary Usage, or by subsequent Acts of Parliament, are now accounted Part of the *Lex non Scripta*, being as it

uncontentious account of the role of custom in an English-style legal system in order to call the theory of tacit legislation into question: the most authoritative English lawyers reworked the idea of the common law to fit the post-Bodin notion of a sovereign legislator, and most contemporary medieval historians would broadly agree with them.[30] So if anything, the role of custom in English law and the response of theoretically acute lawyers to it confirms rather than refutes the theory of tacit legislation by an existing sovereign: rather than treating the continuation of old law as equivalent to the incorporation of custom, they took the incorporation of custom (at least as far as the fundamental principles of common law were concerned) as an example of the continuation of old law.

There is, incidentally, an additional aspect to the role of custom in English law, which to some degree confirms the instincts of Selden and Hale. In Roman law, the theory was both that a custom can acquire legal authority through prolonged use, *and* that a law can lose its authority in the same way – the principle of *desuetudo*, the opposite of

were incorporated thereinto, and become a Part of the Common Law. And doubtless, many of those Things that now obtain as Common Law, had their Original by Parliamentary Acts or Constitutions, made in Writing by the King, Lords and Commons; though those Acts are now either not extant, or if extant, were made before Time of Memory'. Matthew Hale, *The History of the Common Law of England*, ed. Charles M. Gray (University of Chicago Press, 1971), p. 4.

[30.] For one of the most extensive accounts of the role of legislation in the formation of the common law, see Patrick Wormald, *The Making of English Law: King Alfred to the Twelfth Century*, vol. I (Oxford: Blackwell, 1999).

consuetudo.[31] This is perfectly reasonable if we suppose that usage is authoritative; there is no reason why it should work only in one direction. Scots law, as a Roman system, accordingly incorporated the clear principle that a statute could be invalidated by desuetude.[32] But English law never permitted *desuetudo.* In a famous incident in 1818 a plaintiff successfully claimed the right to trial by battle (which had not been exercised since (probably) the thirteenth century), and his claim had to be allowed; Parliament then responded by promptly passing an act abolishing the right. During the discussion of this case at Westminster the English members learned with astonishment that it could not have happened north of the Border, because Scots law permitted desuetude; some of them then proposed a motion for the abolition of desuetude in Scotland, on the grounds that it gave far too much power to the courts. The Scots lawyers resisted, and the principle was maintained as part of Scots law, though it was generally accepted (not entirely plausibly) that the principle could never be used in the case of acts of the United Parliaments, where English conventions would trump Scottish ones.

[31.] Digest 1.3.32.1. See, for example, J. A. C. Thomas, 'Desuetudo', *Revue internationale des droits de l'antiquité* 12 (1965).

[32.] 'As a posterior statute may repeal or derogate from a prior, so a posterior custom may repeal or derogate from a prior statute, even though that prior statute should contain a clause forbidding all usages that might tend to weaken it: for the contrary immemorial custom sufficiently presumes the will of the community to alter the law in all its clauses, and particularly in that which was intended to secure it against alteration; and this presumed will of the people operates as strongly as their express declaration'. John Erskine, *An Institute of the Law of Scotland* (Edinburgh, 1773), vol. I, p. 15 (1.1.45).

I believe that is still the situation in the law of Scotland. The absence of *desuetudo* in England, almost alone among the nations of Europe, is a striking indication of the degree to which – contrary to the conventional view – English law was not fundamentally a customary law, while Roman law was far more open to the role of custom.[33]

A further difficulty for Hart is that if he were correct, the disappearance or delegitimation of an existing sovereign ought not to affect the courts: the old laws should (in principle) continue in their full validity, since they do not depend on the will of the current sovereign. But this has not normally seemed to people to be a straightforward matter: even if the old laws ought to continue in force, the reasons which are characteristically given for this tend not to be Hart's, but rather common-sense considerations of public utility. Sir Matthew Hale provides a striking example of this also. He had been a royalist during the early part of the Civil War, but during the Interregnum Cromwell approached him with an offer to make him a judge. Hale apparently debated with himself 'on the Lawfulness of taking a Commission from Usurpers', but decided that 'it being absolutely necessary to have Justice and Property kept up at all times: It was no Sin to take a Commission from Usurpers, if he made no Declaration

---

[33.] As one might expect, we tend to find enthusiasm for desuetude expressed by theorists opposed to the kind of sovereignty theory whose history I have been tracing. Barbeyrac wrote in its favour (see his note to *De Iure Belli ac Pacis* II.4.5.2), as did Lieber (*Manual of Political Ethics* (London, 1839), p. 242). It is also unsurprising that Hans Kelsen endorsed it (*General Theory of Law and State*, Anders Wedberg (trans.), (Harvard University Press, 1945), p. 119).

of his acknowledging their Authority'. Interestingly, however, he at first refused to sit in capital cases, 'since he thought the Sword of Justice belonging by right to the lawful Prince, it seemed not warrantable to proceed to a Capital sentence by an Authority derived from Usurpers'.[34] A deliberation of this kind seems to be the appropriate response to the problems raised by a revolutionary break in the legal order. Hale believed that the authority of existing laws must *in some sense* be undermined by the disappearance of a legitimate sovereign, though he also recognised that they had to be treated as possessing what we might think of as a kind of provisional authority in order that the legal system should not break down entirely. Either way, his response (and the similar response of many people in revolutionary situations) did not correspond to what Hart might have expected.

The critical issue, however, is not captured by any of these analytical discussions. As I said, the democratic sovereignty theorists believed that only an organised democracy in which we participate has any authority over us. Custom or convention are not enough to legitimate the rules by which we live, since we have not made them in the conscious, intentional and formal way that the theory of democratic sovereignty requires. But equally, the rules made by the long-dead members of a democratic assembly, even if we have succeeded them in the same assembly, cannot have authority unless we make them ours in some fashion, and the theory of tacit legislation is the best way of understanding how we might

[34.] Gilbert Burnet, *The Life and Death of Sir Matthew Hale, Kt* (London, 1681) pp. 36–8.

have done that while simultaneously preserving the principle that the assembly of which we are now members is the only source of legitimation. This is why it has been so pervasive in the tradition I have been reconstructing.

But this in turn has some far-reaching consequences, which are seldom fully recognised. It has been common in recent years for American jurists who call themselves 'originalists' to argue something similar to the theorists I have been discussing; thus Antonin Scalia has emphasised that the Constitution is the product of democratic legislation and should be interpreted by the judges like any other statutes,[35] while Keith Whittington has given a systematic and impressive account of the American Constitution using the very language of sovereignty and government to make the point that the Constitution is the product of genuine legislation by a popular sovereign.[36] But Whittington then argues that because the Constitution is a piece of legislation, it must be interpreted according to the intention of the legislators *in the sense of* the original members of the popular legislature; though like many American jurists, he is evasive about who those members were, as he is ready to talk about 'the founders', despite the fact that (if we take that term to apply, as it usually does, to the members of the Philadelphia Convention) it was not their intentions about or understandings of the text

[35.] Amy Gutmann (ed.), *A Matter of Interpretation. Federal Courts and the Law* (Princeton University Press, 1997), pp. 9–17.

[36.] Keith E. Whittington, *Constitutional Interpretation: Textual Meaning, Original Intent, and Judicial Review* (University Press of Kansas, 1999), pp. 132–5 (sovereign/government distinction), pp. 154–5 (originalism and democracy).

of the Constitution which gave it authority, but (as Lysander Spooner emphasised)[37] those of the members of the ratifying conventions, or even of their electors, if the members were adequately mandated. (Scalia, it should be said, takes the relevant intentions to be those of ordinary language speakers at the time the Constitution was promulgated.)[38] But these arguments give with one hand and take back with the other, as the point of democratic sovereignty is to remove us from the rule of anyone other than *ourselves*; it cannot be to put us back

---

[37.] See his powerful remarks at the beginning of his chapter on 'The Intentions of the Convention' in *The Unconstitutionality of Slavery* (Boston, 1860), pp. 114–16. 'The intentions of the framers of the constitution (if we could have, as we cannot, any legal knowledge of them, except from the words of the constitution) have nothing to do with fixing the legal meaning of the constitution. That convention were not delegated to adopt or establish a constitution; but only to consult, devise and recommend. The instrument, when it came from their hands, was a mere proposal, having no legal force or authority. It finally derived all its validity and obligation, as a frame of government, from its adoption by the people at large. Of course the intentions of the people at large are the only ones that are of any importance to be regarded in determining the legal meaning of the instrument. And their intentions are to be gathered entirely from the words, which they adopted to express them ... In adopting the constitution, the people acted as legislators, in the highest sense in which that word can be applied to human lawgivers. They were establishing a law that was to govern both themselves and their government ... The instrument, therefore, is now to be regarded as expressing the intentions of the people at large; and not the intentions of the convention, if the convention had any intentions differing from the meaning which the law gives to the words of the instrument'.

[38.] *A Matter of Interpretation*, p. 38.

under the rule of the dead.[39] What his position reveals is that even the clearest modern account of the division between sovereign and government lapses into what one might term the Sieyèsian (or the Grotian or Pufendorfian) view of the identity of a 'people', according to which it has a real identity over time, and the past members of the society are as much part of 'the people' as the present ones. But as we have seen, the modern theory of democratic sovereignty was fundamentally opposed to such a view, and with good reason.

Given this fact, what is the government (including in that – as Whittington has correctly stressed – the judiciary) to do? One might say that the American people are very thoroughly asleep at the moment; one might even say, pursuing the Hobbesian analogy, that they are in gaol, so immobilised are they by the conditions of politics in a Union of fifty states, and the peoples of most other modern states are in little better condition. So the vizier can do nothing more than follow the orders he was given the last time the King woke up, as intended by the King at that moment, including the tacit re-enactment of the King's earlier laws. This is, as it happens, the position that Amar has taken up, and I have some sympathy with it; it means that we should interpret the whole of the Constitution as its non-repeal would have been understood at the date of the most recent Amendment (7 May 1992).

[39.] Whittington expressly discusses the 'dead hand' view, and rejects it precisely on the grounds that it must imply that legislative intent is irrelevant (*Constitutional Interpretation*, p. 199). He also rejects the idea of tacit legislation by the current sovereign (pp. 129–31).

But in fact, the modern democratic sovereign is in effect in the third of Hobbes's four cases, the one to do with the dictator.

> [I]f after the election of a *time-limited Monarch*, the *people* has departed from the council with the understanding that it would hold meetings at fixed times and places while the term set for the Monarch is still running, (as *Dictators* were appointed among the Romans), such a one is not to be regarded as a *Monarch* but as the first minister of the *people*, and the *people* can, if it shall see fit, deprive him of his office [*administratio*] even before his term is finished ... [In the same way a] king who has given his power to someone else to exercise, while he himself stays awake, can resume it again when he wishes.

Hobbes thought that in this latter case the sovereign is 'awake', while in the second of his cases, in which 'the *people* leave the assembly after the election of a *time-limited Monarch* with the decision already made to meet at a certain time and place after his death' they are 'asleep'. But the distinction between the two cases is not straightforward, as it is reasonable to think of the people in the third case also as asleep until it gathers to exercise power; as Hobbes presents it, it is simply a matter of a *predetermined* date for the meeting, rather than an ad hoc one. (In this respect his argument contains the same unsatisfactory distinction we saw Bodin make, between the dictator and an elected king, though because Hobbes treated both cases as democracies the distinction is much less significant.) Either way, the people under the American Constitution do not have a specific predetermined date for meeting but are free (in some sense) to meet whenever they choose: though, as I said, the barriers set up to prevent them meeting are currently pretty formidable, they are not yet insurmountable. So it is possible to say that we can know quite a lot about the current sovereign, even before it speaks clearly, and we do not have to rely solely on what it said the last time it gathered; it is quite reasonable to say that the fact that the Constitution has not been amended or repealed by the *present* sovereign means that the present sovereign, with all its other beliefs and commitments, wishes the law to stand.[40] But that in turn means that the government, and especially the judiciary, must take what it knows about those beliefs and commitments into account when it interprets the law. So the approach often described as 'living constitutionalism' turns out to be more closely

---

[40.] This does not at all preclude the possibility that its readiness to let the old law stands is the consequence of a recognition that the messy realities of current politics means that it should not be the object of debate; *politics*, of a perfectly familiar kind, will play its part in the activity of this kind of democratic legislature, as much as in that of ordinary legislative assemblies. A good analogy would be with the Act of Settlement in the UK: no one supposes that its authority for us rests on the authority of a set of half-crazy Protestants in a barely representative body more than three centuries ago. It rests on the understandable unwillingness of the modern Parliament to open up the complicated issues that would arise were the Act to be comprehensively rethought, and that unwillingness is a perfectly justifiable basis for a modern Act. (This analogy has become less forceful since I advanced it in my original lectures, since the Act has been slightly amended by the current Parliament, permitting heirs to the throne to marry Catholics. So the non-repeal of the section requiring the monarch to be a Protestant in 2013 was (so to speak) more 'active' than its non-repeal over the years since 1701. But it was still non-repeal, and not the passing of a new statute).

aligned with the essential character of the democratic sovereignty presupposed by the American constitutions than any other approach.[41]

[41.] This position is to be distinguished from the view that *the founders' intent* was that the Constitution be 'living', and that if we dutifully follow their intentions we cannot be originalists. I think it is true, actually, that their intent was that it be living, but that is irrelevant: it is the facts that we are democrats and that the structures of the Constitution are fundamentally democratic that make it 'living'.

INDEX